GUARDING ⌗ THE ⌗ FÜHRER

Blaine Taylor (*b. 1946*) is the author of twelve histories with illustrations on war, politics, automotives, biography, engineering, architecture, medicine, photographs, and aviation.

The well-read historian is a former Vietnam War soldier and Military Policeman of the US Army's *élite* 199th Light Infantry Brigade under enemy Communist Viet Cong fire during 1966–67 in South Vietnam. He was awarded twelve medals and decorations, including the coveted Combat Infantryman's Badge/ CIB. A later crime and political newspaper reporter, Taylor is also an award-winning medical journalist, international magazine writer, and the winner of four political campaigns as press secretary for county, state, and US Presidential elections, 1974–92.

During 1991–92, he served as a US Congressional aide and press secretary on Capitol Hill, Washington, DC. Blaine lives at Towson, MD/USA.

Previously Published books by Blaine Taylor

Guarding the Führer: Sepp Dietrich, Johann Rattenhuber, and the Protection of Adolf Hitler (1993)
Fascist Eagle: Italy's Air Marshal Italo Balbo (1996)
Mercedes-Benz Parade and Staff Cars of the Third Reich (1999)
Volkswagen Military Vehicles of the Third Reich (2004)
Hitler's Headquarters from Beer Hall to Bunker 1920–45 (2006)
Apex of Glory: Benz, Daimler, & Mercedes-Benz 1885–1955 (2006)
Hitler's Chariots Volume 1: Mercedes-Benz G-4 Cross-Country Touring Car (2009)
Hitler's Chariots Volume 2: Mercedes-Benz 770K Grosser Parade Car (2010)
Hitler's Engineers: Fritz Todt and Albert Speer/Master Builders of the Third Reich (2010)
Hitler's Chariots Volume 3: Volkswagen from Nazi People's Car to New Beetle (2011)
Mrs Adolf Hitler: The Eva Braun Photograph Albums 1912-45 (2013)
Dallas Fifty Years On: The Murder of John F. Kennedy—A New Look at an Old Crime, 22 November 1963–2013 (2013)

GUARDING ⌗ THE ⌗ FÜHRER

SEPP DIETRICH & ADOLF HITLER

BLAINE TAYLOR

FONTHILL

Dedication

*To my world history professor at then Towson State College,
Dr. Armin Mruck, still living as of 2014.*

*Remembering the Dearly Departed: Michael Gallatin, late husband of Divina Celeste Gallatin,
both longtime friends of the author. Gone, but not forgotten! RIP.*

Fonthill Media Language Policy

Fonthill Media publishes in the international English language market. One language edition is published worldwide. As there are minor differences in spelling and presentation, especially with regard to American English and British English, a policy is necessary to define which form of English to use. The Fonthill Policy is to use the form of English native to the author. Blaine Taylor was educated in Towson University, and now lives at Towson, MD therefore American English has been adopted in this publication.

Fonthill Media Limited
Fonthill Media LLC
www.fonthillmedia.com
office@fonthillmedia.com

This revised edition first published in the United Kingdom
and the United States of America 2014

ISBN 978-1-78155-387-9

Typeset in 10pt on 13pt Adobe Caslon Pro
Printed and bound in England

Contents

Acknowledgements

First, thanks are due to my publisher Alan Sutton of Fonthill Media for bringing out this edition for an entirely new generation of readers, and for that I am most grateful, indeed. As always, many thanks to Stan Piet of Bel Air for photographic work and Frank White of Phoenix for computer assistance, both of Maryland/USA.

Following are the various sources of photographs, cartoons, and maps used in this book, both in 1993 and for this new, improved, and updated edition of 2014:

Eva Braun Hitler/EBH, Heinrich Hoffmann/HH, Joachim von Ribbentrop/VR, and SS/LSSAH Albums, all on deposit at the US National Archives, College Park, MD/USA, as well as Captured Enemy Records/CER.

The Anne S.K. Brown Military Collection/ASKB, John Hay Library, Brown University, Providence, RI/USA.

The Blaine Taylor Archives/BT, Towson, MD/USA.

The Imperial War Museum/IWM, London, United Kingdom.

The Hermann Goring Albums/HG, Library of Congress, Washington, DC/USA.

George Peterson, National Capitol Historic Sales, Springfield, VA/USA.

US Army Combat Art Collection/USACAC, Washington, DC/USA.

US Army Signal Corps/USASC Photographer Ray D'Addario at the International Military Tribunal and other Nuremberg Trials, 1945–49.

US Army Military History Institute, Carlisle Barracks, Carlisle, PA/USA.

Professor Peter Hoffmann.

Photographer Hugo Jaeger/HJ

Author's Note

This is a general dual biography of Sepp Dietrich and the men of his Leibstandarte Adolf Hitler Division, as well as of Johann Rattenhuber and his men of the Reich Security Service/RSD in their joint mission of the physical protection of Adolf Hitler, both before and during the Second World War.

This new edition—21 years after the publication of the first—features a better, tighter textual narrative, many of the formerly published photos from 1993, and also new ones selected for this edition that were not available to me then. Several of the new photographs are previously unpublished, and are so identified as such.

I am grateful for this opportunity to present this new edition to another generation of readers seeking to learn more about this time in world history.

Today, figurines of Dietrich, Rattenhuber, and Rommel are sold worldwide, but not yet of Rattenhuber; give it time!

Chapter One

Protecting the Führer:
Josef "Sepp" Dietrich and the
Leibstandarte Adolf Hitler Division

By the time he died at age 74 in 1966, Josef "Sepp" Dietrich had been a highly controversial figure all his life. Sepp was a German Army sergeant in the First World War; Nazi SS bully boy, and early bodyguard for Adolf Hitler in the 1920s; founder of the Führer's élite personal guard squad (later battalion, regiment and division in the decade between 1930–40); division, army and army group commander in the Second World War, and—after the war—a convicted war criminal who served prison sentences under the auspices of both the Allied Powers and his own West German Government.

Virtually alone among the top SS leaders, Dietrich had no official biography on him until English historian Charles Messenger's groundbreaking work, *Hitler's Gladiator*, appeared in 1988. To his former colleagues within the ranks of surviving Waffen SS men, he will always remain in memory what he was in life—their revered, respected "Commander."

To crusty German Army Field Marshal Gerd von Rundstedt, Sepp's overall commanding officer during the epic Battle of the Bulge, Dietrich was "decent, but stupid." And yet Adolf Hitler—whose paladin he was throughout the entire Nazi Third Reich era—entrusted him with the most difficult political and military tasks, not the least of which was the safeguarding of his own life and the lives of the other top leaders of the regime. Indeed, had Dietrich and von Rundstedt won the Battle of the Bulge instead of losing it—and had Nazi Germany won the war itself as well—Sepp most probably would have had a very different postwar career as the Führer's first appointed Waffen SS Field Marshal.

His critics—mostly among the Allies—have been many over the years. States Britain's premiere military author, B. H. Liddell Hart in his 1948 volume, *The German Generals Talk*, "Sepp Dietrich was an SS leader, formerly a rolling stone in various business jobs, who had caught Hitler's fancy by his aggressive spirit. Rundstedt regarded him as responsible for fumbling the crucial part of the (Bulge) offensive."

To Allied officer Milton Shulman in his own 1948 work, *Defeat in the West*:

[Sepp was] short and squat, with a broad, dark face dominated by a large, wide nose. Dietrich resembled a rather battered bartender in appearance. He was a typical product of the Freikorps and the bullying gangs with which Hitler first made his advent on the German political stage. The first Great War interrupted his plans to become a butcher, and after four years of fighting he had attained the rank of sergeant-major. He spent the postwar years at a series of unsuccessful odd jobs and occupied his spare time as an enthusiastic adherent of the Nazi Party.

In 1928, he joined the SS as a full-time member, and in five years rose to the rank of Brigadeführer (Major General) as the commanding officer of Hitler's personal bodyguard. He led the first SS Division (Leibstandarte/Lifeguard) Adolf Hitler in the French, Greek and Russian campaigns, and boasted that by 1943 only 30 of the original 23,000 men in his Division were still alive and uncaptured. In Germany, the Goebbels' propaganda machine had made of "Sepp" Dietrich an almost legendary figure, whose exploits as a fighting man of the people rivalled—if not surpassed—those of that other popular National Socialist personality, Erwin Rommel.

"Crude, conceited and garrulous, his meteoric career was undoubtedly achieved more by his hard and ruthless energy than by his military ability," was Shulman's somewhat pungent conclusion.

The famed "Desert Fox" himself—Field Marshal Rommel—had very little to say about Dietrich in his own, posthumously published postwar memoirs, *The Rommel Papers*. He merely alludes to Sepp's post-D-Day battle action reports to him concerning the total Allied control over the Normandy airspace. Yet it was with Dietrich that Rommel met on July 17, 1944, just a short time before he was put out of action by a British fighter plane attack, and a mere three days prior to the German generals' Bomb Plot attempt on Hitler's life in which many historians believe the Desert Fox was at least partially involved. Was Dietrich also possibly implicated, a great irony for a man the Führer trusted implicitly? (States at least one critic of this notion: "This is a ridiculous idea that 'Sepp' could have been involved in the July 1944 death plot!! Such absolutely unfounded statements should best be left to sensationalist rags!")

John Toland—a mainstream American historian of the Second World War era with such volumes to his credit as *The Rising Sun, But Not in Shame, Infamy*, and *Adolf Hitler*, also took a dim view of Sepp in his 1959 bestseller, *Battle: The Story of the Bulge*:

> When he was told his army commander would be Dietrich, Baron (Friedrich August) von der Heydte was appalled. "Sepp" Dietrich—at best was qualified to lead a division. To von der Heydte, he was an uneducated brute, but Hitler was still rewarding him for his rabid support in the Münich Beer Hall Putsch, and now the butcher from Bavaria commanded a great army of nine divisions.

In addition, it seems Dietrich—like American Union Army Gen. Ulysses S. Grant in the Civil War—liked to "hit the bottle" from time to time, as the aristocratic parachute Baron reported in his conversations with Toland: "At his headquarters near Munstereifel, Dietrich, a big burly man with a rough voice, greeted von der Heydte disdainfully. 'What are your paratroop boys able to do?' 'Anything within reason,' replied von der Heydte, leaning away from Dietrich's whiskied breath."

In fairness to both sides, it should be noted that a great rivalry existed throughout the Second World War between which group of German soldiers was the toughest—Gen. Kurt Student's paratroopers or Dietrich's Waffen SS warriors.

Concedes Toland:

> No insane whim had made Hitler choose Dietrich. The Führer knew his weaknesses, fault by fault, but—as with Rundstedt—Dietrich's name was magic with the troops. Hitler also wanted the great victories of the 6th Panzer Army to be won by a good Nazi.

And one, moreover, commanding Waffen SS men. Indeed, the Führer planned the Battle of the Bulge almost from the very start as a primarily SS offensive; it was to be a victory for the Nazi Party, not the staid, traditional German military establishment that had tried to kill Hitler the previous July.

Not everyone in the conservative, hidebound old Prussian military system looked down on the much-maligned Sepp, however, as the eminent British historian John W. Wheeler-Bennett noted in his 1964 mammoth volume *The Nemesis of Power: The German Army in Politics, 1918-45*. When Field Marshal Günther von Kluge—implicated as part of the July 20th conspiracy—was summoned to appear before Hitler, he chose suicide instead, entrusting his death note proclaiming his loyalty to the Führer to none other than §SS Gen. Sepp Dietrich for personal delivery to the man who had been patron to them both—Adolf Hitler.

As noted in *The Goebbels Diaries, 1939-41*, Nazi Propaganda Minister Dr. Josef Goebbels, in his entry for October 31, 1940, noted: "Chat for a long while with Sepp Dietrich. He is an amiable, solid fellow. Has all sorts of complaints. Nice to chew the fat with an old Party warhorse like him!" Later—on May 21,1941, he stated that Dietrich's conduct in the Greek campaign had been "marvelous," but by the end of the war he, too, was losing faith in Dietrich's military ability, stating in *Final Entries: 1945—The Diaries of Joseph Goebbels* for March 21st: "Even Sepp Dietrich is not in the top class. He is a good troop commander, but no strategist."

And yet, of the four SS army group commanders created by Hitler during the Second World War (the others being SS Reichsführer Heinrich Himmler and SS Gens. Paul Hausser and Felix Steiner), Dietrich had been—and probably even today is considered—the most well known of the group.

Sepp seems to have fared no better in later studies, either. For instance, in the 1982 work by American writer Glenn B. Infield, *Secrets of the SS*, he is called "the most brutal of men," while in his 1977 revisionist history *Hitler's War*, Britisher David Irving described Sepp's military acumen as "at best questionable."

In the 1976 anthology *Hitler's Generals and Their Battles*, editorial consultant Brig. Gen. Shelford Biddwell describes Sepp's early career as:

> farm laborer, waiter, policeman, foreman in a tobacco factory, customs official and petrol pump attendant … Dietrich was not a bad officer; he simply lacked the training and experience to command an army. Göring said of him, 'He had at the most the ability to command a division.'

In his 1976 work, *Encyclopedia of the Third Reich*, author Louis L. Snyder says Dietrich was described by William L. Shirer as:

> one of the most brutal of men. Sepp Dietrich was born in Hawangen, near Memmingen, May 28, 1892 … Burly and tough, he was quick to take offense … Nicknamed 'Chauffeureska' by his patron, he accompanied Hitler on his automobile tours of Germany. Impressed by this hard Bavarian, Hitler found him a variety of jobs, including dispatcher for the publishing house of Franz Eher. In 1930 Dietrich was elected to the Reichstag as a delegate for Electoral District Lower Bavaria. By 1931 he had attained the rank of SS Gruppenführer (Lieutenant General).

Adds Robert Wistrich in his 1982 volume *Who's Who in Nazi Germany*:

> [Sepp was] the son of a poor Bavarian peasant family. Employed in hotels and public houses, then a butcher's apprentice in München, Dietrich joined the Imperial Army in 1911 and served as

a paymaster sergeant during the First World War. After the war he drifted from one job to the next, joined the Oberland Freikorps and was an early member of the NSDAP. A participant in the Münich Beer Hall Putsch, his strong-arm prowess at Party political meetings brought him to Hitler's attention and in 1928 he was made Commander of the Nazi leader's bodyguard. ... during the Second World War, Sepp was one of the few 'old Nazis' to make a name for himself as a soldier, holding commands in Poland, France, Greece, Russia, Hungary and Austria. Though lacking military experience and no great strategist, Dietrich displayed considerable powers of leadership, personal magnetism and a streak of ruthlessness.

Awarded many decorations, including the Oak Leaves with Swords on December 31, 1941 and the Diamonds (Brillianten) to the Oak Leaves in August, 1944, Dietrich's courage and hardness were never in doubt.

Hitler paid him this tribute in February, 1942: 'The role of Sepp Dietrich is unique! I have always given him the opportunity to intervene at sore spots. He is a man who is simultaneously cunning, energetic and brutal. Under this swashbuckling appearance, Dietrich is a serious, conscientious and scrupulous character ... He is a Bavarian Wrangel, someone irreplaceable. For the German people, Sepp Dietrich is a national institution! For me, personally, there is also the fact that he is one of my oldest companions in the struggle.'

"The legend of the military valor;" asserts Wistrich:

was consciously built up by Nazi propaganda during the war, ignoring the atrocities for which he was responsible as a divisional commander in the Kharkov-Kherson district between 1941-43.

In 1988 was published *The Third Reich Almanac* by James Taylor and Warren Shaw, and once again Dietrich strides to center stage in his swaggering SS uniform and high, black polished boots:

In 1928 he became a full-time SS man, and though far from possessing blond Aryan looks, was often chosen as Hitler's personal guard, becoming head of the élite group 'Leibstandarte Adolf Hitler,' distinguished even within the SS for their appearance and arrogance ... a senior commander without staff training or the military background of his fellow commanders. Though without strategic genius, he was undoubtedly an adequate general officer on divisional level. His skills lay in inspiration and leadership.

Coarse, broken-nosed, foul-mouthed, his style of leadership was well-suited to the desperate soldiers he led.

In his superb 1979 study entitled *On the Field of Honor: A History of the Knight's Cross Bearers, Volume I,* LTC John R. Angolia writes of Dietrich's career:

He entered military service in 1911, enlisting in 4 Field Artillery, Regiment 1 at the age of 19. He served first with the artillery, then the infantry, and finally with the newly introduced tank units. He distinguished himself in combat, winning the Iron Cross First and Second Class. When the war ended, Sepp Dietrich was separated from the Army with the rank of Sergeant ... He was noted as being a stern, but fair, taskmaster. His ultimate aim was to train the best political and combat troops possible.

Angolia, the world's leading, tireless chronicler of the awardees of the German Ritterkreuz (RK), or Knight's Cross, and of the Eisernes Kreuz (Iron Cross), notes that Dietrich received his coveted RK:

> on July 4, 1940 while serving as commanding general SS Regiment 'Leibstandarte SS Adolf Hitler' (motorized) for action in the campaign against France. Commanding the same unit, SS Obergruppenführer Dietrich became the 41st recipient of the Oak Leaves for his actions in the Balkan Campaigns. The award was rendered on December 31, 1941.
>
> He became the 16th recipient of the Swords when they were rendered on March 16, 1943 for action on the Russian Front while commanding the LSSAH. Hitler personally presented the Diamonds to his close friend 'Sepp' Dietrich on Aug. 6, 1944…The award was given for action on the Western Front as Commanding General (SS Obergruppenführer und General der Waffen SS) 6th SS Panzer Army. Upon receiving the award, he was promoted to the rank of SS Obergruppenfiihrer [Colonel General, a four-star rank in the US Army] und Panzer-Generaloberst der Waffen SS.

Thus, the publicly known—or declared, as the case may be—record of one of Nazidom's top soldiers throughout the Second World War in Europe, is very little known on the Allied side of the ledger. As personable with his men as Eisenhower, Sepp had the tough exterior of George Patton, yet the concern for his troops' welfare of Omar Bradley. Every bit as much a "political" general in the Second World War as was William C. Westmoreland in Vietnam later, Sepp broke with his Head of State (in wartime!) in a way that "Westy" never would have dared do with Lyndon Johnson.

When Sepp began his Nazi career under Hitler, the SS were merely squads under the overall aegis of the Brownshirted SA, or Stormtroopers, of former Army Captain Ernst Röhm, and when he ended it in 1945, his gray-clad Waffen SS troopers had indeed accomplished what the tactless Röhm had aimed to do in 1934 and failed. That was to achieve a place of equality alongside the regular German Army as a coexistent political armed force upon which Führer and Chancellor Adolf Hitler could depend at all times and in every conceivable situation in both war and peace.

In these pages, we shall therefore explore the actual role that Sepp Dietrich played—or didn't play—in the 1934 "Röhm Purge" of the SA, in alleged war crimes in Russia, and in the asserted Malmédy Massacre of American Army GIs during the Bulge for which he was imprisoned by the Allies. We will also explore his military abilities in the field, such as his little-known triumph over the Greek Army in which he became only one of two SS commanders to receive an enemy surrender during the war. So, too, will his relations with Hitler, Himmler, Röhm, Speer and others be explored, as well as the founding, growth, combat record and destruction of his highly valued "asphalt soldiers," the Adolf Hitler Lifeguard Division. We will explore Sepp's history from parade ground to battlefield to courtroom and on into the grim pages of the history of a terrible epoch that haunts the world still.

Sepp was born the son of Palagius and Kreszentia Dietrich in Swabia, the same area that begat Erwin Rommel. At the time Swabia was a province of the Bavarian Wittelsbach family dynasty, which was second in power in the German Reich created by Otto von Bismarck under the Prussian Royal and German Imperial House of Hohenzollern, the latter meaning "high tax collector" in German. The unification of Germany had come in 1871, 21 years before the birth of Sepp. Four years before his birth had been born the man with whose career he, Dietrich, will be forever linked in history—Adolf Hitler. In 1890, when Hitler was one, youthful Kaiser Wilhelm II had both fired Bismarck from the office of Imperial Chancellor and set out to build a great German High Seas

Fleet, which—added to his already powerful Army—would help bring on the First World War when young Sepp was but 22.

Like Hitler, Sepp was brought up as a Roman Catholic, and he hailed from a family of two other sons (both killed in the First World War) and three daughters, with Josef the oldest child. After completing his eighth grade of schooling, he became a farmhand. Then, in 1907, when 15 he left home for a time to travel in neighboring Austria and Italy, and even learned some Italian. Going on to Switzerland, young Dietrich began work in the Zürich hotels.

Due to be drafted into the Royal Bavarian Army in 1911, Sepp came home to fulfill his military obligation to his country, but within a month a fall from a horse caused him to be mustered out and sent home—a rather incongruous beginning for a military career that saw him reach the rank of four-star general! Returning home to Kempten in Allgau, he became a deliveryman for a local bakery. By the outbreak of the First World War he was five feet six inches tall, stocky, had blue eyes, thinning brown hair and a moustache and had a strong, square jaw that was to be one of his predominant facial characteristics for the rest of his life. He liked to both eat and drink heartily and tell jokes and funny stories.

On Aug. 6, 1914, Sepp joined up again to go to fight for people and Emperor in the 7th Bavarian Field Artillery Regiment, while Hitler was doing the same thing in a Bavarian infantry unit.

In October 1914, Sepp arrived in Flanders on the Western Front under the overall command of the Bavarian Crown Prince Rupprecht, and was sent into action right away with the 6th Bavarian Reserve Artillery Regiment. He fought both Belgians and the British Expeditionary Force, then against the French in the First Battle of Ypres. His unit then took part in heavy night fighting against the Brits once more, in November 1914, as well as against the French infantry.

The taking and retaking of several villages see-sawed back and forth for the remainder of the month until there occurred what neither side had foreseen—the stalling of all mobile operations and the degeneration of the ground fighting into a system of two rival series of trenches. These trenches bedeviled the Western Front (Germany was now fighting the Tsarist Russian forces in the East as well) for the next four years.

As Dietrich's unit was sent to the East, Sepp remained behind as a wounded casualty, with shrapnel in the lower right leg and a lance thrust above the left eye from an Allied cavalryman. (If he could not be a horseman, he at least would be wounded by one!) After recovering from his wounds, Sepp was sent to Sonthofen's Royal Bavarian Artillery School to be trained as an NCO in the 7th Bavarian Field Artillery Regiment once more.

His movements over the next 18 months become difficult to track; this may be because Dietrich—who was later prone to somewhat distort his First World War record—*wanted* it so. In any event, he was wounded again early in 1916 when hit in the right side of the head by an artillery shell splinter from a round that—when exploded—buried him alive in the process. This had occurred during the Battle of the Somme, and in later years Sepp would claim to have served as well against the Italians, as did Rommel, and to have won the Austrian Medal for Bravery as he did the German Iron Cross.

That November, Sepp joined the Bavarian Storm Troop Artillery, a unit utilizing the new Krupp-produced 37 mm cannon. After a reorganization, the unit's weaponry included machineguns, trench mortars and even flamethrowers, putting Dietrich's participation in the war in the forefront of the known military hardware technology of the day.

The Storm Troops themselves were the toughest and élite of the German line infantry units. Many of their veterans joined the postwar Free Corps units and fought in the Communist uprisings of 1919-20, and still later, the Nazi SA Sturmabteilungen units as well.

By 1917, Dietrich was taking part in bitter fighting against the French in the Champagne area, and it was on November 14th that he was awarded the Iron Cross 2nd Class. As Messenger alleges, however, no record can be found for his receiving the First Class Award of the Eisernes Kreuz (Iron Cross.)

On February 19, 1918—in the final year of the war— Dietrich again found himself in the van of military technology when he was transferred to the Bavarian Storm Tank Detachment. During his training outside Berlin, Dietrich's unit gave a demonstration for Kaiser Wilhelm II on February 27th, then was sent into action in the West three weeks later during Gen. Erich Ludendorff's great offensive of March 1918 to smash the Allied front in the Chemin des Dames sector. Depending on whose version of events one believes, Sepp either did or did not fight against French tanks. (In June 1940 he asserted he did.)

After seeing action against British armor at Charleroi, the German tanks were transferred to Cambrai for repair, and their last battle was on November 1, 1918, against the Brits and Canadians. Then the unit was withdrawn to Germany, which by now was in the throes of anti-war revolution, dynastic overthrow and civil war, all events that helped mold Hitler, Dietrich, Hess, Göring and others into the Nazis they later became. Even Sepp's own unit set up a Soldier's Council, and Hitler later might have been embarrassed to learn that his own trusty Dietrich was elected its chairman! He was mustered out of the Bavarian Army, however, on March 26, 1919, and thus forced to start a new career in disadvantageous circumstances.

Sepp joined the Bavarian Police in 1921, yet there seems to be no record that he participated in the anti-Revolutionary counter-movements that were sweeping München and Bavaria at this tumultuous time.

Aside from joining the Bavarian Landespolizei (Land Police), Dietrich also was married in February 1921 for the first time. Later he also asserted that in 1920 he had joined the Oberland Free Corps and traveled to Silesia to fight the Poles. After he was captured in the Second World War, Dietrich would tell his Allied interrogators that he first heard Adolf Hitler speak in 1921 during a speech to some troops, yet stayed aloof from the embryonic Nazi Party in those early days of the patriotic, anti-Red movement in the strife-torn Reich.

And now we confront one of the many obvious contradictions in the life and career of Josef Sepp Dietrich: did he or did he not take part in Hitler's "Beer Hall Putsch" attempt to seize power illegally on November 8-9, 1923?

Here again—as with the possibility of his having joined the Communists earlier—Dietrich may well have taken part in the police efforts to put down the Nazi revolt, again a fact that he would not have wanted known during his heyday in the later Nazi Third Reich. For his part, Hitler may well have known and not cared, since, in his trial for treason held after the abortive revolt, he held out the olive branch of reconciliation to those who had opposed him in hopes of one day uniting to work together; Sepp Dietrich may well have been one of these converts.

After leaving the police force Sepp took the odd jobs previously mentioned, including garage manager of the Blue Buck Filling Station. The garage was owned by a prominent local München Nazi leader, Christian Weber, through whom Dietrich received Nazi Party #89015 on May 1, 1928. This entitled him to wear, after the Nazi seizure of power on January 30, 1933, the Golden Party Membership Badge reserved for the first 100,000 members (of whom even Hitler wasn't Number One, but Seven!)

At this same time Sepp also joined the SS or Schutzstaffeln (Protection Squads), most likely because he was a decorated war veteran, liked to fight and brawl and certainly looked the part to boot. Many years later, during one of his nocturnal chats with his intimates at Führerhauptquartier (Leader Headquarters) on the Eastern Front on the night of February 3, 1942, Hitler gave a good account of these early, rowdy days of the Party, as reported in *Hitler's Secret Conversations, 1941-44*:

> Being convinced that there are always circumstances in which élite troops are called for, in 1922-23 I created the 'Adolf Hitler Shock Troops'. They were made up of men who were ready for revolution and knew that one day or another things would come to hard knocks. When I came out of Landsberg [Prison], everything was broken up and scattered in sometimes rival bands.
>
> I told myself then that I needed a bodyguard, even a very restricted one, but made up of men who would be enlisted without restriction, even to march against their own brothers. Only 20 men to a city (on condition that one could count on them absolutely), rather than a suspect mass. It was Maurice, Schreck and Heyden who formed in Münich the first group of 'tough ones,' and thus were the origin of the SS, but it was with Himmler that the SS became the extraordinary body of men, devoted to an idea, loyal unto death.
>
> I see in Himmler our Ignatius Loyola. With intelligence and obstinacy, against wind and tide, he forged this instrument. The heads of the SA, for their part, didn't succeed in giving their troops a soul … every division of the SS is aware of their responsibility … How Sepp Dietrich could impose his personality!

Thus, Dietrich had joined the SS in the year before Heinrich Himmler. Himmler was a slightly-built, bespectacled chicken farmer from Waltrudering who had never seen active combat service in the First World War, unlike virtually everyone (except Goebbels) in the upper leadership strata of the Nazi Party. This difference—as well as those of temperament and approach—created a lifelong gap between Sepp and Himmler that would never be bridged. In addition to that, even though he was Dietrich's nominal superior in his role as SS Reichsführer (National Leader), "Heini" fumed over the fact that Dietrich always enjoyed instant access to Hitler and, as head of the Leibstandarte, reported direct to the Führer, not to Himmler. Hitler kept it that way, perhaps fearing too much Himmler—control of the SS men responsible for his personal safety and maintenance in power after 1933.

Ironically, Himmler had participated in the "Beer Hall Putsch"—while Sepp had not—but now, in the street brawls, beer hall battles with rocks, tables, chairs, beer steins and fists, it was to men like Sepp Dietrich that Hitler looked for personal protection. The SS was kept small on purpose during these early days of its existence, for the sake of absolute reliability. Thus, when Sepp joined it in 1928, there were only 200 members nationwide, at a time when the Brownshirted SA battalions boasted 72,000.

Promoted Storm Leader on June 1, 1928, two months later Sepp was named commander of the Münich SS Standarte, the élite of the élite in the very capital city of the Nazi Party movement. Immediately Sepp was in close contact almost daily with the supreme leader of that movement, Adolf Hitler, who liked him.

Thus, this was the situation five months later when, on January 6, 1929, the Führer appointed the unknown Heinrich Himmler as SS Reichsführer, leader of a force that now numbered only 280 men. Initially, Dietrich and Himmler got along, and on May 18, 1929, the latter named the former SS Brigadeführer Bayern, in charge of all the Bavarian SS detachments, a major step forward as it later developed.

While working as a packer at the publishing plant of Max Amann, Dietrich was increasingly called upon by Hitler himself to serve with chauffeur Julius Schreck as the élite inner corps of the circle of bodyguards that included Emil Maurice, and what the Führer referred to fondly as his "chauffeureska." In the Reichstag elections of 1930, as we have seen, Sepp was even elected as a Delegate to that national parliamentary body on the Nazi Party ticket. Sepp's movement ever upward in the Party's ranks dates from this moment, even though back at Max Amann's plant he was promoted only from packer to dispatch clerk of the loading dock.

An elected Reichstag Deputy of the people, he also had been promoted within the SS to SS Oberführer Sud, or SS Leader South, on July 11, 1930. Now Sepp was responsible for all SS activities in Southern Germany, the very cradle of the Nazi Party. He had come far within its ranks in just two years, having been the proverbial man in the right place at precisely the right moment in time.

As part of Hitler's inner circle that included his court photographer, Heinrich Hoffmann and first adjutant, Julius Schaub, Sepp was growing in stature within the Party. Now he—a former butcher and Army sergeant—even had his picture published with a son of the ex-Kaiser who sat next to him in the Reichstag.

As Hitler's prominence grew, so, too—in direct proportion to the growth—did Nazi fears for his personal safety, a problem that was now too big for just Sepp and Schreck to handle alone. So on February 29, 1932, there was created the twelve-man SS Begleit-Kommando "Der Führer." These men all were selected personally by Dietrich and presented to Hitler for his approval at the Berlin Nazi Party headquarters in the Kaiserhof Hotel.

These initial dozen men were described by one who knew them as:

> … fine, athletic German types. They had zipped, motorcar overalls over their black-coated uniforms—and wore close-fitting aviators' helmets. Armed with revolvers and sjamboks or hippopotamus whips— terrible weapons capable of knocking a man out with one blow— they looked like men from Mars.

British correspondent Sefton Delmer left a good account of these first SS Begleit Kommando men in action during a 1932 Presidential election trip taken with Hitler on a chartered flight from city to city:

> In the stern nearest the door sat Sepp Dietrich, the gay little fighting cock of a Bavarian ex-cavalry sergeant who was chief of the bodyguard. With him his men—four or five of them there were, but I can only remember Durr by name, a thick-set, flat-nosed, fair-haired boxer with cauliflower ears.
>
> Some of the other men looked strangely delicate for bodyguards—almost effeminate. When they took photographs out of their wallets and began showing them around with remarks like "Isn't he sweet?" I began to wonder whether the Staff Chief Röhm had had a hand in their selection, but delicate though they looked, they were tough, all right—as they showed us a few hours later that evening.
>
> Hitler's leathercoated bodyguards had already leaped out of their car and were lashing out with rubber truncheons and blackjacks. Stones started to fly and pistol shots rang out. Then the Dietrich men were back in their cars, and we went on.

Both Hitler and Dietrich had selected their men well.

Chapter Two

The "Blood Purge" Of June 30, 1934, And Building The Leibstandarte

As the decade of the 1930s opened, the worldwide Great Depression caused the Nazis to become the fastest-growing political party within the framework of the German Weimar Republic. For Josef "Sepp" Dietrich, elected Reichstag Deputy on the Nazi Party ticket in 1930 and now chief of Adolf Hitler's own personal bodyguard—the 12-member *SS Begleit Kommando Der Führer*—it was a heady time of new leadership possibilities. Indeed, the one-time butcher, ex-Army sergeant, strongarm bouncer and gas station manager had come far in his career—and was destined to rise much higher still.

Protecting the Führer from his many enemies was often risky business, as Dietrich learned in 1932 when Hitler ran for the Presidency of Germany against the venerable Field Marshal Paul von Hindenburg of First World War fame. Hindenburg was seeking reelection to a second, seven-year term.

This was a dangerous time for Hitler, who---during a roadside ambush---was hit in the head by a thrown rock, followed by an assassination attempt at Nuremberg that was foiled. Rioting and streetfighting with the rival German Communists became the norm, and at Altona in Hamburg on July 17th, there were 19 killed and 285 wounded therein. Hitler sent Sepp and an advance party ahead to secure an airfield before his own arrival.

By now, both the Führer and Sepp were living at the Nazi Party Münich headquarters, the famous Brown House, which fell under the responsibility of Reichsführer SS Heinrich Himmler. Both men also had apartments elsewhere in the city. In order not to antagonize Ernst Röhm, the powerful Chief of Staff of the SA, Hitler had a guard contingent comprised of both SS and SA members at the Brown House.

Although Hitler lost both the Presidential election and subsequent run-off election between himself and von Hindenburg (there had been other candidates as well in the first contest), Sepp Dietrich had won his own seat in the Reichstag. Sepp was reelected a Deputy in 1934, after the Nazis were firmly entrenched in power.

For a while, Hitler despaired of *ever* achieving power in the Reich, but events came to his rescue unexpectedly. Although he could not win the Presidency outright—and the next election was not due until 1939, assuming that von Hindenburg lived out his term (which he did not)—the Nazis were still the country's strongest political power. The problem for the aging President and his conservative military caste backers was how to deny the Nazis a controlling interest in the Weimar Republic government without unleashing a renewed civil war such as had occurred in 1918-19. All of them abhorred the thought of a civil war, one that would, they feared, result in a Red Communist takeover—a development they dreaded *even more* than a Nazi seizure of power.

At length, it was decided by the President's inner core of top advisors that the only way out was to name Hitler Chancellor of the Reich under von Hindenburg's authority—the very man who had just defeated him in two elections running and who had sworn *never* to appoint Hitler to the government. Nonetheless, it happened on January 30, 1933, and in March the new Reich Chancellor instructed Sepp Dietrich to form a guard for his official Berlin residence, the old Reich Chancellery Building. Sepp duly resigned his post as leader of SS Group North to become head of the new *SS Stabswache (Staff Guard)*. Technically Dietrich was under the orders of Himmler in his capacity as national chief of the SS, but in fact, reported directly to Hitler. This dual authority set-up rankled "Heini" throughout the 12 years of the new Nazi Third Reich, but was one that he was forced to accept.

The new *Stabswache* numbered 117 members and was housed close to the Chancellery at the Kaiserin Augusta Viktoria Barracks. But within a few weeks, attests Messenger, the unit name was changed to *SS Sonderkommando Berlin* and the unit was moved to the old Imperial Officer Cadet School Barracks at Lichterfelde. This direct removal of Sepp's men from under Himmler's wing also soured Sepp's future relations with the Reichsführer SS.

Even though the two men were forced to work together to keep the peace in Hitler's eyes, there grew an intense dislike between them. Sepp testified to the Americans after the Second World War:

> This guy tried to imitate the Führer! His appetite for power just could not be satisfied. On top of this, he was a great hand at hoarding and scrounging. He received money from everywhere and everybody … I had quite a number of rows with Himmler!

Ironically, even Karl Wolff, Himmler's own SS adjutant, later liaison officer with Führer Headquarters, and from 1943, German military governor of Northern Italy's Fascist Salo Republic, took Dietrich's side after the war, again perhaps because—unlike the mousey-looking Himmler—both he and Sepp had been frontline soldiers during the First World War. Said Wolff, "Himmler had nothing in common with the front soldier! His whole bearing was rather sly and unmilitary, but he was very well-read and tried to engage our interest with acquired knowledge, and to enthuse us with the tasks of the SS."

Hitler was well aware of internal leadership bickerings within the top cadre of his black-coated SS. Indeed, Hitler aided, fostered and abetted them to the extent that the SS was never sufficiently able to muster the internal strength to arrest him, the Führer, and take power, much as had the Praetorian Guards time and again in the Roman Empire of antiquity. Hitler knew his history all too well, and thus looked with favor when Himmler selected as his deputies such strong personalities as Reinhard Heydrich and Ernst Kaltenbrunner, both of whom looked upon the Reichsführer as weak-willed and indecisive. Hitler's *modus operandi* was "Divide and Conquer," both in internal, domestic German politics as well as in external, foreign affairs.

Thus, despite the fact that Himmler was later godfather to the Dietrich offspring, the Reichsführer was the only man Sepp ever really hated in his career.

On September 3, 1933, the three existent SS Sonderkommandos were unified under the single heading of *Adolf Hitler Standarte*. Two months later—on the 10th anniversary of the failed Münich Beer Hall Putsch—the Führer renamed it yet again, calling it the *Leibstandarte (Life Guard) Adolf Hitler*—the LSSAH.

The text of their personal oath of loyalty was:

> "We swear to you, Adolf Hitler, loyalty and bravery. We pledge to you—and to the superiors appointed by you—obedience unto death, so help us God!

To grasp the full significance of these remarkable events, imagine the outcry there would be if either the Prime Minister of the United Kingdom or the President of the United States formed an armed, uniformed personal guard of steel-helmeted troops to patrol the grounds and corridors of Number 10 Downing Street or 1600 Pennsylvania Avenue!

And yet, that is exactly what Hitler did in creating the Leibstandarte to protect his person from intra-Nazi Party rivals, disgruntled German Army generals and foreign assassins alike, as well as to solidify his hold on the German government. As his newly named Nazi Propaganda Minister, Dr. Josef Goebbels, accurately predicted, "No power on Earth will get us out of there (the old Reich Chancellery) alive!"

Sepp also angered Himmler and other Nazi Party stalwarts—particularly SA Chief of Staff Röhm—when he developed close relations with the field gray-clad German Army, which the Brownshirts seemed instead to delight in taunting. Röhm, in fact, made no secret of his ambition to see the SA replace the existent Army as the official bearers of arms of the nation—despite the fact that he—like Hitler, Sepp and Göring—had served with distinction within it.

Röhm felt that a Party Army would, in the end turn out to be more loyal to the Nazi regime (he was proven right, a decade after his death, however) and that he should be the new Minister of Defense in command of that army. Hitler, who feared Röhm's growing personal power within the regime, would never permit that to happen. Nor did he completely disagree with the concept of an entirely Nazi private army (something later achieved in fact by Himmler and even—to a certain extent—by Göring, with his paratroopers and Luftwaffe Air Force Field Divisions), but felt that the time was not yet ripe for such a move. The Party was not yet strong enough within the populace to challenge the Army, and the Army had the guns and the troops with which to overthrow the regime if matters came to that.

Sepp wisely recognized the way the wind was blowing within the old Reich Chancellery, as did Göring, Goebbels, Rudolf Hess, and later Himmler, but not Röhm. Sepp also adopted military terminology in the Leibstandarte. The officers were called offiziere rather than führern, although this did not last very long. Dietrich liked to use Battalion, Kompanie and Zup instead of the Nazi paramilitary Sturmbann, Sturm and Truppe. Himmler tried to get Dietrich to use the latter terms, but without success. On October 1, 1933, he appointed Sepp commander of *SS Group East*, but this rather transparent bribe did nothing to induce the stubborn Sepp to change his mind.

As the first year of Nazi power drew to a close, the Liebstandarte had grown from a mere company to two battalions, each with two line companies of armed infantry as well as support companies of machinegun and transport troops—indeed, the very nucleus of the later Waffen or Armed SS in embryo. The Leibstandarte was beginning to assume ever more openly the status of the regime's "asphalt soldiers," performing changing of the guard ceremonies daily and guarding the Führer everywhere he went, particularly in public at the gigantic Nazi indoor meetings and outdoor rallies. The steel-helmeted, jackbooted troops also formed honor guards for visiting foreign leaders, such as Benito Mussolini of Italy in 1937 and Neville Chamberlain of Great Britain the following year.

The unit's band was established in August 1933 under conductor Hermann Müller-John. The unit's overall force was 835 men, with fully 110 troops deployed on guard duty at Berlin daily. Besides the personal homes of both Himmler and his deputy Reinhard Heydrich, 40 percent of the SSLAH's strength was stationed at Hitler's Berlin Reich Chancellery, while others guarded the Reich Capital's trio of airfields: Staaken, Templehof, and Johannistaal, besides their own Lichterfelde barracks.

It irked Himmler that he was not in command of his own personal security troops.

Again, Hitler evidently *knew* what he was doing in establishing such a relationship with his close confidante Sepp Dietrich in that the arrangement would enable them to arrest both the Reichsführer SS and the later Reichs Protector of Bohemia and Moravia at a moment's notice. Considering Himmler's later plots against Hitler and peace moves in 1945, this seems to have been both a wise and well-justified decision.

In addition to the Reich Chancellery in Berlin, the Brown House in Münich and Hitler's Prinzregentstrasses apartment there, Sepp was also responsible for protecting The *Berghof*—the Führer's high Alpine chalet in the Bavarian Alps overlooking the village of Berchtesgaden and the nearby Austrian border. (This location was considered handy in the Party's pre-1933 days out of power, when a quick getaway from the authorities might prove necessary—it never did, however and Dietrich maintained an SS compound there behind the Führer's residence.

As the Nazi Party solidified itself in power, so, too, did Sepp Dietrich. By now Sepp was not only an elected Reichstag Deputy, but also a member of the Reich State Press Chamber and a judge of the Labor Front's Supreme Disciplinary Court.

With the new posts and added salaries, Sepp's former somewhat Bohemian lifestyle improved as well, with residences still at the Münich Brown House and at Lichterfelde. Sepp also became an award-winning cross-country rally race car driver to boot and, as Messenger notes, "was awarded the SA Sports Badge in gold and likewise the German Reich Sports Badge, also in gold." His main occupation during these prewar years in power, however, was in turning the Leibstandarte into a finely tuned, crackerjack military machine and parade unit—and in this goal he succeeded completely, as even his worldwide enemies still admit to this day.

The original entry standards made the Leibstandarte an all-volunteer outfit, with young men between the ages of 17–22 to start with, a minimum height of between 1.80 and 1.84 m (5 feet 11 inches—6 feet and ½ an inch) and very physically fit as well. Indeed, later Himmler would boast that "until 1936, we did not accept a man in the Leibstandarte if he had one filled tooth!" The men even had to prove Aryan (i.e., non Jewish) ancestry as far back as 1750 for officers and 1800 for enlisted men.

From November 9, 1933, onwards, all members had to be in the SS, but as late as March 1934, there were 181 members out of a total of 968 who were not members of the Nazi Party! All of this was overlooked by both Hitler and Dietrich, though relations between the Army and the SA continued to worsen dramatically, Röhm declared his future intentions openly in speech and print, and the Army Commander, General Werner von Fritsch, and War Minister, Gen. Werner von Blomberg, ordered their men not to cooperate in military training for the still paramilitary—but, increasingly, armed—SA.

The Army feared an SA putsch that might drive Hitler out of office and allow the SA to seize power, while Hitler worried about an Army revolt that would destroy not only Röhm and the SA, but also the rest of the Nazi regime he had worked so hard to build. Göring saw Röhm as his number one rival to make himself second only to the Führer in the regime (he had ambitions to be the next War Minister, too), while Goebbels wanted to be on whichever side won. Hess sided with Hitler unconditionally and the Himmler/Heydrich team saw an opportunity for growth for the SS if Röhm was removed and the SA downgraded.

Thus, as the shadows of 1934 lengthened into mid-year, unwittingly Sepp Dietrich and his Leibstandarte asphalt soldiers would find themselves at center stage for perhaps the single-most controversial aspect of his long career, with the exception of the alleged Malmédy Massacre participation a decade later.

On June 17, 1934, Sepp accompanied Hitler to Italy on Hitler's first trip out of Germany since becoming Chancellor, to meet the man the Führer most admired in the world—Fascist Duce (Leader) Benito Mussolini, who then did not share the fondness. On their return, Blomberg confronted Hitler on June 21st, stating that the Army would declare martial law and act against Röhm unilaterally if Hitler himself did not do so, and soon. As history records, Hitler struck reluctantly, but completely, on June 30,1934, with Sepp Dietrich as one of his lightning rods.

There have come down to us many accounts of what happened after Hitler and Dietrich flew to Münich in the pre-dawn hours of that first fateful day of a murderous weekend in Nazi history that proved to be such a watershed for the regime. Hitler ordered seven men to be shot, but at least 82 were, and possibly many, many more. Several were private scores settled by Göring, Himmler, Heydrich and the others following the initial killing.

Let us briefly examine the available literature on the event.

State James Taylor and Warren Shaw of Dietrich's role in *The Third Reich Almanac*, "With the rank of SS Major General, he was detailed for special execution work, leading a squad in the Röhm Purge." Robert Wistrich asserts in his *Who's Who in Nazi Germany*, "On July 4, 1934, he was given the rank of SS General for his prominent role in the Röhm Purge. As Chief of the Staff Guard, it was Dietrich who led the assassination squad which murdered Ernst Röhm and other SA leaders, some of whom were formerly personal comrades."

In his *Encyclopedia of the Third Reich*, author Louis L. Snyder asserts:

He [Dietrich] took an important part in the Blood Purge of 1934. At that time, Hitler drew up a list of conspirators and dispatched Dietrich to the Ministry of Justice in Berlin to shoot the traitors. 'Go back to the barracks,' Hitler ordered, 'select an officer and six men and have the SA leaders shot for high treason!' Dietrich complied. The doomed men protested. One cried out, 'Sepp, my friend! What is happening? We are completely innocent!'

Dietrich replied, 'You have been condemned to death by the Führer! Heil Hitler!' The men were executed on the spot. The incident illustrated Dietrich's philosophy of life: 'Human life matters little to the SS!' He regarded it as his overwhelming duty to protect the person of Adolf Hitler.

Writer Glenn L. Infield gives this version of events in his book *Secrets of the SS*:

Supported by SS members of Sepp Dietrich's Leibstandarte SS Adolf Hitler, the Führer arrived at the hotel in Bad Wiesee and personally directed the arrest of his old friend Röhm. The only concession Hitler made was to order Röhm taken to Stadelheim Prison in Münich unharmed; most of Röhm's associates who were at Bad Wiesee were executed on the spot.

For two days, Hitler fluctuated between exiling his old friend or executing him. Finally, he decided that Röhm—if permitted to live—would never change his ways … Nor would the generals ever accept the SA commander in their ranks—and Hitler needed the generals on his side. Himmler, of course, favored killing his rival, despite the fact that they had once been close companions.

On July 2nd, Hitler gave Sepp Dietrich the order to execute Röhm. The Führer made one concession to his old friend—he gave him the chance to die the "honorable" way. He ordered a pistol put in Röhm's cell and the SA commander left alone for 10 minutes with SS Brigadeführer Theodor Eicke administering the *coup de grace* with a bullet in the head.

The Röhm Purge set the stage for SS ascendancy … The story of the SS was written in blood from the day of the Röhm Purge.

In *Hitler's Secret Life: The Mysteries of the Eagle's Nest*, Infield enhanced this account:

On June 30, 1934, Hitler arrived at the Münich-Oberwiesenfeld airfield shortly after 4 a.m., stepped into his armored car, and with an escort of six trucks headed for Wiesee, where Röhm was vacationing. Röhm was sound asleep in the Pension Hanslbauer when Hitler arrived to confront him. For once, he was alone in bed.

Hitler screamed accusations at him, accusing the half-asleep Röhm of plotting to overthrow the NSDAP (Nazi) regime, then ordered him taken to Stadelheim Prison in Münich. In what he considered a heroic gesture, Hitler ordered that Röhm be given a gun so he could die a "good soldier." Röhm spat on the gun. "If Adolf wants me dead, let him do it!" Sepp Dietrich, leader of the SS Obergruppe Ost, did it.

Author Nikolai Tolstoy, in his book *Night of the Long Knives*—as the purge subsequently became known—states that Dietrich:

… played his part in blackening Röhm and the SA to Hitler. … On July 2nd, two SS guards acting on Sepp Dietrich's orders, entered Röhm's cell. Stripped to the waist, he rose as if to say something, but his words were silenced by a noise familiar to him all his life—the crack of pistol shots. An expression of gross contempt on his face, he slumped dead to the ground.

French author Max Gallo gives a much more detailed rendering of this incident in his 1972 work *The Night of the Long Knives*—so far, overall, the best full treatment in its entirety:

Eicke chooses two absolutely reliable SS: Sturmbanführer Michael Lippert and Gruppenführer Schmauser. The three men check their weapons and head to the Stadelheim Prison … At 2:30 p.m., Eicke, Lippert and Schmauser arrive … A prison guard is ordered to take the three SS officers to Röhm's cell—Number 474. Röhm, still naked to the waist, has apparently lost his will. He watches Eicke come in, watches him put a copy of the *People's Observer* on the table. It reports the dismissal of Röhm and lists the names of the executed SA leaders. Eicke also places a revolver on the table, loaded with a single bullet. Then he leaves …

What Röhm had seen was more than a tragic vision or nightmare. He remains sitting in his cell: he has not moved. After 10 minutes, SS Lippert and Eicke open the door. "Röhm, make yourself ready!" Eicke shouts. Lippert, his hand trembling, fires twice. Röhm still has time to murmur, "Mein Führer, mein Führer," before a third bullet kills him.

From the accounts given thus far, therefore, the actual role of Sepp Dietrich himself seems clouded with contradictory testimony, as, indeed, was much of his entire career.

Stadelheim Prison was under the jurisdiction of Bavarian Nazi Justice Minister Dr. Hans Frank, who initially would permit no executions without a legal warrant in hand. This was overuled later by Hitler on the authority of Reich President von Hindenburg, and thus the killing commenced. Sepp later testified at his 1957 Münich trial that he left after the fourth or fifth shot, the slain SA leaders being friends of his.

The Berlin massacre was ordered by the troika of Göring, Himmler, and Heydrich, and carried out by the SSLAH at Lichterfelde commanded by SturmbannFührer Martin Kohlroser. In 1943, Eicke was killed by Red Army fire in Russia, while Lippert stood trial with Sepp in 1957.

Hitler astounded the newly promoted SS Obergruppenführer Dietrich with the assertive question, "Do you know *you* were also on the list?"—apparently put there by his enemy, Himmler. Charles Messenger also asserts that everyone remotely connected with the shootings was sworn to an oath of secrecy, one that was maintained, moreover, until the Dietrich–Lippert trial 23 years later.

Out of the events of that single weekend, the real bedrock of future SS power was established. The SS itself was removed from under SA control and made directly responsible to Hitler, as Sepp had always been. The SA was defanged and sunk to the level of being merely the Army's future manpower pool rather than the other way around, which had been the late Ernst Röhm's intention. The 25 SS men promoted by Hitler also received ceremonial daggers to mark the historic nature of the occasion, but Dietrich, believes Charles Messenger, "remained shocked over what had happened for several days."

Ernst "Putzi" Hanfstaengl, like Sepp a Bavarian and an early intimate of Hitler (Hanfstaengl left Nazi Germany for American exile in 1937 when his own life was threatened), later recalled that:

> Dietrich as good as admitted that he had been at Wiesee with Hitler, but he was not talking. I really think that even he was shattered by what he had taken part in. "You have no idea," he muttered. "Thank your lucky stars that you were not around! I got my orders signed, but I had to practically force him (Hitler) to put his signature on them."

Fast forward now to the 1957 trial, when Dietrich was charged by the West German government with manslaughter for the deaths of the six SA men, and Lippert with the same charge for the murder of Röhm, since both were acting under "orders" from higher authority. The trial began on May 6th. Dietrich shouldered his own responsibility, while Lippert claimed he remained outside the death cell while only the conveniently-dead Eicke went inside to shoot down Röhm. Eight days later, both men were found guilty, and sentenced to 18 months in prison. Dietrich began serving his sentence on Aug. 7, 1958, at Landsberg Prison, where he had been imprisoned earlier by the Allies after the war crimes conviction, and where—in 1923–24—Hitler and Hess had co-authored *Mein Kampf.*

Because of the onset of a severe heart condition, Dietrich was released once more, on February 2, 1959, but all that was decades in the future when—in the immediate aftermath of June 30, 1934—the German Army agreed "to provide a division's worth of arms and military equipment for the SS. Out of this would arise the Waffen SS." Thus—irony of ironies!—Röhm was barely dead when Himmler and the SS were on the way to recognizing one of the SA's most cherished ambitions!

In September 1934, there was made the official announcement of the formation of the armed *SS-Verfügungstruppe (SS Special Purpose Troops)* or *SS-VT* for short and two units were located, one in Hamburg and the other in München. Simultaneously Himmler reorganized all the concentration camp SS guards into the SS Totenkopfverbande (SS Death's Head Units) under none other than Theodor Eicke. These three units, including Heydrich's SD, were now placed under the general heading of the Allgemeine—or General—SS.

At this point, Himmler tried again to bring the still-independent SA within the purview of his SS-VT, but Hitler, to Dietrich's delight, again vetoed the idea. Brought in to administer the SS-VT were three men who—alongside Sepp—would later write the combat historical record of the Waffen SS across the length and breadth of conquered Europe—Paul Hausser, Felix Steiner and Willi Bittrich. All three men would become high-ranking SS generals in the wartime years to come.

Meanwhile, back at the Reich Chancellery, Sepp's boys were getting restless, as there was really nothing of interest for them to do, so they resorted to loud radio playing, pranks, and riding up and down in the Reich Chancellery elevators.

Nevertheless, as before when the Führer for years overlooked the rampant homosexuality within the ranks of the SA, so now, too, did he cast a blind eye toward these harmless pranks as he led his famed asphalt soldiers into the newly acquired Saar region. This was the first of his bloodless acquisitions in 1935.

At the head of almost 1,600 men (including a motorcycle detachment), Dietrich led the way into the delirious Saarland, and paraded his Leibstandarte there for the next five days. Hitler granted his beloved LSSAH several distinctions at this time: "Only the Leibstandarte was allowed to wear white accoutrements with its black uniform and bear the SS runes on the collar tab without a unit number. According to his eldest son, Dietrich personally designed the Leibstandarte's uniform."

Dietrich was enormously popular with his men, even after his death.

Everything was not as well in Sepp's personal life. He was experiencing problems with his wife of 14 years, Betti Dietrich, partly because she couldn't have children and also due to Sepp's wandering eye for other women. He met and fell in love with the 22-year-old daughter of a friend, Ursula Moniger, but Betti Dietrich refused to grant Sepp a divorce. The latter couple had their first son, Wolf Dieter, out of wedlock in 1939, but were unable to be married until January, 1942. Her parents never held this against Sepp apparently, but it is somewhat surprising that Hitler—a notorious prude—even though he maintained a mistress for 13 years before marrying her—allowed Sepp to go on in this way, since he had acted so strongly to keep the Goebbels' marriage together when it was about to break apart due to the mutual affairs of both Josef and Magda. For his part, Himmler could say little, since he maintained a wife *and* a mistress until his suicide in May 1945.

Once again, though, Hitler let his faithful Sepp slide, as he needed him to command his asphalt soldiers in the conquest of one European country after another in the coming years.

By now, however—in February 1936—Sepp and the Leibstandarte were sharing the overall responsibility for the Führer's security with Rattenhuber of Heydrich's SD, an arrangement that proved harmonious when introduced at the 1936 Winter Olympic Games held at Garmisch-Partenkirchen.

As a formal member of the Führer's inner circle and personal staff, Dietrich had authority over both his chauffeur Julius Schreck (and, after his death in an auto accident in May 1936, Erich Kempka, until the end of the war nine years later), as well as over his personal pilot from 1932–45, Col. Hans Baur.

As the showpiece unit of the Nazi regime, the Leibstandarte was gaining worldwide fame as an élite unit—on par with the French Foreign Legion in France, the Coldstream Guards in England, the United States Marines in America and the Bersaglieri in Italy.

The Nuremberg Rallies held in September each year during the 1930s also entailed a large Leibstandarte commitment, as did the commemoration of the 1923 Putsch in München. There is no doubt that the Leibstandarte by now had gained a reputation second to none for the standard of its drill and turnout.

By the end of 1936, the LSSAH possessed both trench mortars and armored cars, and Dietrich met Col. Erwin Rommel—author of the book *Infantry Attacks*—when the latter came to lecture the officers of the Leibstandarte in November 1937.

Relations between the Army, the LSSAH and the SS-VT remained good throughout this period, even though it always rankled the former that Hitler insisted on being guarded by the LSSAH alone—even when on maneuvers reviewing his own Army. He would never trust the Army again since it had forced him to suppress his SA, and the Führer one day would exact a terrible revenge. These events were far in the distance, however, as the Führer prepared to lead his armed forces into the Second World War.

Chapter Three

From Leibstandarte to Waffen SS
The Death's Head Legions at War

By May, 1938, SS Generals Josef "Sepp" Dietrich and Paul Hausser were feuding over the formation of the fourth SS-VT Standarte in newly Nazi-occupied Vienna, named *Der Führer*. With the backing of Dietrich's nominal boss, SS Reichsführer Heinrich Himmler, the former retired German Army officer was demanding that the obstinate Sepp supply a cadre for the new unit from the élite Leibstandarte Adolf Hitler, which the latter refused to do. He was backed in this decision by his longtime patron and protector, Hitler himself, and so Himmler once more had to eat humble pie at Sepp's hands, while Hausser was refused the right to even inspect the LSSAH without the Reichsführer present.

Continuing his build-up of close ties with the regular, establishment German Army, Sepp also developed a harmonious relationship with Nazi Germany's future panzer wizard, Gen. Heinz Guderian. Earlier in the year Guderian had been the one detailed to tell Dietrich that the LSSAH would participate in the peaceful invasion of Hitler's homeland—Austria—within 48 hours!

Guderian recommended that the SS vehicles should enter what became known in Nazi lingo as the Ostmark bedecked with both flowers and greenery, to show that the Nazis indeed came in peace.

The Leibstandarte duly crossed over into Austria at 2 p.m. on March 12, 1938, headed for Linz, Hitler's boyhood home, and then to the old Austro-Hungarian Empire capital of Vienna. There it held back the throngs of cheering Viennese who hailed Hitler's arrival and then paraded in front of the man who had left the city down and out before the First World War.

Back in the now-expanded Third Reich, the Führer planned his next move—*Operation Green*—the proposed German invasion of Czechoslovakia, again pairing the successful Guderian–Dietrich team. Since the Austrian venture, Dietrich's troops in the campaign wore the new *feldgrau* (field gray) combat uniforms copied from the Army, only with SS runes and other markings. At the end of September 1938, the LSSAH went for a training exercise at Grafenwöhr. Their absence from the capital played a key part in persuading the gathering anti-Nazi movement of Army officers, clerics, labor leaders, conservatives and others to prepare to mount a putsch to overthrow the Nazi regime if war with the West looked imminent—much as Hitler feared would happen when he struck first against the SA dissidents in June 1934.

The Münich Conference took place instead; with war averted, Hitler had been given the German-speaking Czech Sudetenland for free and the conspirators scattered.

Six months later—during a blinding snowstorm—the Leibstandarte took part in the Führer's occupation of the rest of Czechoslovakia with Gen. Erwin Rommel in charge of security once the drive on Prague began. It was a process to be repeated again in September 1939, as the asphalt soldiers got their first taste of a shooting war in Poland.

Parade ground troops, SA murderers and occupiers of peaceful countries though they might be, how would the LSSAH do in actual combat, wondered military analysts the world over. In Poland, as in the previous operations, Sepp's men were placed once more under Army command, and now the former NCO of the First World War began the Second as a commanding general in the field.

Willi Bittrich was assigned to Sepp to help initiate him into modern warfare; previous to this, Dietrich had motorized war classes in 1936 at the Army command HQ at Zossen outside Berlin and a panzer course two years later at the Windsdorf Tank School. Still—as he related after the war—Bittrich quickly grew exasperated with him: "I once spent an hour and a half trying to explain a situation to Sepp Dietrich with the aid of a map. It was quite useless—he understood nothing at all!" was his lament.

Nevertheless, the LSSAH performed quite well during *Case White*, Hitler's code-name for the conquest of Poland, although their natural elan and zeal for combat made their casualties somewhat higher than they might otherwise have been. In the early days of the invasion, the SS troopers fought stiff Polish Regular Army resistance over a number of towns and villages. In one battle, Sepp's own forward command post was almost cut off, but, reinforced, he went on to win the day. By September 9th, his unit had been transferred to be in on the German drive on the Polish capital of Warsaw.

Already, the LSSAH was gaining a reputation for burning enemy villages and, during the remaining battles, for being trigger-happy, wiping out the Polish forces on the Vistula and around the city of Modlin. Dietrich himself was at Guzów, where Hitler arrived to review his Leibstandarte on September 25th. By the time Warsaw fell two days later, the LSSAH had lost 108 killed, 292 wounded, fourteen lightly wounded, three missing in action and fifteen accidental deaths, states Charles Messenger. There were also other rumblings, as German diplomat of the old school Ulrich von Hassell noted in his diary entry for October 19th: "I hear that Blaskowitz, as commander of an army, wanted to prosecute two SS leaders—including rowdy Sepp Dietrich—for looting and murder." Meanwhile, in the rear areas, Eicke's Death's Head units were shooting Polish intellectuals and Jews.

Nothing came of it, however, and Sepp and the LSSAH returned to the Reich after a period of occupation duty in the new Reich Protectorate of Bohemia and Moravia—the old, dismembered Czechoslovakia. For seven years Czechoslovakia remained a virtually SS-run state, particularly after 1941 under Reinhard Heydrich and his successor, SS Police Gen. Kurt Daluege. Then it was back to Germany, where the strange events of the Münich Beer Hall blast of November 9, 1939, occurred, in which Himmler's actual role is still obscure to this day.

Dietrich had been in the hall with Hitler when the Führer unexpectedly cut short his normally lengthy speech and left, Sepp in tow. A few minutes later, a bomb exploded very near the speaker's platform. It would surely have killed Hitler had he remained. A Communist—Georg Elser—was arrested, but he was not executed until 1945, fueling rumors over the years that Himmler and Heydrich had put him up to it, then protected him when the plot misfired. Was this an SS plot to remove Hitler and thus avert a war with the West that both Hermann Göring and the Army generals feared Nazi Germany could not win? We may never know for sure.

Nevertheless, Himmler's ambitions for his own, private Nazi army—separate and apart from the Wehrmacht—took another leap forward when, in March 1940, on the eve of the great Western Offensive, Hitler ordered that the SS-VT be renamed the Waffen (Armed) SS. As for the LSSAH, it was upgraded to regimental status as a fully motorized infantry unit, complete with an infantry gun company and an assault gun battery.

The LSSAH took no part in either the Danish or Norwegian campaigns of April, but instead were held for the invasions of Holland and France the following month. In Holland, Sepp's men crossed rivers and seized important bridges—not all of them intact, though—and almost killed Luftwaffe paratroop Gen. Kurt Student by accidental fire while he was busy negotiating a ceasefire with the Dutch Army in Rotterdam.

Student recovered enough to lead the first and only German mass paradrop of the war at the Battle of Crete (while the LSSAH was in Greece) and—like Sepp—later in the war commanded an army. He died in 1978.

Before he did so, however, Student issued a statement that "he never suggested by a single word that he was hit by a shot from members of the Waffen SS." Messenger feels, after thorough research, however that Dietrich's men were, indeed, the accidental culprits. Ironically, had they succeeded in killing Student, the Battle of Crete would probably not have happened, as Student was the operation's creator, father and executor from start to finish, and after it Hitler forbade such a repetition.

In Holland, Dietrich found himself first under the orders of Gen. Hausser, then transferred to France under Guderian once again, a situation more to his liking, no doubt. By the time of his 48th birthday on May 28th, Sepp and his Leibstandarte were engaged in attacking the retreating British Expeditionary Force trapped on the beaches at Dunkirk.

During one ambush, Dietrich and Max Wünsche found themselves diving through a large drainage pipe under heavy enemy small arms fire before arriving at Guderian's headquarters. The latter later wrote that Sepp "soon appeared … covered from head to foot in mud, and had to accept some very ribald comments on our part!"

For their part, the British were astounded by the frontal attack of the LSSAH on their defenses: "The infantry attacked in large numbers and—in some cases—shoulder to shoulder! In the rear, they were urged on by cries of 'Heil Hitler!' Large numbers were undoubtedly mown down by our fire." Later, Dietrich himself entertained some captured British officers (as did Rommel, in North Africa), but here the first SS atrocities against prisoners of war were reported.

Between 80–90 British soldiers were killed by the SS men in a barn:

> They were double-marched to the barn, and thrust at with bayonets on the way. Wounded and unwounded alike were then herded into the barn. Capt. Lynn-Allen immediately protested. He was answered with taunts, and several hand grenades were thrown among the crowded troops, killing and wounding many of them. Survivors were taken outside to be shot, in batches of five. After this had happened twice, those left behind refused to come out: whereupon the Germans fired indiscriminately into the barn until they judged that none were left alive. They judged wrongly, a few men *did* survive.

These survivors were unwittingly exchanged back to Britain in October, 1943, to tell their tale.

Meanwhile, also in the 1940 campaign, 98 out of 100 captured British Royal Norfolk Regiment troops were gunned down by men of the *Totenkopf* at the French village of Le Paradis. Both atrocities resulted in postwar trials. While the British were allowed to escape across the Channel, Sepp's men eventually reached the celebrated body of water and took a symbolic swim. That was the closest they ever got to conquering England.

Adopted as the unit's logo for display on all vehicles was a white skeleton key, translated as *Dietrich* in German!

As post-battle reports came into his headquarters, Sepp determined that he had lost 111 killed and another 390 wounded during the 1940 campaign. Sepp rated his opponents thus:

The British were a formidable enemy, and superior in their equipment. They were variable. Often they fought very courageously, while at other times they hardly resisted at all! Their equipment— compared with that of the German Army—was satisfactory. The German troops made good use of the battle experience gained in the Polish campaign, and the supply system of the German Army was satisfactory everywhere.

In his 1983 book *Die Leibstandarte im Bild* (*The Lifeguards in Pictures*) former SS veteran/author Rudolf Lehmann shows a photo of Dietrich speaking in full uniform with the caption, "At the regimental battle HQ, the commander declares the campaign is finished and honors the memory of the soldiers of both sides who were killed."

Sepp also issued this Order of the Day to his truppen:

I, as your Regimental Commander, am proud of you and grateful that I have been allowed to lead this Regiment, the only one in the German Army with the Führer's name!

Hitler, too, was pleased at how his asphalt soldiers had made war thus far, and added to Dietrich's twin Iron Crosses won in Poland the coveted Ritterkreuz (Knight's Cross) of the Eisernekreuz on July 4, 1940. The official citation read:

Obergruppenführer Sepp Dietrich, through independent resolve in his sector during the gaining of the bridgehead over the Aa Canal near Watten decisively influenced the speedy pursuit of operations in Northern France and further—as before, in Poland—has demonstrated special personal bravery and close comradeliness with panzer and motorized formation headquarters.

The Leibstandarte proceeded to Paris, although it did not parade in the French capital, as did the German Army. After a time of renewed occupation duty at Metz, the LSSAH spent the summer months of 1940 preparing for *Operation Sea Lion*—the projected cross-Channel invasion of England that never materialized.

At both Christmas 1939 and 1940, the LSSAH had been honored by having their Führer as a special dinner guest, and in the spring of 1941—even as the planning for the coming merciless campaign against the Soviet Union was moving ahead full-steam—he called upon them once again. He commanded them to take part in the German blitzkrieg in the Balkans under the command of Army Field Marshal Sigmund List in *Operation Marita*.

Advancing rapidly into Greece, the SS men met house-to-house resistance in the village of Bitola, then headed on to face the British at the entrance to Klidi Pass, at Vevi. In three days of very heavy fighting, the LSSAH lost 37 killed, 98 wounded and two missing. But they had captured 450 prisoners and a number of weapons, including 8 light tanks.

Meanwhile, at Klissura Pass, SS Sturmbannführer Kurt Meyer found the path of his men blocked by stubborn members of the Greek 20th Division using machineguns. Wrote Meyer later:

In my distress, I feel the smooth roundness of an egg hand grenade in my hand. I shout at the group. Everybody looks thunderstruck at me as I brandish the hand grenade, pull the pin and roll it precisely behind the last man. Never again did I witness such a concerted leap forward as at that moment! As if bitten by tarantulas, we dive around the rock spur and into a fresh crater. The spell is broken. The hand grenade has cured our lameness. We grin at each other, and head forward toward the next cover.

That afternoon the Pass was taken with 600 Greek prisoners to boot, for only 9 dead and 18 wounded. At Kastoria, Meyer later took another 1,200 POWs and 36 guns, thus routing the Greek forces into the Pindus Mountains. By April 20th—the Führer's 52nd birthday—Sepp's men were blocking the Greek retreat through Katarra Pass, and it was now that one of the pinnacles of his military career was reached. Sepp received a message from there stating:

> Greek delegate offers surrender of whole Greek Army, General Tsolakoglou … holds the Delegation, keeps the Army under surveillance and requests Commander send back instructions.

Without waiting for word from Field Marshal List, Sepp sent this terse message: "Commander on the march and underway." He accepted on behalf of Nazi Germany and Fascist Italy the surrender of fully sixteen Greek Army divisions.

Sepp's spectacular foray into the hitherto-unknown (for him) realm of international diplomacy got Hitler into hot water with Southern Axis Pact partner, Benito Mussolini, on whose behalf the German-Greek campaign had been fought in the first place. Mussolini demanded—and got—a separate, harsher surrender of the Greeks to the Italians, but to the disgust of Sepp Dietrich, who even sent LSSAH troops to the Albanian border to keep the Italians from negating the deal he had so quickly cut with the valiant Greeks.

Back in Germany, Sepp received a mild but firm dressing-down from a miffed Adolf Hitler: "You are a good, brave soldier, but no diplomat—and still less a politician! You forgot that we still have a friend called Mussolini!" (Mussolini had joined the war on the side of the Axis the previous year.)

But before this, Dietrich's men had pushed on to the Corinth Canal to try to prevent the British from escaping from Greece in a "second Dunkirk." Despite the efforts of Kurt Meyer and others to cut them off (including a seized fishing boat expedition to capture the Greek port of Patras), the British once more made good their exit by the Royal Navy under fire.

One of those captured—Sir George Kennard—gave the LSSAH this tribute: "Over the entire fighting, they had been brave, chivalrous and—toward the end—they would go out of their way, at considerable risk to themselves, to take prisoners rather than take lives." Perhaps the SS had been stung by the 1940 record in France in this regard.

For this superb performance under fire, Sepp Dietrich received plaudits from many sides. SS Gen. Kurt Daluege, commander of the German Police under Himmler, mentioned "The great joy here in Berlin once again at what one, an Old Fighter [from the Party], is able to perform without staff training." German Army Field Marshal Wilhelm Keitel enthused about how "Sepp Dietrich roared through them with his division!" His loyal aide Max Wünsche stated:

> If our men had not been motivated, and if Sepp Dietrich had not been at the right places at the right times during the decisive phases, with his orders and decisions, the campaign would've gone a different way.

And so, in a truly Herculean effort, Sepp Dietrich had managed to plant the Nazi swastika on the heights of the fabled Greek Mount Olympus, then paraded his unit past Field Marshal List in

Athens on May 3, 1941. Awards and promotions were now showered down upon the officers and men of the LSSAH.

States Charles Messenger: "The campaign in Yugoslavia and Greece was the maturing of the Leibstandarte. There was undoubtedly delight among circles closest to Hitler at its performance" no matter what the Führer might tell Sepp *vis-à-vis* the angry Duce. When, once again, the unit was transferred back to the Czech Protectorate on May 8th, it was for rest, refitting and relaxation. The next day the unit received a visit from a glowing Reichsführer SS Heinrich Himmler, as noted by the unit historian, Rudolf Lehmann, in his 1987 work, *The Leibstandarte 1 SS Panzer Division*:

> He issued several promotions, and it was probably at this time that the Standarte received permission to call itself "SS Division LSSAH." The first letterhead bearing this designation which has been found is dated May 15, 1941.

Adds LTC John R. Angolia in his excellent work, *On the Field of Honor: A History of the Knight's Cross Bearers* volume 1: "SS Obergruppenführer Dietrich became the 41st recipient of the Oak Leaves for his actions in the Balkans campaigns. The award was rendered December 31, 1941." By that date, however, the LSSAH was already heavily committed in the Russian campaign that had opened with a bang on June 22nd.

In their book *The Third Reich Almanac*, authors, James Taylor and Warren Shaw assert:

> The Waffen SS were not taken very seriously as a fighting force at this time, but in the bitter battles of the Eastern Front, the SS rapidly dissolved the disdain of the establishment generals. For this change of attitude to the Waffen SS, Dietrich could claim a large part of the credit.
>
> After the Leibstandarte was decimated in the battles of 1942, it was refitted and returned to the front at the beginning of the following year, fighting most effectively on the Donetz, and at Kharkov.

Adds Angolia:

> Sepp Dietrich and his men fought long, hard and often with great casualties during their fight on the Eastern Front until they were transferred once again to France.

In his 1970 Memoirs: *Inside the Third Reich*, Albert Speer recalled the difficulties of psyche the SS combat troops had to face in Russia in this vivid passage:

> Sepp Dietrich, one of Hitler's earliest followers and now the commander of an SS tank corps hard-pressed by the Russians near Rostov in the Southern Ukraine, was flying to Dnepropetrovsk on January 30, 1942, in a plane of the Führer's air squadron.
>
> I asked him to take me along. My staff was already in the city, organizing the task of repairing the railroads in southern Russia … Huddled close together, we sat in a Heinkel bomber refitted as a passenger plane. Beneath us the dreary, snow-covered plains of Southern Russia flowed by. On large farms we saw the burned sheds and barns. To keep our direction, we flew along the railroad line. Scarcely a train could be seen; the stations were burned out, the roundhouses destroyed. Roads were rare, and they, too, were empty of vehicles.
>
> The great stretches of land we passed over were frightening in their deathly silence, which could be felt even inside the plane. Only gusts of snow broke the monotony of the landscape—or, rather,

emphasized it. This flight brought home to me the danger to the armies almost cut off from supplies … it snowed and snowed. Railroad and highway traffic had come to a total standstill.

Indeed, as Messenger points out, Hitler had prepared for the Leibstandarte "a test on an altogether different scale than the blitzkrieg campaigns of the past 20 months" prior to crossing the long frontier of the USSR on that fateful morning of June 22, 1941.

This new campaign—called *Barbarossa*—was set to be another such lightning strike designed to knock Russia out of the war by autumn, much as had Sepp's first campaign under the Kaiser in France a generation previously, and—like that occasion, too—now the quick war dragged out to a length of four years. When it was over, Germany would be overrun, Hitler and Himmler dead, the SS defeated, disgraced and disbanded, the Nazi regime obliterated and a dismayed Sepp Dietrich in prison awaiting the trial of his life.

None of that was foreseen, however, as "the Commander" gaily led his men across the broad Russian plains in the initial heady days of conquest of the Nazi crusade against the Bolshevik Soviet Union. In this campaign, Dietrich came for the first time under the command of the most venerated Field Marshal in the Wehrmacht, Gerd von Rundstedt, who—with Army Group South—was charged with invading the Soviet bread basket/grain basin in the Ukraine, taking Kiev and shoving on towards the Donetz Basin. Despite massive surrenders by the Russians and great victories at the outset of the campaign, Sepp's men learned at length to respect their Slavic foe—whom Nazi racial ideology had taught them to hate and view only with disdain as subhuman trash not worthy of an SS man's attention. The Leibstandarte advanced first on Uman and then to Archangelsk, where—after a week's bitter fighting—it helped take 100,000 prisoners, an unheard-of number. Still, after its first three weeks in combat, the SS was moved to the realization that, for them, this was a new type of war.

In the West, when enemy troops were surrounded, they generally surrendered, but here, in the East, the Russians many times either fought to the last man or broke out of the pocket to fight another day. Moreover, the LSSAH soon suffered 683 killed and wounded and over 100 vehicles destroyed, leading one SS man to wonder aloud in a daze that the Russians "are the best fighters we have ever met!"

At Rostov an LSSAH man would write home later:

It is not possible in words to describe winter on this front! There is no main battle line, no outposts, no reserves—just small groups of us depending on each other to hold defended points … We are here in the sunny south, how frightful it must be for the comrades up north! Here, life is paralysed … you would never believe the lavatory procedures … and the food … We live on a sort of thick soup made of ground buckwheat and millet. We have to strip the fallen—theirs and ours!—for warm clothing. I don't think I will ever be warm again, and our tame Ivans say that this is a mild winter! God help us!

In a talk given in 1982 and released in booklet form as *Epic: The Story of the Waffen SS*, the Belgian Rexist volunteer Leon Degrelle leaves a vivid picture of this period as well:

If Hitler had been able to start the campaign in time, as it was planned, he would've entered Moscow five weeks before, in the sun of early fall, when the earth was still dry. The war would've been over, and the Soviet Union would've been a thing of the past. The combination of the sudden freeze and the arrival of fresh Siberian troops spread panic among some of the old Army generals. They wanted to retreat to 200 miles from Moscow. It is hard to imagine such insane strategy!

The freeze affected Russia equally, from West to East, and to retreat 200 miles in the open steppes would only make things worse. I was commanding my troops in the Ukraine at the time, and it was 42 degrees centigrade below zero! Such a retreat meant abandoning all the heavy artillery, including assault tanks and panzers that were stuck in the ice. It also meant exposing half a million men to heavy Soviet sniping … Can you just imagine in 1941 half a million Germans fighting howling snowstorms, cut off from supplies, attacked from all sides by tens of thousands of Cossacks? I have faced charging Cossacks, and only the utmost superior firepower will stop them. In order to counter such an insane retreat, Hitler had to fire more than 30 generals within a few days.

It was then that he called on the Waffen SS to fill in the gap and boost morale. Immediately, the SS held fast on the Moscow front. Right through the war, the Waffen SS never retreated. They would rather die than retreat.

At least some of the above is vintage Nazi wartime propaganda and needs qualification, particularly from a man who Hitler said would be the kind of man he would want for a son. First, even if the Nazis had succeeded in taking Moscow in late 1941, the war would have gone on—even from behind the Ural Mountains in far-off Soviet Asia, if necessary—just as Tsar Alexander I had continued to resist Napoleon after the French had taken the capital in 1812. To believe that the war would have ended with the fall of the Soviet capital in 1941 is just wishful thinking on the part of the Nazis and their apologists, even now.

Second, if the Waffen SS did not retreat, how did at least some of them survive the war? Not all of them, surely, were ordered back to the Western Front, as was the Leibstandarte on at least two occasions.

Third, to be fair to the Germans—and to discount Russian testimony that the 1941–42 winter was a "mild" one—I quote an impartial source, author Alan Clark, who noted in his superb 1965 study, *Barbarossa: The Russian-German Conflict, 1941-1945* that it was "the worst winter for 140 years." I believe him.

Prior to unleashing his legions on the Soviet Union, Hitler had called his generals to the Berghof to lecture them on how he wanted the war on the Eastern Front to be fought mercilessly, with no remorse and no pity. The Russians were subhumans, fit only for destruction. Red Army Commissars were to be shot on sight.

There is no doubt that the SS Einsatzgruppen murdered hundreds of thousands of Jews and others behind the lines in mass, open-air executions. This brutality often extended to the fighting soldiers at the Front, as well as to the conduct of the harsh anti-partisan operations to the rear.

It has since been acknowledged that German Army troops also committed atrocities previously always attributed to the SS alone.

Messenger discounts the many rumors of Sepp Dietrich ordering reprisal executions of captured Russians—"We owe it to the title on our sleeve," he said. And I leave this open to the readers' own judgment. By October 16, 1941, Sepp's land-based artillery was shelling Soviet gunboats on the Don River and had captured the city of Taganrog. It was here that the asphalt soldiers felt their first taste of the coming Russian winter, with even Sepp suffering first and second degree frostbite to the toes of his right foot. Von Rundstedt then ordered the first German retreat of the war from Rostov (for which an angry Hitler fired him for the first of many times in the war). By Christmas, the Leibstandarte occupied its first defensive positions east of Taganrog on the Sea of Azov, staying there until June, 1942.

Incensed, Hitler himself flew to Mariupol to talk with Sepp, and the latter not only defended Von Rundstedt and the other Army generals, but claimed that he had initiated the Rostov retreat. By now, even the formerly doubtful German Army generals were singing the praises of their comrades-in-arms the LSSAH, as Gen. Eberhard von Mackensen—son of the famed Field Marshal Hussar of the First World War—wrote to Himmler on December 26, 1941.

> I can assure you that the Leibstandarte enjoys an outstanding reputation … Every division wishes it had the Leibstandarte as its neighbor, as much during the attack as in defense. Its inner discipline, its cool dare-deviltry, its cheerful enterprise, its unshakable firmness in a crisis (even when things become difficult or serious), its exemplary toughness, its camaraderie (which deserves special praise)—all these are outstanding, and cannot be surpassed. In spite of this, the officer corps maintains a pleasant degree of modesty. A genuine élite formation that I am happy and proud to have under my command and, furthermore, one that I sincerely and hopefully wish to retain.

It was a view that, in general, was maintained by the Army throughout the remainder of the war. On New Year's Eve, Sepp flew to Hitler's principal wartime military headquarters—the Wolfsschanze at Rastenburg in East Prussia—to receive from Hitler's own hands his Ritterkreuz Oak Leaves. He then spent the month of January 1942, in Berlin, being honored and feted everywhere, staying at the New Reich Chancellery.
Hitler exulted:

> "What care he takes of his troops! He's a phenomenon in the class of people like Frundsberg, Zeithen and Seydlitz [all famous Prussian generals under Frederick the Great]."

Goebbels now made sure that "the Party's general" was brought front and center in the Nazi media to help downplay the terrific losses on the Eastern Front in the popular mind, and long feature articles about Sepp appeared in both the *People's Observer* and the house organ of the SS itself, *The Black Corps*. At his annual birthday celebrations on January 12, 1942, Göring introduced Sepp to his guests as "The pillar of the Eastern Front!" Dr. Goebbels added of the SS:

> For them difficulties exist only to be overcome. Sepp Dietrich is a real comrade, and makes one think of a Napoleonic general. If we had 20 men like that as divisional commanders, we wouldn't have to worry at all about the Eastern Front! He told me in great detail how the bourgeois generals on the Southern Front lost their nerve, and how this weakness of character naturally communicated itself to the troops.

His old friend Guderian had been fired by Hitler, and it is to Sepp's credit that—in this dark time of career disgrace for the "panzer general"—he took the time to call from the Reich Chancellery to console him. "Indeed, Dietrich was one of his few visitors at this time."

January was also an important month for Dietrich's personal life. On the 19th he married his second and final wife, Ursula, a happy union that lasted the rest of his life, in good times and bad, for 24 years.

On the 30th—the ninth anniversary of the Nazis coming to power in 1933—Josef "Sepp" Dietrich returned with Albert Speer to the embattled Russian Front for whatever further adventures awaited him there. He was not to be bored!

Chapter Four

Hitler's Gladiator:
Sepp Dietrich in Russia and the Bulge

On May 28, 1942, SS Obergruppenführer Joseph "Sepp" Dietrich celebrated his 50th birthday, a time when many men begin thinking of their retirement years—but not Sepp! He visited his men of the SS Leibstandarte Adolf Hitler in their winter rest positions on the Sea of Azov in the Soviet Union.

Told there were food shortages, he took two SS troopers back with him to his Divisional headquarters—and they returned hardly able to carry all the food.

His soldiers therefore loved him, and as a birthdaygift, the Führer presented Sepp with a tax-free check for 100,000 Reichsmarks. With this sum, his salary and Ursula's dowry, for the first time Sepp was able to provide for his family in the way he wished—but they were far away as he prepared the LSSAH to take part in Hitler's summer 1942 campaign in the Soviet Caucasus.

Suddenly, in July, the Führer—worried about a possible Allied "Second Front" invasion of France that Josef Stalin was loudly demanding of his Western partners—ordered the Leibstandarte to entrain on the 11th. They went by rail to Fontainebleau, Napoleon's old palace outside Paris, where they arrived in time to parade down the Champs-Élysées, goose-stepping proudly past a reappointed Field Marshal Gerd von Rundstedt as Supreme Commander West and Sepp's old military nemesis, SS Gen. Paul Hausser, now Commander of the SS Panzer (Armored) Corps.

On Aug. 19th, Hitler's fears seemed somewhat justified when an Allied raid on Dieppe on the coast of France was repulsed. Although it took no part in it, the Führer ordered the Leibstandarte sent to Normandy just in case. The Division passed the autumn of 1942 in reorganization and refitting and was placed under the aegis of Hausser once more when Hitler sanctioned the formation of the First Waffen SS Corps headquarters in France, which also included *Das Reich* and *Totenkopf* Divisions. In December—after *Das Reich* occupied Vichy France and the threat of an immediate Second Front seemed to dissipate with the Allied landings in North Africa instead—Hitler ordered the entire Hausser Corps back to the Eastern Front once more.

On December 10th, the Führer changed the title of Sepp's unit as well, now calling it the rather unwieldy SS Panzer Grenadier Division Leibstandarte Adolf Hitler. Hitler increased as well its artillery regiment to four battalions with guns ranging in caliber from 105–150 mm. In increasing its numbers to 21,000 men, though, the rigidly maintained SS racial purity at last went by the board. Now even Russian and British volunteers found their way into its ranks!

The LSSAH left France with an alleged 7,000 reported cases of gonorrhea sustained, but in an apologetic report to an irate Himmler, Sepp claimed the number was only 244 cases. From there, it was on to Kharkov in Russia with Hausser, for what was to prove to be the last successful German offensive of the war, even as the German Wehrmacht's regular 6th Army under Field Marshal Freidrich von Paulus was surrendering to the Reds at Stalingrad. When, at length, Hausser was forced to retreat from Kharkov in the face of Red Army counter-attacks, Sepp manfully stepped forward and defended the decision of his old rival to the Führer. When asked what reserves he had left behind him, Dietrich gruffly replied, "400 kilometers of wind!"

Nevertheless, when Kharkov fell to the LSSAH and other SS troops on March 14, 1943, it was another milestone in Sepp's career, winning for him the Swords to the Knight's Cross and leading Goebbels to note in his diary:

Sepp Dietrich enjoys the Führer's unlimited confidence. He considers him one of our best troop commanders and expects miracles from him. He is, so to-speak, the Blücher of the National Socialist movement.

Goebbels alludes to the popular Marshal Geberecht von Blücher of the Napoleonic Wars, affectionately known as "Old Forward" to his men, whom he, in turn, called "My Children."

Hitler ordered Goebbels to stage a public relations build-up for Sepp as a Nazi hero on par with what had previously been done for Erwin Rommel, by now a defeated Field Marshal about to be expelled from Tunisia. Again, there were radio broadcasts, newsreel clips in public theaters and feature articles in the press, all heroically extolling Sepp's military virtues. Noted Goebbels, "He is not to be classed as a mere 'also ran' among the generals."

Sepp's second son was born that month, on the 20th, and was named Lutz, with Himmler as his godfather(!) The prudish Reichsführer SS never recognized the first son, Wolf Dieter, whom he evidently classed as a bastard.

Previous to these events, the 1934 killer of SA Chief of Staff Ernst Röhm—SS Gen. Theodor Eicke—was killed in an air crash on February 26th. This fact probably was noted with at least some grim satisfaction in private by Sepp Dietrich, nine years after the tragic purge of June 30th.

When the Soviets retook Kharkov for good in August 1943, they charged the Waffen SS with war crimes and atrocities. That December the Soviets held trials for the SS men they had in captivity for allegedly throwing an incendiary grenade into a hospital and shooting the wounded down as they tried to escape the flames. Four SS were found guilty and hanged. The Soviets also claimed that Dietrich and six others were guilty, and would be charged under the criminal laws of the USSR when and if they were ever caught.

This led the Western Allied intelligence services to brand Sepp a war criminal and in June 1944—on the eve of the D-Day landings in Normandy—one of the top 33 prime figures in the Nazi state, as well as "the most prominent figure in the Waffen SS." Thus, the 1943 Hitler/Goebbels PR blitz was to have unfortunate consequences for Sepp Dietrich after the war.

Meanwhile—ironically!—Dietrich took no part in the massive Zitadelle (Citadel) offensive at the Battle of Kursk—the largest tank conflict in history—in July 1943, and after a decade of commanding the LSSAH in all its various forms, relinquished that post to its second commander, Theodor Wisch.

To mark the true ending of the Dietrich era, Rudolf Lehmann wrote of him:

Our old Commander—to us under him "Obersepp," was no strategic genius, but a leader of the highest quality of soldiers and of men … he possessed a special sense for what would become crisis points, especially how to favorably develop them. His very rare and then very short speeches to his men did not contain any strokes of genius … but they came from the heart, and they went from heart to heart. This man had an extraordinary charisma.

Somebody who experienced him can only recall with astonishment and admiration how he set himself up against a human wave in a night of crisis, during which everything fled towards the rear. With the collar of his coat turned up … uttering incomprehensible sounds … he managed not only to stop the wave of men but to reverse its direction. Also, his warning to his troop leaders will never be forgotten: "Bring me my men!"

On June 23, 1943, Hitler promoted him with a unique rank-SS Obergruppenführer und Panzergeneral der Waffen SS, with Col. Fritz Kraemer from the regular Army as his new Chief of Staff to succeed Lehmann. Kraemer stayed with him throughout the war, even into the postwar Malmédy Trial. Dietrich's new command was the 1st SS Panzer Corps, headquartered at Sepp's old post of Berlin-Lichterfelde.

It must have seemed like old times for Sepp Dietrich, and yet he was dismayed by what he had seen on the Russian Front. To this simple, blunt and straightforward old soldier, it seemed that the Third Reich could, indeed, lose the war, particularly after Stalingrad, Kursk and Kharkov. When Himmler learned that Sepp had stated publicly that, because of sheer numbers alone, it would not be possible to defeat the Russians, the Reichsführer SS sent him a written rebuke: "Whatever you think about the war in the East, I know best! … We are sure that the Russians can and will be defeated!"

Nevertheless, Himmler himself—egged on by his own SS aide, Gen. Walter Schellenberg—was at this point considering a possible SS coup to remove the Führer, make peace in the West and turn the Reich's full force against the Red Army. Even more astonishing is this comment of Messenger's in *Hitler's Gladiator*: "Gen. Henning von Tresckow … a key participant in the plots against Hitler, is supposed to have told Carl Goerdeler in August 1943 (Field Marshals) von Manstein and von Kluge and (Gen.) von Küchler would support an anti-Hitler coup and that Hausser and Dietrich would go along with it." If true, this means that Hitler's fear of his SS Roman-style Praetorian Guard was indeed justified.

At the end of July 1943, Sepp and the LSSAH were ordered to Innsbruck in Austria preparatory to being sent to Northern Italy in the wake of the Italian Royal Family/Fascist Grand Council overthrow of now-ex-Duce Benito Mussolini. In command of the overall German efforts was to be none other than Field Marshal Erwin Rommel, Dietrich's fellow Swabian.

It was decided to send the Leibstandarte to secure the Brenner Pass on the Italian-German frontier in the South Tyrol, the scene of the famous March 1940 Führer/Duce meeting at the railway station there, but on Aug. 14th, the Leibstandarte instead was sent on to Verona in Northern Italy in case of an Allied landing there, again under Hausser's orders, with headquarters at Merano. It was a long time since Sepp had first come to Italy with the Führer in June 1934, and—another irony!—after SS commandos under Capt. Otto Skorzeny rescued Mussolini on September 12, 1943—it was LSSAH men who guarded the freed Duce, soon to be leader of Hitler's rump state in Northern Italy—the Salo Republic.

At Milan, the ex-Duce gave a speech that—according to a Goebbels diary entry—Dietrich told the Propaganda Minster could only be done "under the protection of German arms, otherwise he would be booed off the stage!" As October 1943 came to a close, the LSSAH was returned once more to the Eastern Front, since the expected Allied landing had occurred in the South, and not in the North, of Italy. Prompt Hitler/Dietrich action had helped keep at least part of the Italian boot in the Axis, where it would remain until Himmler's SS representative there, Karl Wolff, surrendered it in May 1945.

For Sepp there now came a new assignment—1st SS Panzer Corps again, but this time in Normandy (where he had last been in 1942.) In April 1944 he was delighted to be joined there once more by his beloved LSSAH Division, back from renewed fierce fighting in Russia, with the Germans now in full withdrawal.

Here, he was once more working with both Field Marshals Rommel and von Rundstedt in preparing for the expected Allied landings. Like everyone else in the Third Reich, however, he was startled when they took place in Normandy (and not in the expected Pas de Calais) on June 6, 1944, and like Rommel was away from his command at the time—in Brussels. Hitler believed that the Normandy landings were only a ruse—with the real landings to still come at the Pas de Calais but, to be safe, Dietrich launched an attack from Caen to push the Allies back into the water.

But—just as Rommel had predicted, based on his own harrowing experiences in North Africa—Allied air superiority over Göring's Luftwaffe now played havoc with German attempts to counter-attack. At 1st SS Panzer Corps HQ, Dietrich and Kraemer found even their own telephone lines cut by incessant Allied bombing, and Rommel now placed the counter-attack under the command of an Army officer, Panzer Gen. Baron Geyr von Schweppenburg. This still nettled Sepp after the end of the war when he testily said to his Canadian jailers, "What did Rommel know of war? He constantly had himself photographed by Dr. Berndt, his publicity man, for the newspapers back home! All he could do was stand on a tank, baton in hand and shout, 'I am the King of Africa!'" This was a fanciful view at best, but one shared by many of Rommel's fellow generals in the Wehrmacht. Like them, Sepp looked down on the man even von Rundstedt called "The Field Marshal Laddie" because he hadn't seen a day's combat in Russia.

Over the next six weeks, both SS and Wehrmacht troops were consistently ground up in the Allied meat-grinder, which made all inter-service wrangling academic. States author Robert Wistrich in his *Who's Who in Nazi Germany*, "In Normandy he [Sepp] was given the task of containing the Anglo-American beachhead, but proved unable to throw back the Allied forces."

Somewhat kinder, writer LTC John R. Angolia states in his book *On the Field of Honor: A History of the Knight's Cross Bearers* volume I:

> His units took part in a two-month, bitterly contested battle in the vicinity of Caen—a battle that rightfully earned the designation "Diamond Dust of Caen"—due to the cost in lives that it took to capture the city. Making up for what he lacked in brilliant generalship, Dietrich lead his men by example. Hitler recognized the bravery of the SS troops by making Sepp Dietrich the 16th recipient of the Diamonds. He personally made the award on Aug. 6, 1944, and promoted Dietrich to the next higher grade.

In his 1948 study, *Defeat in the West*, author Milton Shulman paints this very interesting view of the new Rommel–Dietrich relationship. The latter protested to the former about the "wasteful" use of his armored troops as infantry, unable to advance because of Allied air attacks. 'I am being bled white and I am getting nowhere!' Rommel replied, 'You must attack.' Receiving this answer, Dietrich raised his hands and moaned, 'But with what? We haven't enough troops! We need another 8–10 divisions in the next day or two or we're finished!'" His weary troops therefore were placed at Caen to hold the line while Hausser—back yet again from Russia—tried a counter-attack.

As this, too, floundered, there began a series of meetings between the Field Marshal and the SS Obergruppenführer and their respective staffs that remain cloudy and vague in their intentions. It has been asserted that what was discussed was the possibility of Rommel securing an armistice on the Western Front that would halt that fighting, thus allowing the Axis to deploy all its forces on the Eastern Front alone, against the Red Army. Reportedly, Sepp agreed to obey whatever orders his field marshal superior gave him.

States at least one critic, "This 'revisionist history's' pure bunk!" These were two experienced soldiers whom many feel were nonetheless inexperienced politician/diplomats, but whom I believe knew well enough what they were discussing. They were dancing about with vague words, bandying about high treason at least and murder at worst. Both well knew their fates if they were either found out or failed, but—as fate would have it—an Allied British Typhoon aircraft intervened, thus changing the history of the Second World War at a key moment.

Rommel's staff car was strafed on the way back, and the Field Marshal was thrown onto the road by the force of the blast. His chauffeur was killed, with the famed "Desert Fox" sustaining serious head injuries that removed him from the July 20th Plot a mere three days later and took him out of active duty until the end of his life that October.

Fortunately for him, Sepp Dietrich was never implicated in the subsequent Bomb Plot, of whose survivors Himmler was put in charge of eradicating by a vengeful, but very much alive, Adolf Hitler. The existing evidence seems to indicate that Sepp was prepared to let the conspiracy take its course—as, indeed, was Himmler—at least in its formative stages, when, apparently, Sepp knew about it through his SS spies. Still shocked by the Nazi Blood Purge of a decade earlier, Sepp Dietrich meant to be on the winning (in this case, surviving) side, no matter what.

On the day of the explosion at Rastenburg, Sepp attended a military conference in France with German Army Field Marshal von Kluge. It is very possible that both of them were awaiting word of Hitler's death from the Wolfsschanze, when what they got instead late that night was a telephone call from Heinrich Himmler ordering him to move his Panzer Corps on Paris and suppress the revolt there—since the bomb had not killed Hitler and the Führer, though wounded, was still alive.

Even as late as 1978, Spiedel told Messenger that Dietrich had stated the SS would remain aloof once *Operation Valkyrie*—the takeover plan—had gotten underway. "Hitler will have to be wiped out!" he declared. In addition, from his contacts within the SS brotherhood, Sepp knew, too, about what was happening to the Jews at places like Auschwitz by his brother officers, the Death's Head units, whom he now disdainfully called "Those swine!" He meant to survive both the Nazi regime and any subsequent Allied postwar criminal trials—and did.

As for the Allies, mysteriously, their pressure let up in the West for four days after July 20th, but the battle resumed in earnest on the 25th—when it can be supposed they, too, realized the plot had failed.

Summoned to East Prussia to receive his Diamonds on Aug. 6th, Sepp got only two minutes with the Führer. He began with, "Mein Führer, I would like to speak to you about what happened in Normandy …," but sensing that what he was about to hear would be unpleasant, Hitler cut him off with, "Don't bother me with these details now! I'm too tired." He was still reeling in shock from the events of July 20th.

On the 9th, Dietrich took command of the 5th Panzer Army, and ordered to attack in the Avranches area against the Allies. Sepp for the first time asserted, "There was only one person to blame for this stupid, impossible operation—that madman, Adolf Hitler! It was a Führerbefehl—a Leader Order. What else could we do?"

Said one Panzer Lehr division officer of Sepp at this time, "He was no soldier, but he was a realist!" Another asked Dietrich why he didn't approach Hitler personally about the military situation—not aware that he'd already tried in vain. Sepp answered: "If I want to get shot, that's the way to do it!" One supposes in this case that the man of June 30, 1934 knew what he was talking about.

His new commander in the West since Rommel's wounding and von Rundstedt's subsequent firing by Hitler—again—was German Army Field Marshal Günther von Kluge, but he, too, was replaced by Hitler on August 16th by the man known as "Hitler's fireman," tough Field Marshal Walther Model. In his suicide note, von Kluge referred to his burly Waffen SS subordinate as a man "whom I have come to know and appreciate as a brave, incorruptible man in these difficult weeks."

Model ordered Dietrich to mount a four Panzer division counter-attack across the Seine River on the 23rd, but it, too, was repulsed by the rampaging Allied armies, now driving on Paris. Meanwhile, Sepp had taken over the 7th Army from Gen. Paul Hausser, who had been wounded in the fighting of the surrounded German forces in the Falaise Pocket, and this placed Dietrich in charge of over 100 miles of the Western Front. Later, Model ordered him to relinquish the command of the tattered 5th Panzer Army to Gen. Heinrich Eberbach, and on September 11th he was relieved as well in the creation of a German armored reserve by famed Panzer Baron Hasso von Manteuffel and ordered to return to the Reich to receive a new assignment from the Führer he now thought "mad."

After the war, Sepp's assessment of the Battle of Normandy was that it was the toughest fighting of his long and varied combat career. He'd lost many valuable Waffen SS top commanders there as well, among them both Fritz Witt and Michael Wittmann killed, Theodor Wisch seriously wounded, and both Kurt Meyer and Max Wünsche captured.

The shadows were lengthening for Sepp Dietrich, the LSSAH and the Waffen SS as the year 1944 drew to a close, but there was still much hard, bitter fighting ahead, both in the West and the East.

Reporting to the Führer on September 14th, Hitler named Sepp commander of the 6th Panzer Army, and he also had a chat with Nazi Party Reichsleiter and Secretary to the Führer Martin Bormann about the Normandy campaign and the events of July 20th. By now, even Sepp was on some thin ice politically, especially since Rommel was under suspicion and the Field Marshal's Chief of Staff, Gen. Speidel, was under arrest by the Gestapo as well.

As before with Guderian when he was in disgrace after Moscow in 1941, so now, too, Dietrich cast caution to the wind and went to visit his one-time rival, commander and friend, Erwin Rommel. It was to be their last meeting, since the Desert Fox took poison in mid-October to save himself from trial for treason and his family from SS persecution. His reward was a State Funeral ordered by Hitler at which von Rundstedt delivered the eulogy. Speidel survived the war to become, in 1959, chief of all NATO ground forces as a General in the new West German Bundeswehr, at least in part because Sepp had argued for his life with Hitler and won.

Meanwhile, Sepp was busily reorganizing his shattered troops into a new command, the purpose of which he had no idea. As Chief of Staff, Dietrich had Gen. (Alfred) Gause, whom he knew from Normandy. The two corps commanders were respectively General Lieutenant der Waffen SS Hermann Preiss and Willi Bittrich, who had recently done well in the defense of Arnhem against the British airborne attacks. Wilhelm Möhnke, who had distinguished himself in the last weeks of the campaign in France, now commanded the Leibstandarte, and Sepp's old Chief of Staff, Fritz Kraemer, had the "Hitlerjugend," or Hitler Youth Division.

What none of them would know for several weeks yet was that Hitler had decided to pool all his reserves on the Western Front for a surprise armored attack in the Ardennes region to start on December 16, 1944—three months to the day he conceived the operation. It was hoped this attack would shatter the Allied armies, take the port of Antwerp (from which they were being supplied) and force the Anglo-Americans to consider a political solution to the war that would leave the Nazi regime in power and free to face the Soviets in the East, perhaps even with help from the West.

Central to the entire plan was Sepp Dietrich and his SS Panzer troops. Their main thrust was to be supported by both von Manteuffel's 5th Panzer Army and German Infantry Gen. Erich Brandenburger's 7th Army, with overall command of the operation going once again to Field Marshal Gerd von Rundstedt! Ironically, in some circles the operation came to be known as "The Rundstedt Offensive," but—after the war—he denied all prior knowledge of it. Initially a great success in denting the Allied positions, it came down to history as the Battle of the Bulge, the greatest campaign in the history of the US Army, whose main foe was SS Gen. Josef "Sepp" Dietrich.

Also ironically, reportedly none of the German commanders involved in the execution of the plan believed it would succeed, but out of fear of being shot by Hitler as malingerers, they went ahead with it anyway. At the end of October 1944, Sepp came to Hitler's headquarters, where present to receive his Knight's Cross from the Führer was the Belgian commander of the volunteer *Wallonia* SS Brigade, Léon Degrelle, (1906–1994), later a fascist author writing in exile from Spain. Degrelle has left this vivid portrait:

> The Führer's lieutenant—Martin Bormann, round, plump and pasty-faced—debated noisily with Gen. Sepp Dietrich of the SS, who arrived in a glider(!) from the Western Front. His legs wide apart, his face as red as a turnip, Sepp expatiated at length on the strength of the Anglo-American air force and on the ravages of the strafing planes, but he wasn't especially worried. He gave everyone great thumps on the back, drank cognac with every breath and went back to his room at 5 oclock in the morning, vigorously supported by four giants of the guard.

At home, his third son, Gotz-Hubertus, was born on November 23, 1944, and again, his hated "boss," SS Reichsführer Heinrich Himmler, served as the Dietrich family godfather.

That same day, Sepp was present at a meeting between the Führer and all the top generals—Army and SS—who were to be involved in the coming battle. Hitler discussed the plans he'd already informed them of on October 22nd, even though, after the war, Sepp told the Americans he knew nothing about the attack until December 12th—a mere four days before it was to be launched. Sepp was, by now, certain it could not work, as he told Canadian Army officer and later author Milton Shulman as a prisoner in 1945:

> "I grew *so big* with these plans," sarcastically commented Dietrich, flinging out his arms and puffing outs his cheeks. "I had *merely* to cross a river, capture Brussels and then go on and take the port of Antwerp—and all this in the worst months of the year, December, January, February—through the countryside where snow was waist-deep and there wasn't room to deploy four *tanks* abreast, *let alone* six *armored divisions*, when it didn't get light until 8 a.m. and was dark again at 4 p.m., with divisions that had just been reformed and contained chiefly raw, untried recruits—and at Christmas time!"

Not only did Sepp feel that the planned parachute drop behind enemy lines by Baron Friedrich von der Heydte was bound to fail (it did, miserably, the last such German jump of the war), but also he had no faith in SS LTC Otto Skorzeny's *Operation Greif*, in which German commandos in American Army uniforms would penetrate US lines and—it was later rumored—attempt to kill Allied Supreme Commander Gen. Dwight D. Eishenhower. Of Skorzeny himself, Sepp later told the Americans that he was "a shady character, always in with Himmler on any dirty work!" During the famous meeting with the stiff para Baron who later testified that Sepp was drunk, von der Heydte asked for carrier pigeons in case his radios failed, to which Dietrich loudly retorted, "What do you think I am—running a zoo?"

The final briefing of the campaign got off to a bad start when the commanders met in two sessions, December 12th and 13th at the Führer's Eagle's Nest HQ in the Taunus Mountains north of Frankfurt, originally built for the 1940 Western offensive. Later, von Manteuffel would recall that:

> … the seating accommodation was inadequate and the SS generals politely left the chairs to their senior Army colleagues, while they stood. This created the impression on some of the Army generals that an SS officer was posted behind each Army officer's chair. This was certainly a misunderstanding.

The attack ultimately failed, although, for a time, it scared the hell out of the U.S. Army top brass, with no less than Gen. George S. Patton, Jr., thundering to Ike, "We can still lose this war!" But, in reality, the actual result was a foregone conclusion due to the ultimately hopeless position of Nazi Germany being crushed like an eggshell in a disastrous two-front war. The Führer's only valid hope was that the postwar Cold War would start a few years before it actually did; in this, however, he was simply too far ahead of his time.

Of the Bulge, Louis L. Snyder states in his *Encyclopedia of the Third Reich*: "When Dietrich's army stalled, Hitler's offensive collapsed." States Brig. Gen. Shelford Bidwell in his book *Hitler's Generals and Their Battles*:

> The Ardennes operation left behind 76,890 American casualties and 81,834 German, and though American losses in tanks and aircraft were greater—733 to 324 and 592 to 320—the German losses were now almost irreplaceable.

As David Irving noted in his 1977 study, *Hitler's War*:

> Hitler … decided that if he was not to lose the initiative entirely, he must … pull out Sepp Dietrich's 6th SS Panzer Army to establish a tactical reserve while he could, for there was no knowing what the enemy might do with the divisions he could now release from the Ardennes battlefield. This order—Hitler's tacit admission that he had lost the Ardennes gamble—was issued from the Eagle's Nest at 2 a.m. on January 8, 1945.

The Battle of the Bulge was over.

Remaining from it, however, to haunt Dietrich for the rest of his life, was the Malmédy Massacre of American Army prisoners of war on a snow-covered field in Belgium by troopers from the command of Waffen SS Col. Jochen Peiper—who would himself be murdered in still-unexplained circumstances while he was living incognito in France in 1976—32 years after the Bulge. According to Richard Gallagher's 1964 investigation of the incident on December 17, 1944, *Malmédy Massacre*, "At the height of the Battle of the Bulge, 115 American POW's were shot down senselessly by a Nazi tank detachment,"—Dietrich's SS men.

As noted by author Charles Whiting, Sepp himself—who was not present—learned of the shootings only from Allied press reports five days later—on the 21st. His own official investigation denied that it ever happened.

Apparently it did, considering the 1940 events in France, as well as the atrocities in Russia, as noted earlier. At any event, at the postwar Malmédy Trial 74 SS men, including Sepp, were brought to heel for the crime.

At the time of these events, naturally enough, Dietrich was concentrating on winning the battle at hand, and, indeed, was flushed with the thrilling feeling of Nazi victory once again, as in that heady year of 1940. Asserts Léon Degrelle:

Sepp Dietrich showed me the Tongres-St. Trond area on the map, west of Leige. "See!" he said. "It's here that I'll corner them!" Then, with glittering eyes, he put his big thumb under the name of Aachen, the holy city of the Empire. "Aachen!" he exclaimed. "Aachen! In the month of January, I will be in Aachen!"

(Aachen had been the first city of the German Reich taken by the Western Allies back in September 1944.)

In the wake of the SS failure to take the key road junction of Bastogne, there was much Army criticism of Hitler's selection of Sepp to be the spear-point of the offensive, Sepp's handling of the attack and the combat conduct of the SS men. So, when January 1945 arrived, Dietrich found himself not in Aachen on the Western Front, but instead sent to fight the Russians once more, this time on the ground of Germany's junior Axis Pact partner, the Hungary of Regent Adm. Nikolaus Horthy.

Dietrich passed through Berlin on his way to Hungary in mid-February, and held what he didn't realize would be his last meetings with both Hitler and Dr. Goebbels. Goebbels recorded in his diary "Obersepp's" criticisms of the Führer's military decisions, noting, tartly, "Dietrich is in no position to judge." It was also now that the LSSAH changed commanders for the final time, from Wilhelm Möhnke to Otto Kumm.

The attack to relieve surrounded Budapest, the Hungarian capital, began on March 6th, but stalled, as Sepp noted later:

The terrain, which was supposed to be frozen hard … was wet and marshy … now 132 tanks were sunk in the mud, and 15 Royal Tigers were sunk up to their turrets, so that the attack could be continued only by infantry. Considerable losses of men followed.

Requests on the 11th and the 14th to halt the attack were denied by Führerhauptquartier, but the massive Red Army counter-attack two days later made this a moot point anyway. The subsequent Waffen SS/LSSAH retreat sent Hitler into a rage. Goebbels now noted in his diary:

Our SS formations have put up a wretched show in this area. Even the Leibstandarte is no longer the old Leibstandarte, since its officer material and men have been killed off. The Leibstandarte bears its honorary title in name only.

The Führer has nevertheless decided to make an example of the SS formations. He has commissioned Himmler to fly to Hungary to remove their armbands. This will, of course, be the greatest imaginable disgrace to Sepp Dietrich! The Army generals are rubbing their hands at the blow dealt to their rivals. The SS formations in Hungary not only failed to carry their offensive through, but withdrew and, in some cases, pulled out … Sepp Dietrich is to be pitied, Himmler, too, however, since he—the Head of the SS with no war decorations— now has to carry out this severe punishment in the face of Sepp Dietrich, who wears the Diamonds.

At the Führer Conference where Hitler announced the decision, Hitler raged, "If we lose the war, it will be Dietrich's fault!" This was a reprimand of his Waffen SS that Himmler suffered in silence. Was he secretly happy at Sepp's fall from grace at last? Only Luftwaffe Reich Marshal Hermann Göring (himself in hot water with Hitler) stood up to the Führer on Sepp's behalf Guderian balked at taking the reprimand to Sepp, and Himmler didn't fly out after all, since—as Goebbels correctly noted—"Dietrich … is not the sort of man to take such a humiliation lying down."

So, in the end, the bad news was sent to the tough SS man by radio to his 6th Panzer Army headquarters stating simply:

> The Führer believes that the troops have not fought as the situation demanded, and orders that the SS Divisions *Adolf Hitler, Das Reich, Totenkopf* and *Hohenstauffen* be stripped of their armbands.

After the war, Sepp told Shulman that, when he received this order, he first got drunk, then slept it off for the next three hours. Upon awakening:

> "I asked myself, 'Am *I* crazy or are *they* crazy?' I'm not crazy, therefore, they must be!" Calling the four divisional commanders together, Sepp angrily threw down the order in front of them on the table with the fiery words, "There's your reward for all you have done the past five years!"

He told them not to pass the order on to the men, and also to keep on their own armbands, then sent a note to Hitler threatening to shoot himself if the Führer insisted on the order standing, a missive greeted by a week's silence from the FHQ. Miffed, Sepp sent back all his own decorations, then was summoned to Vienna for a personal dressing down from Himmler.

There, as the meeting began, the Reichsführer SS received a phone call from Hitler ordering him to take all the decorations from the 6th Panzer Army officers as well. Himmler is supposed to have retorted over the line, "I would have to drive to the Plattensee to take the crosses off the dead. A German SS man cannot give more than his life for you, mein Führer!"

An angry Sepp ripped off his Iron Cross, throwing it to the floor, there later retrieved by an aide who returned it to him when his temper cooled.

One widely-reported tale of this entire affair is that the outraged officers of the Leibstandarte themselves—the élite of the élite of Adolf Hitler's SS men—sent their decorations in a chamber pot to the Reich Chancellery Bunker in Berlin where Hitler was now holed up in his last command post. The pot allegedly also contained a human arm with the LSSAH armband attached in a gesture of supreme defiance by the men to the man they were sworn-to protect with their very lives for the past 12 years of the Third Reich, a state now in its last death throes. The truth probably lies somewhere in between all these fantastic accounts but, as Messenger asserts, "A number of Dietrich's decorations, including his Knight's Cross with Oak Leaves, Swords and Diamonds, are in the possession to this day of his eldest son, Wolf Dieter."

Dietrich was never himself after this affair, but after the fall of the Hungarian oil fields on April 2, 1945, it had blown over sufficiently for Sepp to be ordered to defend Vienna from the Red Army with the four SS divisions at his command. He now served under the overall command of the Austrian Alpenkorps General, Dr. Lothar Rendulic. Sepp set up headquarters in the home of the city's Nazi Gauleiter and former Hitler Youth Leader Baldur von Schirach, who asked him how many tanks he had for the defense of Vienna. With his characteristic humor and penchant for speaking bluntly, Sepp answered impishly, "We call ourselves the 6th Panzer Army because we only have six tanks left!"

Keenly aware of the fate of Röhm in 1934, Dietrich was taking no chances of a vengeful Hitler now, in the middle of April 1945, ringing his next castle command post with machineguns and loyal LSSAH men—loyal to him, that is. As he told a visiting von Schirach, "I have set up this hedgehog position just in case Adolf wants to wipe me out for not defending Vienna!"

Now the Russians were in the city itself, and when Otto Kumm went to receive a decoration at Sepp's own headquarters, he reports that, "The very moment that he gave it to me, the door was opened and someone was shot dead just in front of it!" It was high time to leave or surrender, but on the 13th, Dietrich was ordered to form a line of defense west of the city to hold the Russians from proceeding further westward, which he was actually able to do.

Out of touch with his chief, Gen. Rendulic, Sepp sent the *Hohenstauffen* and *Hitlerjugend* divisions westward, too, where they surrendered to George Patton's 3rd Army, while Hitler moved *Das Reich* to the Czech Protectorate for reinforcements there. The LSSAH covered the retreat route for the rest of the 6th SS Panzer Army—away from the Red Army and toward the West, as no SS man in his right mind wanted to surrender to the Russians!

Certainly not Sepp Dietrich, and the German surrender of May 8, 1945 found him safely in American-occupied Austria at Zell Am See south of the dead Hitler's retreat at Berchtesgaden at OKW Sud HQ, under the command of Gen. August Winter, his last formal chief. He left Zell Am See to fetch his family at Sonthofen and bring them to safety as well, and thus he and Ursula found themselves surrendering to Master Sgt. Herbert Kraus of the US 7th Army's 36th Infantry Division—the same unit, in about the same time, place and circumstances that captured his friend and patron of years past, Hermann Göring.

As a former sergeant himself, Sepp Dietrich must have seen the mocking irony in his situation, but he had, nonetheless, survived the greatest war in history as well as escaped Hitler's possible wrath. Would he now be able to escape the Allied hangman's noose as an accused war criminal?

Ultimately, he did, but he spent almost 11 years of his remaining 21 in Allied and German imprisonment for his Nazi and SS activities during the period 1928–45. Forthright as always, he told his captors:

I could have put a slug through my brains if I wanted to, but I have a responsibility for which I must take a stand. I want to speak for the men I once led. I never signed any order providing for the massacre of the Jews or the burning down of churches, nor have I ordered the pillaging of occupied places. I therefore want to clarify things and stand up for my men.

His views on the top Nazis his questioners found very interesting as well:

Hitler knew even less than the rest! He allowed himself to be taken for a sucker by everyone. Göring was a lazy bastard—a clown. Heydrich was a great pig, but Kaltenbrunner was a decent fellow who had to do a lot of things that he did not like to do. He had many a heated argument with Himmler.

As for his views on the Russians, whom he knew as both former allies and opponents, Sepp called them:

… a very intelligent people; good-natured, easy to be led and also adapted in technical matters …
I spoke to many Russians. They like it better under Stalin than under the Tsar.

Like Göring, he was questioned at length by American Army Lt. Rolf Wartenburg. He was put in the rather unenviable position of having been extolled by the dead Nazis and now ridiculed by his surviving German Army counterparts, as well as accused by the Americans of complicity in the Malmédy Massacre—and yet he survived them all.

Urging the Americans, British and Canadians to build up a common front against Communism (which, indeed, he, unlike Hitler, lived to see in NATO), Dietrich also talked wistfully about starting over again in Canada with the 25,000 Reichsmarks he had managed to save during the war. In November 1945, he was sent to Nuremberg as a possible witness there, but was never used, and so in March 1946 was transferred to the former SS camp at Dachau for the Malmédy Trial, in which he would take the stand as one of the accused.

During the trial, the SS men remained faithful to each other, refusing to turn state's evidence even in their rather dire straits, facing as they were literally the hangman's noose. The trial opened May 16, 1946—more than a year after the end of the war itself. Accused of "letting his men run riot," Dietrich was given a life sentence, to be served at the old Landsberg Prison in Bavaria, where Hitler had written *Mein Kampf* during his stay a generation earlier. The trial ended on July 16th, and Sepp arrived at Landsberg the next day, while his American-appointed defense counsel, Willis Everett, continued his efforts to free Dietrich for what he considered "a miscarriage of justice."

Still suffering somewhat from the frostbite he had got in the winter of 1941-42 on the Russian Front, Sepp was put to work in the prison's bookbinding shop, and in 1948 was allowed visits from Ursula and the boys. The coming of the Berlin Airlift crisis, followed by the Cold War and the hot Korean War led to an easing of the formerly hostile view taken by the Western Allies of the defeated Germans. After the creation of the new German Federal Republic of West Germany, the Allies became desirous of admitting German troops into the new North Atlantic Treaty Organization as a bulwark against threats from Stalin from the East. Ultimately, this led to the creation of the Bundeswehr, complete with air, sea and ground forces, all of which Sepp lived to see with amusement, but parole for him was rejected time and again.

In the United States, the Red-baiting era of US Senator Joseph McCarthy of Wisconsin was in full swing, and "Tail Gunner Joe," as he was called, unwittingly came to the aid of another "Joe" Sepp Dietrich—when he opened investigations into certain legal irregularities in the conduct of the Malmédy Trial at which Sepp had been convicted and sentenced. Thus, after his fourth parole application was accepted, Sepp was released on October 22, 1955, following more than a decade in prison—only to stand trial for the Röhm Purge events and to be sent back to Landsberg once more, and then to be released again.

Reunited with his family at last, Sepp spent time with them hunting and working in the SS veterans relief association. At one of their gatherings in August 1959, Dietrich was met with "enthusiastic applause lasting several minutes." He had never been forgotten by his men, now prospering under the West German economic "miracle" of the 1950s. The American author John Toland met and interviewed him for his book, *Battle: Story of the Bulge*, and found him "content to be with his family and former comrades and … to stay well clear of politics."

States Charles Messenger: "When his end came, it was quiet. On Apr. 21, 1966, he died of a massive heart attack in his bed," the day after what would have been Adolf Hitler's 79th birthday. In former years on Hitler's birthday Sepp Dietrich—in martial-looking regalia, black uniform, steel helmet, polished boots and dress sword—would lead "his boys" (also thus resplendent) stomping down the Wilhelmstrasse. They would parade past their beaming Führer, who would be standing bolt upright in his gleaming Mercedes-Benz touring car as he proudly watched his "asphalt soldiers" goosestep by.

All of this seemed very far away, indeed, from the world of 1966, from the Beatles, LSD, Bobby Kennedy, and also the Vietnam War, where once again Communists were waging a brutal war against soldiers from the West.

Time, too, has softened the historical verdict on Sepp Dietrich, who served 10 years in prison as a model prisoner.

He was the *only* top Nazi leader, indeed, to receive a funeral at which atop his casket was placed a German steel helmet, a sword, and a flag bearing the old Prussian Iron Cross, if not the Nazi swastika—which was then and still is banned from public display under German law. His Ludwigsburg services were attended by 6,000 people, mainly former Waffen SS wartime veterans like him. Gen. Bittrich delivered a short eulogy.

One thinks that the "Nazi Blücher" would have understood and been pleased.

Chapter Five

SS Gruppenführer Johann Rattenhuber and the Reich Security Service

Up until early 1936, the primary responsibility of protecting the person of German Reich Chancellor and Nazi Party Führer Adolf Hitler resided mainly in the hands of one of his earliest bodyguards, SS Gen. Josef "Sepp" Dietrich. But during the Winter Olympics held at Garmisch-Partenkirchen that February, however, it began to be shared with SS Gruppenführer Johann Rattenhuber and his Reich Security Service—and, indeed, other groups and individuals, too.

As 1936 wore on, increasingly Hitler's security fell to these men. Sepp's black-coated SS Leibstandarte gradually moved upward in size from squad to platoon to company, then from battalion to regiment and eventually, during the Second World War, to full-scale Waffen SS Division status, with Sepp rising to the exalted rank of a Panzer Army Group Commander.

In his excellent 1979 study entitled *Hitler's Personal Security*, author Peter Hoffmann concluded that the main danger to the Führer throughout the 12 years of the Nazi Third Reich and the decade prior to 1933 was not from hostile Communists and others bent on assassination, but rather from the crush of friendly crowds at such Nazi rallies as the annual Nuremberg extravaganzas. As for the assassination attempts, he concludes, most of those that failed did so because of fateful accidents, while other people—who were better-placed to try to kill Hitler because of their daily proximity to him—failed to try, either out of personal loyalty or refusal to sacrifice one's own life, a certainty in view of the many guards available to the Führer.

Nonetheless, from the earliest recorded attempt in 1921 to Albert Speer's plot to gas the Führerbunker in Berlin in 1945, there are at least 51 known, alleged or suspected attempts—and there may have been more that no one (not even Hitler!)—knew about, with culprits ranging from disgruntled SA men and German Army generals to cranks. Even before Hitler came to power on January 30, 1933 as German Reich Chancellor, he was the target of attacks, particularly in the middle of the fierce beer hall brawls between Nazi toughs and their mortal political foes, the members of the German Communist Party (which the Third Reich outlawed in 1933).

During a famous November 1921 brawl, shots were fired both at the speaker's podium and also from it, as Hitler himself returned fire with the personal pistol that he carried until he shot himself in 1945. The fighting below him featured fists, beer steins, table and chair legs, plus brass knuckles, enabling Hitler to continue speaking, before the police arrived to shut down the hall.

Although the SA toughs were there for protection, they were not Hitler's formal bodyguards. A unit of these---the first SS---was formed, and its earliest members included drivers Schreck and Emil Maurice, student Rudolf Hess, first official bodyguard and professional butcher Ulrich Graf, beer hall bouncer Christian Weber, and even Hitler's own World War I unit sergeant and later Nazi publishing tsar, Max Amann.

Dietrich was not among this original group, taking his valued place later. After 1933, Hitler's personal swearing in of his elite guards took place at night in Münich's Feldherrnhalle on the anniversaries of November 9, 1923. The units evolved from the *Ordnertruppe/Stewards, Order Troop* to the *Saalschutz/Assembly Hall Protection*, then into the *Schutzstaffel/SS Protection Squad.*

During the renowned November 4, 1921 Battle of the Münich Hofbrauhaus, Hess and Maurice were both badly injured.

When former pilot, ace and *Pour le Merite* holder Capt. Hermann Göring took over the SA in March 1923, he set up a formal Stabswache (Staff Guard) to protect the Führer. By May it numbered 20 men, reorganized into the Stosstrupp Hitler (Hitler Assault Squad, or Shock Troop), complete with "black bands," now with 100 men.

These were men with whom Hitler took over the Burgerbraukeller Beer Hall on the evening of November 8–9, 1923 to launch the famous "Beer Hall Putsch" in Münich. The next day, Hitler led them in a march through the city that culminated with their being met by a cordon of armed Weimar Republic policemen who opened fire.

"Hitler … was definitely being fired at. (Max).

Scheubner-Richter, who was walking next to him, was killed instantly, apparently pulling Hitler down with him. Graf threw himself in front of Hitler as the Leader was going down, and that inflicted serious injuries upon his bodyguard." Apparently, these men took their duties seriously, and this was nine years before the Party came to power and they could be rewarded, although—admittedly—they didn't know that at the time.

In the wake of the failed Putsch, Hitler was tried, convicted and jailed for plotting to overthrow the legally constituted government, while the Party, the SA and the Stosstrupp all were banned. Upon the Führer's release from prison, in late 1924, he declared that he would henceforth work within the law to achieve power legally (and did), and thus was allowed to reform his outlawed formations.

Over the next 20 years, the SA would have as its leaders, in succession, Capt. Franz Pfeffer von Salomon, Capt. Ernst Röhm and Viktor Lutze (after Röhm's murder in 1934 and until his own death in an auto accident nine years later).

And yet, the SA remained a wild and wooly organization, and the revolt of its Berlin membership in August 1930 embarrassed him, especially when the regular police had to be called upon by the Nazis to restore order within their own ranks. Hitler personally took over the SA as Party and Supreme SA Leader on September 2, 1930, but only after he had personally come to Berlin from Münich to put down the revolt of the SA by the force of his personality.

"He confronted first the troopers and the rebellious leaders. All were extremely hostile, and one SA leader is said to have grabbed and shaken Hitler by the necktie, to the great horror of Hess, who could not prevent it."

The shakeup also placed the SS directly under Hitler and then the SA, with Röhm reporting to Hitler (when the former resumed control in 1931) as Chief of Staff of the SA. Still Hitler felt both his position challenged and his life threatened within his own political movement, a situation that would exist for another three-and-a-half years, until the Blood Purge of June 30, 1934.

The reborn Stabswache, in 1925, numbered eight men, then it was renamed the SS, with Julius Schreck its most prominent member. At Schreck's funeral in May 1936, following an auto accident, the SS Reichsführer (National Leader) Heinrich Himmler called him "Adolf Hitler's first SS man," and perhaps rightly so. As for the growing SS itself, their story has been told earlier in this tale via their growth as the SS Leibstandarte Adolf Hitler (LSSAH).

Himmler was originally one of Röhm's men, and a standard-bearer during the 1923 Putsch on the barricades in Münich; on January 6, 1929, Hitler named him Reichsführer SS, a post he would hold almost for the rest of his life, until his fall from power and later suicide in May, 1945. The SS grew slowly under Röhm, but he did also create—on February 25,1931— the SD, or Sicherheitsdienst (Security Service) "for the protection of the leaders of the Party, and to turn over to the Reichsführer SS command of this new security service as well as giving him responsibility for the 'protection of the Hitler rallies in the entire Reich territory.'"

After a second SA revolt—in April 1931 under Capt. Walther Stennes—the latter was fired by Hitler, and the Führer once again saw the need for a powerful security group for himself in time of danger. During the same month, a young German naval officer named Lt. Reinhard Heydrich was forced by Admiral Erich Raeder to resign his Naval commission for "conduct unbecoming to an officer and a gentleman." Heydrich had a great interest in women and pursued sex with the same self-driven desire for achievement he applied to everything else. He had many sexual relationships and in 1930 was accused of having sex with the unmarried daughter of a shipyard director—thus leading to Raeder's action. According to popular Nazi legend, this was as a result of his refusal to marry her. With his Naval career wrecked, his fiancée, Lina von Osten, an enthusiastic Nazi Party member, suggested he join the Nazi Party and look into the SS organization which at that time served mainly as Hitler's personal bodyguard and had about 10,000 members.

While these events were unfolding, Hitler was becoming increasingly concerned for his own safety. Already, several attempts had been made on his life: "He had a … close shave in 'Red' Thuringia in 1923, and once in Leipzig, people were taking shots at his car. On March 15, 1932, shots were fired at a train in which Hitler, Goebbels and Frick rode from Münich to Weimar. On July 30, 1932, an assassination attempt was made against Hitler in Nuremberg, and in June he had barely escaped an ambush on a road near Stralsund." In the Presidential Campaign of 1932, he was "often standing up in his open Mercedes car as he rode through teeming and hostile mobs."

By now, Sepp Dietrich and the LSSAH were in their early form, but around Hitler's immediate person as well there were "old followers and bodyguards such as Schaub, Brückner, Otto Dietrich, Hanfstaengl, Schreck, Kempka, Gesche, Gildisch and others."

Early in January 1931, Hitler installed his Nazi Party offices in the newly bought Brown House at 45 Brienner Strasse, and here were placed both SA and SS men "in three groups of 20 each, plus three in reserve for each group." States Hoffmann, "From 8–10 security men were always inside the building, in a guard room, ready to be called out to assist those on post. At least six men constantly guarded the building entrance and a park area behind the house. At night, two men patrolled the park … the guards around the Brown House did carry gas pistols which could temporarily disable." (They were forbidden by law to be armed with lethal weapons in these early days before the Party came to power.) Ironically, there was a Nazi plot within the Brown House framework in March 1932 to have Röhm and other SA leaders assassinated, led by the Supreme Party Judge, Walter Buch—the father-in-law of later top Hitler aide Martin Bormann—that fizzled out before the intended victims could be shot down.

The following month, the German Green Police occupied the building for a full day, something that was repeated later in the year, immediately before the appointment of Hitler as Chancellor. Following that event, however, as the head of the German Government, Hitler was entitled to official protection for the first time.

There were several rumors of assassination attempts, even some secret ones inspired by Himmler "who feared he might miss the boat in the general power-grab … Himmler was still in Münich and without a major government post, but enough of the threats were real." Hitler feared that he might be shot down by a rifleman perched opposite the Reich Chancellery balcony in Berlin.

"In the early months of 1933, the police were tipped off about assassination plots at least once a week. They would learn that some anonymous person planned to hand Hitler a bunch of flowers and through the flowers squirt a poison into his face. Another plan was to have a doctored fountain pen explode in his hand." There were numerous rumors of subterranean bombs dug into the cellars of government and other public buildings. There were reports, too, of riflemen and stealthy assassins lurking about the Chancellery grounds. "Hitler—was informed of many of these plots, and they worried him, but time and again he was driven to take great risks, as if under compulsion like a self-destructive gambler. There were at least seven assassination plans that came to the attention of the authorities in 1934 and 1935."

On June 30, 1934, Hitler finally took action to smash the upper leadership cadre of the SA and to kill Röhm and other Storm Troop leaders. Hitler was egged on by Himmler and Göring, although he probably truly believed there was an SA plot to murder him, under the direction of SA Standartenführer Julius Uhl, as he later told the Reichstag on July 13, 1934 in defense of his preemptive actions against the Sturmabteilungen.

Meanwhile, Himmler's SS began to secretly penetrate Göring's creation, the Gestapo—the Secret State Police, and by Apr. 20, 1934, the Führer's 45th birthday, had managed to effectively take it over. Then, step by step, Himmler acquired more and more of the German provincial police forces, and thereafter his rise was meteoric.

"Himmler reached a peak in his career on June 17, 1936, when Hitler decreed that the Party office of SS Reichsführer be institutionally combined with that of Chief of the German Police. Other peaks were to follow as the SS became a new quasi-revolutionary army through numerical increases, via the foundation of the Waffen SS, and when Himmler became Reich Minister of the Interior in 1943 and, nominally, Commander-in-Chief of the Home Army on July 20,1944," in the aftermath of the failed Army Bomb Plot to kill the Führer. After that, Himmler found himself undone when, in actuality, he became commander of Army Group Vistula. Having few real military skills, he could nonetheless not have stopped the Red Army in 1945 anyway.

In March 1934—a year after Sepp Dietrich had formed his LSSAH to officially guard Hitler in Berlin and at his various other residences—Himmler had stuck his pudgy finger in the pie called "Führer Security" when he announced the formation of the Führerschutzkommando (Führer Protection Group) or Kommando Z.BV (Special Task Group). Thus enters the story for the first time the name of a lesser-known figure than the legendary Sepp, but one vital still for Hitler's well-being over the next 11 years.

"The personnel files of the Führerschutzkommando commander, Police Captain Johann Rattenhuber, show that he was in command from March 15, 1933, but as late as December 28th, Rattenhuber's letterheads describe him as Adjutant to the Commander of the Political Police in Münich (i.e. Himmler); in November 1934 his letterhead read Gestapo-Führerschutzkommando. Only in 1935 did Rattenhuber's Führerschutzkommando become a separate Reich agency; and was now called Reichssicherheitsdienst," asserts Peter Hoffmann.

In some respects, the careers of Dietrich and Rattenhuber were alike. Born in 1897 he, unlike Sepp, graduated from a secondary school, joined the Army in 1916 during the First World War and was commissioned a Second Lieutenant just as the war was ending, late in 1918. "He served in a Free Corps until March 31, 1920, then joined the Bavarian Provincial Police [where served Sepp] in Bayreuth, was promoted to lieutenant in 1925, and to Captain in June 1933. His appointment was not based on any Party merits [as had been Sepp's]. He did not even become a Party member until May 1, 1933."

Still, during 1933-34, the working relationship of Hitler's own, hand-picked security detail chief (Dietrich) with that of Himmler for the Führer (i.e. Rattenhuber) was at best confusing and always murky: "In its earliest days, the Führerschutzkommando, which was composed mostly of Bavarian criminal police officers, could operate only in Bavaria, where Himmler's authority was undisputed.

"In the Reich Chancellery, the criminal police officers of the Berlin Police IA Department were forced into the background by Hitler's personal SS Begleit-Kommando (SS Escort). Hitler refused to allow any bodyguards to accompany him in the early months of his rule, but Himmler's criminal police Führerschutzkommando tried to follow him around surreptitiously. One day in the spring of 1933 in München, Hitler noticed another car following his own and that of his SS Escort, and he instructed his driver, Kempka, to increase the speed of his supercharged Mercedes so that the strange car could not keep up. It developed that the 'strange car' carried Himmler's policemen!

Hitler, however, retained a strong aversion to policemen of any kind, apparently derived from his experiences in the Years of Struggle. It was not until the spring of 1934 that he finally accepted the professional criminal police guards, so that they were enabled to operate in the entire Reich territory."

By 1935, there were 18 members of the Führerschutzkommando, including its commanding officer. On February 13, 1935, there was held a special conference among the various bureaucracies involved in the daily protection of Hitler the Party Leader and Führer, and Hitler the government Chancellor, to try to sort out the growing, overlapping mess.

"The details included four criminal police officers salaried by the Presidium of Police in Berlin; four gendarmes paid by the Reich Ministry of the Interior; 31 men from the SS Leibstandarte Adolf Hitler whose salaries were paid by the Reich Ministry of the Interior; and 15 Führerschutzkommando officers from the criminal police forces of the various provinces and paid by them."

After many more such meetings and much inter-bureaucratic haggling as to which group would fall under whose budgetary preserves, it was agreed on March 29, 1935 that "the Führerschutzkommando budget and the operating costs for the Reichssicherheitsdienst (Reich Security Service, or RSD) … were to be listed together in the budget of the Reich Ministry of the Interior." Himmler continued these tangles with the Minister, Dr. Wilhelm Frick, for another eight years, until he himself succeeded and supplanted his Nazi rival as Minister of the Interior.

And yet, in October 1935, Hitler had appointed Himmler Chief of the RSD for the entire Reich, and on the surface thus responsible for the protection of Hitler and all other top government figures as well. But, just as Sepp always had and always did remain directly responsible to Hitler alone, so now, too, did Hitler tweak his ambitious Reichsführer's administrative nose yet again by absorbing Rattenhuber and his men within his own orbit of Reich Chancellery power!

"Rattenhuber was still the commander and took most of his orders, especially for day-to-day operation, directly from Hitler through one of his aides Brückner, Bormann, Schaub) … The immediate RSD commanders were Rattenhuber and his deputies, Detective Inspector of Criminal Police (Peter) Högl and Police Inspector (Paul) Kiesel. All took orders directly from Hitler, Hess, Bormann or Brückner. Himmler tried many times, even via his position as Chief of German Police, to gain full control of Hitler's RSD bodyguards, but Martin Bormann got a good deal further toward this goal."

Why? Why was controlling the Führer's guards so important to all these high Nazi leaders? The reason was simply as a means of having protective access over the man who ruled the Reich, a fact of which Hitler was acutely aware from the start. He eliminated the SA threat to his rule by murder, proceeded to neutralize the conservative faction/military menace systematically until it was for all practical purposes totally negated by the time war broke out on September 1, 1939, and never allowed the SS to grow beyond a point where he felt it was out of control. Indeed, until the last day of his life, the SS men within his own, private circle owed their allegiance to him, the Führer, never to their "own" Reichsführer SS, and Hitler even fired Himmler before the end of the war for entreating with the enemy. Even though he always addressed Himmler as "the loyal Heinrich," he never entirely trusted his own, handpicked Reichsführer—and for good reason, as it turned out.

Even as the war went from bad to worse, Hitler—as with the LSSAH before it—never relinquished control over the RSD: "In January 1942, (Dr. Hans-Heinrich) Lammers contemplated alleviating the burden of Hitler's many official duties, seeing that the Führer's health was deteriorating rapidly, but Hitler firmly insisted on signing every RSD man's appointment document in his own hand in every case. Again, in 1944, it was emphasized that, while the Reichsführer SS was 'Chief' of the RSD and Rattenhuber was his deputy as commander, the Führer had reserved for himself personally the command of the RSD. The RSD had become a separate Reich agency not subordinated institutionally to any other Reich authority (Ministry of the Interior, Chancellery, Reichssicherheitshauptamt, or RSHA), but only to the Führer himself."

As an avid student of history throughout his life, Hitler was perfectly well aware that the Roman Emperors had often been overthrown by their own Praetorian Guards, that Napoleon's police chief, Joseph Fouché, had plotted against him, and in his own time had witnessed the fall of his Axis Pact partner—Italian Duce Benito Mussolini—taken out of power by an internal palace coup; he had no intention of allowing that to happen to himself. Whatever else the man may have failed at, he succeeded in maintaining internal power within his regime until the very moment he shot himself with his own pistol on Apr. 30, 1945.

Moreover, both elements of the LSSAH and RSD detachments were also "assigned" to Himmler, Göring, Goebbels, von Ribbentrop, Frick, Walther Darré (Minister of Food), Hess (Deputy Führer) and, as the later war expanded throughout Europe, to all of the Führer's various satraps ruling in his name in foreign capitals. He could, therefore, order the arrest of all of them by telephone, telegram or teleprinter (as he did in the case of Göring in April 1945).

Thus, gradually, the RSD began weaving its own network of responsibilities for Hitler's cars, planes, trains, private homes, government residences and, during the war, his many far-flung military headquarters. The growth of the RSD was not as rapid or as large as that of its (at first) seemingly parallel organization, the LSSAH under Sepp Dietrich, but while the latter went off to fight Hitler's foreign wars as his SS representatives, the RSD remained behind to accomplish their joint and original task: to protect the Führer.

"In 1935; there were 45 RSD officers (not counting crews of Hitler's planes), some 20 of whom were detailed for Hitler's security … By 1936, there were 56 positions in the RSD, and in the draft budget for 1937, there were 100. By 1939, there were some 200 RSD men, and about 400 by the end of the war." Dietrich's LSSAH men received their field gray Waffen SS uniforms in March 1938, as they spearheaded the peaceful Nazi annexation of Hitler's former homeland, Austria, into the Third Reich, but, conversely, Rattenhuber's RSD men remained in the somber SS black until war broke out on September 1, 1939. When not on field duty before the outbreak of war, it should be clarified—such as on guard at the Reich Chancellery or parading down the Wilhelmstrasse for the Führer—the LSSAH retained for wear their own black SS uniforms, made distinctive from those of the Allgemeine SS by the exclusive use of white belts and cross-belts.

According to one knowledgeable source, "true, the LSSAH did wear the black, but they never wore the white belts apart from guard or parade duty! The ordinarily SS black uniform did not bear the exclusive sleeve band or shoulder strap logo which identified members of the LSSAH when off duty or on the street."

In addition to the LSSAH and RSD detachments guarding the Führer, there was also the so-called Führer Escort Detachment, or Führer-Begleit-Kommando, which was derived thus: "For trips and public functions, between 5–11 members of each of the RSD and SS Begleit Kommando, were combined to form the Führer-Begleit-Kommando." To the outsider, this must seem somewhat confusing, "but RSD and SS-Begleit-Kommando … moved in separate groups, even in separate cars, when they were combined as Führer-Begleit-Kommando, and each had a keen consciousness of being different, of having special and different duties," states Hoffmann.

And that was not all! "There had been since 1935 an internal Sicherheitsdienst (Security Service) in the Reich Chancellery for doorman and surveillance service … in 1939, a new SicherheitsKontroldienst (Security Control Service) was set up in the new Berlin Reich Chancellery and adjoining buildings … it began operations December 12, 1939, and its responsibilities included patrolling the Chancellery, the Presidential Chancellery [of the late von Hindenburg], the Private Chancellery of the Führer, and the Supreme SA Leadership Office … The patrols should be manned by experienced craftsmen who could intelligently keep under surveillance any construction repair work in the buildings."

Rattenhuber was also placed in charge of these men, who were armed with Walther PPK 7.65 mm pistols and flashlights. As for the Führer's pilot, Col. Hans Baur, and his air personnel, Peter Hoffmann states that they "were not integrated into an existing security force such as RSD or SS Escort … instead, they were given commissions as police officers, so that, in fact, still another independent group directly responsible to the Führer was created. Rattenhuber did not command it immediately, and Himmler had as much or as little authority over it as over the RSD and the operations of the SS-Begleit-Kommando."

This assertion seems at variance with that of Dietrich's biographer, Charles Messenger, in *Hitler's Gladiator*, penned some nine years after Hoffmann's 1979 *Hitler's Personal Security*. In Messenger's version, Sepp and the LSSAH maintained organizational control over Col. Baur and his men, but in the bureaucratic jungle that Hitler and his "centrist" Nazis seemed to delight in creating and re-creating for themselves, it is possible that maybe even they did not know for sure!

Then there was the Führer-Begleit-Battalion (Führer Escort Battalion) of the regular Army's Greater Germany Armored Division (Panzer Division Grossdeutschland), whose responsibility it was to safeguard the Reich Chancellor's Führerhauptquartier during wartime.

Initially called the *Kommando Führereise/Leader Trips* in June 1938, it guarded Hitler in the Sudetenland in October 1938, and in Prague in March 1939. As of Aug. 23, 1939, the unit was named *Frontgruppe der FHQu.Truppen,* later as *Führer-Begleit=Battalion,* and as of November 1939---as with the later, wartime *Führer-Begleit-Battalion*---its forerunners were commanded to January 1940 by German Army Col. Erwin Rommel.

By now, I suppose, the reader is thoroughly confused—and who wouldn't be? Pity the poor men who were charged with making all this work and with not butting heads into each other, willingly or not. Undeniably—and perhaps completely understandably!—the many and varied differences between and among these men and units led to friction and clashes over authority and jurisdictions. They displayed disparate training and backgrounds, but all were devoted to the safety and wellbeing of their "Chief"---as they called him---Hitler.

The SS were mainly political soldiers, while the RSD was the most standout unit, it being comprised of professional police officers much like the then and still current US Secret Service, trained to halt attacks before they happened, if possible. Like the *SS-Begleit-Kommando,* the RSD and all the others stood by Hitler daily, in all types of hazards and weather as well.

All were prepared to die for Hitler if necessary.

But how did all this work in actual practice?

Chapter Six

Guarding the Head of State

The practical aspects of guarding Adolf Hitler in his various capacities as Head of the German State, Chancellor of the German Reich, Supreme Commander of the Wehrmacht and Führer of the Nazi Party (and with it the SS and SA) was truly a daunting task for both of the men charged with its accomplishment—RSD Gruppenführer Johann Rattenhuber and SS Oberstgruppenführer Josef "Sepp" Dietrich. Before the German declaration of war against Poland in September 1939, this involved protecting the Führer in his various official and private residences throughout the Third Reich itself—as well as traveling from point to point by car, train and plane. After September 1, 1939, was added the responsibility of guarding Hitler the Warlord at his many wartime military headquarters scattered across Europe in Germany, Belgium, France and Russia.

As a starting point there were his official and private residences prior to the outbreak of the war. These included first the old and new Berlin Reich Chancelleries, the former occupied from the date he achieved governmental power—January 30, 1933, until he vacated it for the latter six years later, in January 1939. This latter building—although grandiose in the extreme—was meant only as a temporary residence, to be replaced by a third, even more grand structure in 1950, after the Nazis had won the Second World War and perhaps even the Third World War—the latter against her former Axis Pact partners, Fascist Italy in Europe and Imperial Japan in the Far East.

Even in 1939, as the "new" Berlin Reich Chancellery was being dedicated, the Führer was thinking of the unbuilt Führer Palace, still 11 years away! He discussed this future project in detail with his prewar architect, Albert Speer, according to the latter in his 1969 autobiography, *Memoirs: Inside the Third Reich.*

> He said he might be forced to take unpopular measures, and then there could be an insurrection. One had to be prepared for this possibility: all buildings on the square where the new Führer Palace was to stand were to have heavy steel shutters and doors, all bullet-proof, and the entire square was to be closed off with steel gates.
>
> The Palace itself would have no windows at all, the only openings being a huge, heavy steel door and a door onto a small balcony, five stories above the crowds, from which Hitler could receive ovations. The barracks of the Leibstandarte … were to be moved close to the Palace, but the Army's Berlin Guard Battalion barracks were to be located even closer.

There was reason to worry, too, as despite the vigilance of the combined SS and RSD detachments, on January 11, 1937, at 2:30 p.m. in full daylight—an unemployed salesman climbed over the

Vossstrasse fence and even got into the old Reich Chancellery through an open toilet window, carrying a gas pistol. Unemployed for five years, he sought a meeting with Hitler; arrested, he was let go without charges being filed. On the following February 14th, butcher Franz Kroll tried to force his way into Hitler's rooms at the Chancellery. Drunk, he was turned over to the Berlin police. There were several more such incidents as well, all deflected in time, plus the usual accidental shots from SA and SS guards themselves, toying with their loaded weapons.

The 1935 balcony added to the Old Chancellery and built for Hitler by Speer was reinforced with 8 mm steel plates under its concrete façade. This was eclipsed by the more magnificent New Berlin Reich Chancellery where one was able simply to walk up to him for a casual chat—so safe did Hitler feel within the confines of his official Berlin residence.

Indeed, his very presence there was advertised to the public by the flying of his own personal standard (designed by him, incidentally). It flew from a flagpole atop the building whenever the Führer was in residence (as, indeed, it flew wherever he was present officially).

Yet there were constant lapses in security from the first to the last days of the Third Reich's 12-year existence, and people always seemed to be losing their passes—including even Sepp Dietrich and the Führer's own personal SS valet, Heinz Linge. On March 16, 1939, a SS sentry was found asleep on guard duty, a condition seemingly the bane of sentries the world over.

The coming of the war and the November 8, 1939, attempt to kill Hitler at the Bürgerbräukeller beer hall in Münich by a carpenter-built time bomb tightened up security a great deal at Hitler's many residences. These included his apartment on Prince Regent Street in Münich, his suite of rooms at the Kaiserhof in Nuremburg, where he stayed during the annual Nazi Party Rallies each September, and at The Berghof, his alpine retreat overlooking the village of Berchtesgaden in the Bavarian Alps, as well as at the official Party structures in Münich, the old Brown House and the newer Führerbau.

Wartime air raids were seen as possible enemy penetrations of their security defenses, so RSD men ensured that all gates and doors were locked during them to prevent any intruders gaining access. No RSD men could leave their posts until even after dropped incendiary bombs had been extinguished, and also not until the Chancellery's roof-mounted anti-aircraft batteries actually returned fire! During such events, relief guards were dispatched on the half hour.

Interestingly enough—so far as is known, at any rate—no Allied assassination attempt was ever tried against Hitler or any other Nazi leader, with the exception of SS Gen. Reinhard Heydrich, who was successfully attacked in his car while on the way to his office one morning by Czech parachutists, and the failed attempt by British commandos to kill Afrika Korps leader Field Marshal Erwin Rommel at the latter's headquarters in 1941. No bombing attack was ever made on any of Hitler's homes and headquarters—even by the Soviets—throughout the war, nor any commando assaults on any of them either.

Asked to assess the security of the Wolf's Lair military headquarters in East Prussia in September 1943, following his successful rescue of the imprisoned Mussolini from a mountain-top prison, SS Maj Otto Skorzeny alarmed Rattenhuber's RSD men when he said it would be both entirely possible and feasible to penetrate it. Indeed, construction of new bunkers and fence perimeters went on there even after Hitler left it for good in November 1944 as the Red Army approached.

On March 11, 1942, two telephone cable workmen in overalls simply walked into the Reich Chancellery, stating that they were looking for a fellow worker. Notes Hoffmann somewhat humorously:

They talked to two of the guards, who directed them to other entrances without accompanying them so that the two laborers roamed the basements of several parts of the building until they were finally stopped by a third guard in an inner court.

Hitler maintained the Münich apartment from 1929-45, and Sepp Dietrich lived there, too, after 1934. It consisted of nine rooms, two kitchens, two storage rooms and two bathrooms. When Hitler was actually there, the RSD had 14 men posted, but it was always occupied and watched by security men even when he was absent, with seven on duty and 14 assigned at all times, with the roof patrolled as well.

The Führerbau—north of the Brown House on Arcisstrasse in Münich—came on-line in 1937. This, too, was guarded at all times, whether or not the Führer was present.

The Berghof—in addition to being under the watchful eyes of both Dietrich and Rattenhuber— also fell under the construction aegis of Martin Bormann, first in his capacity as Rudolf Hess's deputy assigned to the Führer's entourage, and then—after the Deputy Führer's 1941 flight to Scotland—in his own right as Reichsleiter and, after 1943, as Secretary to the Führer. Hitler first began staying in the Berchtesgaden area during 1922-23, when the old building was the modest Haus Wachenfeld. After 1933 it was rebuilt and added onto as the ever-grander Berghof, a construction project that kept Bormann busy right up until the end of the war. It is significant to note that the British finally bombed the entire area once (including the home of Luftwaffe Reich Marshal Hermann Göring) on Apr. 23, 1945, when it was already clear that Nazi Germany had lost the war. Hitler wasn't present, although Göring and his family were in their private air raid shelter and survived the aerial attack.

At first, even after 1933, life tended to be somewhat more relaxed in this beautiful mountain setting. On his daily alpine walks while he was in residence, Hitler could easily have been successfully attacked, just as the British wartime SOE planned in its *Operation Foxley* that was never implemented, however. A series of concentric fences surrounded the entire area of "Hitler's mountain," and was maintained up to May 1945.

And yet, until at least 1937, 2,000 people daily came to be seen and received by him in long lines on the grounds, watched by vigilant SS men. One who had virtual constant access to Hitler in order to photograph him as his court lensman, was Heinrich Hoffmann of Münich.

At least one known instance of an armed assassin in an SA uniform in 1933 is on record. Hitler was also stalked there in late 1938 by Swiss theology student Maurice Bavaud. By the end of the war, only 30% of Bormann's work-force at Berchtesgaden which by then numbered in the thousands— were native Germans.

Still, there was the Platterhof SS Barracks above the Berghof where were housed the ceremonial guards of the LSSAH, and an extensive series of bunkers underneath the various structures, linked by underground tunnels and lifts. Over all of these structures there was the lofty Eagle's Nest on the towering Kehlstein, built by Bormann for presentation on Hitler's 50th birthday, Apr. 20, 1939. The Führer visited it only a few times, because he found it difficult to breathe there and felt uneasy in taking the elevator that had been blasted out of the solid rock.

From the earliest days of the Nazi movement, Hitler preferred traveling in big, heavy, expensive Mercedes-Benz touring cars and several of his original SS bodyguards had been his drivers, members of his inner circle of "chaffeureska." After taking power in 1933, "he rarely rode in his car without having it followed by a carload of SS Escort men, plus a carload of RSD after 1934. Hitler usually sat next to the driver (except on ceremonial occasions) with one of his valets, usually Krause or Linge sitting behind him. They were armed, and during the war they carried machinepistols.

Hitler joked to his personal SS valet Heinz Linge of his SSBK commander, "Linge, I am glad that Gesche does not sit behind me—he might shoot me in the back!" At lunch at Führer Headquarters on May 3, 1942, Hitler asserted, "As far as possible, whenever I go anywhere by car I go off unexpectedly and without warning the police. I have also given Rattenhuber ... and Kempka, my chauffeur, the strictest orders to maintain absolute secrecy about my comings and goings, and have further impressed on them that these orders must still be obeyed even when the highest officials in the land make inquiries ..."

Hitler always used his own armored Mercedes-Benz touring cars whenever possible, rejecting those of his field commanders whom he visited, having both his own vehicle and those of his RSD bodyguards sent on ahead whenever necessary.

Hitler trusted not even his own Party leaders or his generals and marshals, and with good reason, since plots to remove or kill him germinated from within both groups on several occasions.

Before coming to power on January 30, 1933, Hitler owned at least four known vehicles, and during the years of the Third Reich, another 44 cars were ordered from Daimler-Benz for use by the Reich Chancellery and its various bureaus. The Leader Convoy was called in German the Führerkolonne.

Rattenhuber mandated that his field men retire at age 50 because of the duty strain upon them. Drivers were instructed to smash with their own cars any vehicle that obstructed that of Hitler's. Unknown vehicle drivers could be blindsided at night by rear-mounted searchlights that were standard equipment on all his cars, it has been reported.

Careless pedestrians might even be run down, as, indeed, one woman was, accidentally. FBK and RSD men both rode on the sideboards of Hitler's car, and also cleared the way by running alongside it when necessary through crowds.

Still, Hitler insisted on standing up in his cars as he entered cities and reviewed troops, seeming to tempt fate. There are no recorded attempts at his being shot at during these times, although at least Maurice Bavaud contemplated attacking him with a pistol during one of the Münich Feldherrnhalle marches.

For longer ground trips, Hitler preferred to travel by rail, both before and during the war. He went into both Austria and Prague by car, but by train to the Czech Sudetenland and to visit Mussolini once in 1938 and twice in 1940, as well as to see both French Marshal Phillippe Pétain and Spanish Generalissimo Francisco Franco that same year.

Hitler used Special Trains as Chancellor. During 1937-39, new coaches were constructed for the permanent Führer Special Train. All cars were built of welded steel---excluding their windows---and topped 60 tons' weight. By January 1939, two *Führersonderzug/Leader Special Trains* existed: one for prewar travel, and the other for wartime, reportedly.

The wartime Special was known as *Führerhauptquartier/Leader Headquarters*, and was later codenamed, ironically, *Amerika*, in August 1939, for the invasion of Poland and beyond.

Hitler banned advance publication and/or even Railway notification to deter assassins, but this created chaos for German *Reichsbahn* re-scheduling of other trains when the Führer Special came on. When unused, the Führer Special was stationed at Berlin's Tempelhof repair depot.

Rattenhuber---and not the now combatant Sepp Dietrich---was in charge of the Führer's travel safety. Heavily armored, the Special Train had state-of-the-art radio communications, and its own anti-aircraft guns, but the safest air defense tactic was the closest railroad tunnel; Hitler never resorted to this, however.

Amerika was Hitler's mobile headquarters twice: in the Polish campaign of September 1939, and again for the April 1941 *Operation Spring Storm* against Yugoslavia, and also *Operation Marita* versus Greece and its Crete, being parked at the Monichskirken, Austria railway platform that can still be seen today.

In 1945, the Führer Special Train was captured, and Hitler's personal Pullman #10206 was blown up by the Allies upon capture, allegedly. According to the English publication *After the Battle*:

> The rest of the train traveled to Saalfelden and remained there until the end of May; then it went on to Pullach near München, where it was taken over by the American Army. Most of the carriages were used by American and British military authorities, and returned to German authorities in 1950, 1951 and 1953. One of the carriages was still used in the Federal Chancellor's Special Train in the 1960s.

If Franklin Roosevelt used trains extensively during the American Presidential campaign of 1932 for the first time in a major way, so, too, did Adolf Hitler employ aircraft in his two efforts to defeat the aged Marshal Paul von Hindenburg for re-election as President. The Nazi propaganda slogan was "Hitler Over Germany," and he would swoop down on several German cities daily from the air to make political stump speeches. His pilot in all these flights was the civilian Hans Baur. The two men got along well from the start, and after 1933 the, Reich Chancellor got Baur into Luftwaffe uniform as his only personal pilot until the very end of the war—when he refused the then Colonel's offer to fly him to safety out of burning Berlin and the clutches of the Russians.

Baur, a Nazi Party member since 1921, was eventually not only Hitler's pilot, but also in charge of the official Government Flight, which consisted at one time of some 40 aircraft—a small Luftwaffe in itself. At the beginning, however, it included a modest six Junkers Ju-52 transport planes. Later it also encompassed models by Focke-Wulf that were bigger and much faster, complete with a special parachute chair to eject Hitler from a plane attack if need be.

Hitler preferred travel by both car and rail to that by air, fearing thunderstorms, lightning strikes, and being downed over water, since he was a non-swimmer, plus other aerial hazards, such as crashes and mechanical failures.

Hitler rarely traveled by water, his official State yacht *Grille* notwithstanding.

There was at least one known assassination attempt against him on his plane, when a time bomb was placed aboard it in Russia by one of the German Army officer plotters. It failed to go off, however, and was retrieved before it was discovered. One should also bear in mind that three top German officers died in air crashes during the war: Luftwaffe ace and first General of the Fighters Werner Mölders in 1941, Todt Organization chief and Reich Minister of Munitions Dr. Fritz Todt in 1942, and Alpenkorps Gen. Edouard Dietl ("The Lion of Narvik" in Norway in 1940) in June 1944 in the frozen north. Considering all the thousands of air-miles he logged flying with Hans Baur during 1932-44, Hitler was indeed lucky not to have suffered a similar fate—not to mention being shot down by an enemy fighter, as was Imperial Japanese Combined Fleet Admiral Isoroku Yamamoto on Apr. 18, 1943 in the Pacific.

Just as with his travel arrangements, Hitler's public appearances were also rigidly controlled events, as were his informal teatime "bull sessions" with his cronies at such watering holes as the *Kaiserhof* in Berlin and the two cafés he favored most when in München, the *Heck* and the *Osteria*.

There were also a series of annual events he generally attended, both Nazi holidays and official governmental observances. These included, January 30th, the taking of power, parades in Berlin; February 24th, Party Founding Day, meeting held at München's *Hofbräuhaus*; March 21st, Heldengedenktag (Heroes' Memorial Day), parade and commemoration ceremonies in the Reich capital; Apr. 20th, the Führer's birthday, day-long celebrations and parades in Berlin; May 1st, honoring the labor movement, Berlin events; September, week-long Nuremberg Party Rally; November 8th–9th, Beer Hall Putsch commemorative meeting at Bürgerbräukeller, followed the next day by a ceremonial march through downtown München.

At all of these events, in addition to the security forces already discussed, the local Gauleiters were in charge of security arrangements within their own districts. This setup drove first Sepp—and later, Rattenhuber—to distraction, particularly since Hitler never wanted the local police to protect him, and trusted only his own LSSAH, FBK and RSD forces.

Generally, when speaking in halls or at outdoor rallies, when riding through crowds or towns in his car or when walking, the Führer was completely and totally surrounded by his SS and RSD men, although people—children and women especially—could and did frequently break through these cordons to shake his hand, salute him or hand Hitler the seemingly ever-present bouquets of flowers that caused his guards so much worry.

The SS men had strict orders of what to do when guarding him, particularly at public events. They were not to salute as he passed, for instance, but told to keep their eyes either on him and/or the crowd. During the Winter Olympic Games, there were even SS men present on skiis. Carloads of burly guards followed him during all motorcades, while others lined the routes, linking arms and even holding each other's belts to keep back the surging crowds. When Hitler addressed the Nazi parliament, the Reichstag, in Berlin's Kroll Opera House (after the fire of February 27, 1933, that gutted the former building), over 4,000 SS men guarded his route from the Reich Chancellery to the speaker's platform.

Despite all these arrangements, Hitler believed he could be "eliminated at any moment by a fool, insane person or assassin," particularly by a sniper firing with a rifle fitted with a telescopic sight from a tall building. In addition, as he once told his aides:

> Imagine that, while we are gathered here, a truck passes through the Wilhelmstrasse. Right in front of the Reich Chancellery, it has a flat tire or other breakdown. The driver leaves to get help, and meanwhile the truck—loaded with dynamite—blows up and buries us under the ruins of the Chancellery!

Notes Peter Hoffmann: "This was precisely the opportunity offered to the drivers of the commanders-in-chief of the Army, Navy and Air Force, or of some of the other dignitaries who were driven into the courtyard." None ever tried this, though.

He was also vulnerable on the usual reviewing stand site during his Berlin parades—in front of the Institute of Technology on Berlinerstrasse. Indeed, as war looked ever more likely, the Berlin-based British military Attaché, Col. Mason-MacFarlane, even urged his government officials to shoot Hitler at that spot:

> I had strongly urged that Hitler should be assassinated. My residence in Berlin was barely 100 yards from the saluting base of all the big Führer reviews. All that was necessary was a good shot and a high-velocity rifle with telescopic sight and silencer. It could have been fired through my open bathroom window from a spot on the landing some 30 feet back from the window.

Although the idea was feasible, London vetoed it. Perhaps it was rejected because it was still peacetime; in war, it was the British who sent the Czech paratroopers to kill "Hangman" Heydrich, as well as the commandos to slay "Desert Fox" Erwin Rommel.

Asks Hoffmann, "What if one of the many machinegunners passing in review had suddenly turned his weapon on Hitler's stand and opened fire?" And what of the SS guards themselves? Were they not possible suspects? All of these were possibilities, except that Hitler developed an extremely close, personal relationship with each and every one of his guards and—as we have witnessed—personally approved all their individual appointments. When asked to retire prematurely some of the older men from the force, Hitler would not hear of it, declaring that he would keep these loyal men with him at his side and in his employ as long as he lived—and was as good as his word, too.

Asserts Peter Hoffmann, "Hitler himself once singled out the Nuremberg Party Rally as the event where he was exposed to the greatest degree of danger," especially at the 1934 event immediately following the Röhm Purge. As journalist William L. Shirer noted in his *Berlin Diary* for September 9th:

> Hitler faced his SA Stormtroopers today for the first time since the bloody purge … There was considerable tension in the stadium, and I noticed that Hitler's own SS bodyguard was drawn up in force in front of him, separating him from the mass of the Brownshirts. We wondered if just one of those 50,000 Brownshirts wouldn't pull a revolver, but not one did.

Hitler was well aware, too, that few of his immediate associates with whom he was in daily contact, would simply have the guts to walk up and shoot him point-blank, even though—until von Stauffenberg's bomb went off at Rastenberg on July 20, 1944—there was no screening of personnel for concealed weapons. It was considered inconceivable that a German officer would violate either his own oath or Hitler's tacit trust in this way.

Indeed, Chief of the German General Staff Col. Gen. Franz Halder met Hitler oft times with a loaded pistol, intent on shooting him. Neither he—nor anyone else in the inner circles, for that matter—ever attempted such a thing, despite daily opportunities to do so over the course of several years.

It cannot be denied that Hitler was an extremely lucky man as regards premonitions about leaving the scene of impending danger to his person. During the late 1920s he on numerous times told his chauffeurs to drive off, and later found out that something had happened just after he left. On November 8, 1939, he left the Bürgerbräukeller just moments before the planted bomb exploded. At the Berlin Zeughaus (Armory and Museum) on March 21, 1943, he scurried through an exhibition in great haste, as if he somehow knew there was an assassin lurking with a lethal weapon stalking him. Indeed, there was, an Army Colonel with a bomb in his pocket who meant to take his own life while killing the Führer. Hitler guessed right, and the bomb was never used.

Perhaps most ironic of all, the only attempts that came really close to succeeding were by those Hitler suspected least, his own Army officers. Von Stauffenberg had planned to explode his briefcase bomb at The Berghof a few days prior to the actual detonation at Wolfsschanze on July 20, 1944, but declined because both Göring and Himmler were absent from the Führer Conference and the conspirators initially wanted to kill all three men at once. It was only after it appeared unlikely that they would, in fact, be able to accomplish this goal that it was decided to strike at Hitler alone at Rastenburg.

This same attempt would have been possible at any of Hitler's many wartime headquarters. There is an interesting passage on them found in the introduction to *Hitler's Secret Conversations, 1941-44* by the British historian H. R. Trevor-Roper (who in 1947 published *The Last Days of Hitler*):

Hitler's life, during the war, was spent, in general, at his military headquarters. At first, during the Polish campaign, these headquarters were in his Special Train, stationed near Goglin; later, during the same campaign, he transferred them to a hotel in Zoppot. At the beginning of the Western campaign, his headquarters were in a cramped bunker near Bad Nauheim, which he called Felsennest, or "Eyrie;" later, as victory followed victory, he moved to Bruly-le-Pêche in Eastern France.

His quarters there were named Wolfsschlucht/"Wolf's Lair" (he had an odd liking for the name Wolf, which he had himself assumed when in hiding in the days of struggle for power.) … Thereafter, he divided his time between a new headquarters in the Black Forest (Tannenberg) and his Special Train. Then in July 1941, he moved to East Prussia to direct the greatest of all his campaigns, the knock-out blow in the East.

For over three years, his headquarters remained in the East, generally in East Prussia, once (during the triumphant advance in the summer of 1941) in Russia itself. Then, in November 1944, Field Marshal Keitel persuaded him to leave that insalubrious spot, among dreary pine forests, in which he had so nearly been assassinated and in which he had lived, for the last year, night and day, a troglodyte existence. …

This East Prussian headquarters was at Rastenburg, and Hitler called it Wolfsschanze. His temporary Russian headquarters was at Winnitza in the Ukraine, and was called "Werwolf."

In the end, Hitler defeated all the security measures he had ever implemented on Apr. 30, 1945, when he took his own life.

And what of Johann Rattenhuber of the RSD? He, along with most of the surviving occupants of the underground Berlin Führerbunker, escaped from the burning Reich Chancellery after Hitler's suicide—only to be captured by the Red Army and imprisoned within the Soviet Union for the next 10 years; released, he returned to Germany and died in 1967, shortly after Sepp Dietrich.

Bibliography and Other Suggested Additional Reading

Anyone delving into the SS will find a vast treasure trove of books, memoirs, studies, monographs and other volumes. The search for information in this field is truly varied and rewarding. The following list represents those works that I consulted for the present volume:

Biographies

Eva Braun: Hitler's Mistress by Nerin E. Gun, Meredith Press, New York, 1968.

Hitler's Gladiator: The Life and Times of Oberstgruppenführer and Panzergeneraloberst der Waffen SS Sepp Dietrich by Charles Messenger, Brassey's Defense Publishers, London, 1988.

SS Oberstgruppenführer und Generaloberst der Waffen SS Paul Hausser, 1880-1972 by Mark C. Yerger, John Fedorowicz, Winnipeg, 1986.

Student by A. H. Farrar-Hockley, Ballantine Books, New York, 1973.

Leibstandarte Histories

Hitler's Guard: The Story of the Leibstandarte SS Adolf Hitler, 1933-1945 by James J. Weingartner, Battery Classics, Nashville, 1979.

Hitler's Bodyguards by Alan Wykes, Ballantine Books, New York, 1974.

The Leibstandarte/I—1 SS Panzer Division Leibstandarte Adolf Hitler by Rudolf Lehmann, J. J. Fedorowicz Publishing, Winnipeg, 1987.

Die Leibstandarte im Bild by Rudolf Lehmann, Munin-Verlag GmbH, Osnabrück, 1983.

Collected Biographies

Defeat in the West by Milton Shulman, E. P. Dutton and Co., Inc., New York, 1948.

German Commanders of World War II by Anthony Kemp and Angus McBride, Osprey Publishing, London, 1982.

Hitler's Generals, Edited by Correlli Barnett, Grove Weidenfeld, New York, 1989.

Hitler's Field Marshals and Their Battles by Samuel W Mitcham, Jr., Scarborough House, Publishers, 1990.

Leaders and Personalities of the Third Reich by Charles Hamilton, R. James Bender Publishing, San Jose, 1984.

Encyclopedia of the Third Reich by Louis L. Snyder, McGraw-Hill Book Company, New York, 1976.

Who's Who in Nazi Germany by Robert Wistrich, Bonanza Books, New York, 1982.

On the Field of Honor: A History of the Knight's Cross Bearers, by LTC John R. Angolia, R. James Bender Publishing, San Jose, Volume 1 (1979); Volume 2 (1980).

Medals, Badges, Militaria, Etc.

The Iron Cross: A History, 1813-1957 by Gordon Williamson, Blandford Press, Dorset, 1987.

The Prussian Orden Pour le Mérite: History of the Blue Max by David Edkins, Ajay Enterprises, Falls Church, 1981.

Basic Nazi Swords and Daggers, by Peter Stahl, Die Wehrmacht Military Publications, Stanford, 1972.

SS Regalia by Jack Pia, Ballantine Books, New York, 1974.

Third Reich Militaria by Robin Lumsden, Ian Allen Ltd., London, 1987.

Military Uniforms of the World in Color by Preben Kannik, Macmillan Co., New York, 1968.

Army Uniforms of the Second World War by Andrew Mollo and Malcolm McGregor, Blandford Press, Dorset, 1977.

German Uniforms of the Third Reich by Brian Leigh Davis and Pierre Turner, Arco Publishing Co., Inc., New York, 1980.

Orders, Medals, Decorations and Badges of the Third Reich by David Littlejohn and Col. C. M. Dodkins, R. James Bender Publishing, San Jose, 1968.

Combat Medals of the Third Reich by Christopher Ailsby, Patrick Stephens, Wellingborough, 1987.

German Uniforms of the Second World War by Christopher Ailsby, Patrick Stephens, Wellingborough, 1987.

Uniforms and Badges of the Third Reich/Volume II–*SA, NSKK, SS* by Rudolf Kahl, Military Collectors Service, Holland, (no date).

Volume I–*NSDAP* by Rudolf Kahl, Military Collectors Service, Holland, (no date).

Flags and Standards of the Third Reich: Army, Navy and Air Force by Brian Leigh Davis, Arco Publishing Co. Inc., New York, 1975.

Hitler's Teutonic Knights: SS Panzers in Action by Bruce Quarrie, Patrick Stephens, Wellinborough, 1986.

Weapons of the Waffen SS: From Small Arms to Tanks by Bruce Quarrie, Patrick Stephens, Wellinborough, 1988.

German Tanks of the Second World War in Action by George Forty, Arms and Armor Press, New York, 1987.

Buildings And Cities

The Reichs Chancellery and the Berlin Bunker: Then and Now, After the Battle, Battle of Britain Prints International Ltd., London, 1988.

Hitler's New German Reich's Chancellery in Berlin, 1939-45 by Ray Cowdery, Northstar Maschek Books, Switzerland, 1987.

Obersalzberg: The History of a Mountain from Judith Platter Till Hitler by Josef Geiss, Verlag Josef Geiss, Berchtesgaden, 1983.

Hitler and Münich by Brian Deming and Ted Hiff, Verlag Anton Plenk, Berchtesgaden, (no date).

The Eagle's Nest: From Adolf Hitler to the Present Day by Andrew Frank, Anton Plenk, Berchtesgaden, 1985.

Obersalzberg After the Battle, Battle of Britain Prints International Ltd., London, 1975.

Events

To Die for Germany: Heroes in the Nazi Pantheon by Jay W. Baird, Indiana University Press, Bloomington, 1990.

Night of the Long Knives by Nikolai Tolstoy, Ballantine Books, New York, 1972.

The Night of Long Knives by Max Gallo, Harper and Row, New York, 1972.

The Nuremburg Party Rallies: 1923-39 by Hamilton T. Burden, Frederick T. Praeger, New York, 1967.

Memoirs

Inside the Third Reich: Memoirs by Albert Speer, Macmillan, New York, 1970.

Hitler's Secret Conversations, 1941-44 Signet Books, New York, 1953.

General Information

Hitler's Personal Security by Peter Hoffmann, The MIT Press, Cambridge, 1978.

The SA: A Historical Perspective by Jill Halcomb, Crown/ Agincourt Publishers, Overland Park, KS, 1985.

The Biography of the Third Reich by Verlag Erwin und Sivia Fabritius, Berchtesgaden, (no date).

The Nazis by George Bruce, Hamlyn, New York, 1974.

Quest: Searching for Germany's Nazi Past by Ib Melchior and Frank Brandenburg, Presidio Press, Novato, CA, 1990.

General SS Histories

The Order of the Death's Head: The Story of Hitler's SS by Heinz Hohne, Ballantine Books, New York, 1971.

Hitler's SS by Richard Grunberger, Delacorte Press, New York, 1970.

The History of the SS by G. S. Graber, David McKay Co., Inc., New York, 1978.

Secrets of the SS by Glenn B. Infield, Stein and Day, Publishers, New York, 1982.

The SS Third Reich Series, Time-Life Books, Alexandria, 1988.

A Pictorial History of the SS 1923-45 by Andrew Mollo, Stein and Day, Publishers, New York, 1976.

Army of Evil: A History of the SS by Adrian Weale, Nal Caliber, New York, 2010.

Waffen SS Histories

Campaign in Russia: The Waffen SS on the Eastern Front by Leon Degrelle, Institute for Historical Review, Torrence, CA, 1985.

Waffen SS in Russia by Bruce Quarrie, Patrick Stephens, Wellingborough, 1988.

Epic: The Story of the Waffen SS by Leon Degrelle, Institute for Historical Review, Torrance, CA, 1983.

Waffen SS: The Asphalt Soldiers by John Keegan, Ballantine Books, New York, 1970.

Black Angels: A History of the Waffen SS by Rupert Bitler, St. Martin's Press, New York, 1979.

Waffen SS by Martin Windrow, Hippocrene Books, Inc., New York, 1974. Revised Edition by same author, 1982.

Waffen SS Uniforms in Color Photography by Andrew Mollo and Peter Amodio, Europa Militaria, Windrow and Greene, London, 1990.

Waffen SS in Action by Norman Harms and Ron Volstad, Squadron/Signal Publications, Carrollton, TX, 1973.

Shock Troops: The History of Elite Corps and Special Forces by David C. Knight, Crescent Books, New York, 1983.

Waffen SS: Fighting Élites by Keith Simpson, Gallery Books, New York, 1990.

The Waffen SS: A Pictorial Documentation by Herbert Walther, Schiffer Publishing Ltd., West Chester, PA, 1990.

Waffen SS: An Illustrated History by Adrian Gilbert, Gallery Books, New York, 1989.

The 12th SS Armored Division by Herbert Walther, Schiffer Publishing Ltd., West Chester, PA, 1989.

The 1st SS Armored Division by Herbert Walther, Schiffer Publishing Ltd., West Chester, PA, 1989.

The Waffen SS 1939-45: Hitler's Élite Guard at War by George H. Stein, Cornell University Press, Ithaca, 1966.

Hitler's Samurai: The Waffen SS in Action by Bruce Quarrie, Patrick Stephens, Wellingborough, 1986.

Waffen SS by Brian L. Davis, Blandford Press, New York, 1985.

Uniforms, Organization and History of the Waffen SS by Roger James Bender and Hugh Page Taylor, San Jose, CA, Volume 1 (1969); Volume 5 (1982).

Dictionary

Langenscheidt's German-English Dictionary Pocket Books, Inc., New York, 1968

Lieutenant General (Obergruppenführer in the General
SS) Josef "Sepp" Dietrich wearing 1933-34 style eagle and
swastika cap emblem and black General SS uniform. He had
an exciting, varied career, from private in the Great War to
army commander in the Second, from butcher to bodyguard,
from cavalryman to political soldier, from party thug to
accused war criminal, from husband and father to jailbird.
(Photo from the Heinrich Hoffmann Albums, US National
Archives, College Park, MD/USA)

1914

Above left: Unfortunately, no good photographs of Sepp's service before or during the First World
War have been found. According to his biographer, Charles Messenger, "He himself for many years
liked to have it believed that he joined the 1st Bavarian Uhlan Regiment ... In fact, he joined the
4th Field Artillery Regiment 'Konig' at Augsburg in 1911." In this wartime photo, German lancers
stand guard over French peasants, probably suspected of being "Franc Tireurs," the First World War
equivalent of today's terrorists or partisan fighters. (HG)

Above right: Messenger asserts that Dietrich claimed he saw service from 1911 right up until the
outbreak of war in August 1914. "The truth was less glamorous. Dietrich joined his regiment on
October 11, 1911, but a month later, on November 17, he was invalided out of the Bavarian Army
after a fall from a horse. Like young men all over Europe, the stocky Dietrich re-enlisted upon the
outbreak of war, on August 6, 1914, in the 7th Bavarian Field Artillery Regiment. By the fall, the
war of movement bogged down, and both sides dug in, initially in pits like this. When they became
connected, the trench system from the days of the American Civil War was re-born 50 years later.
Here is a German infantryman in his "home." (HG)

On February 22,1918 Dietrich participated in a tank warfare demonstration held in a French village for His Imperial Majesty, Kaiser Wilhelm II, seen here (right, center) in spiked helmet. In conversation with his eldest son and heir to the throne Crown Prince Wilhelm (wearing Death's Head Hussars' busby shako), is the Crown Prince's Chief of Staff von Knobelsdorf (left). (HG)

Dietrich's unit went into combat in October 1914, almost as soon as it arrived in Flanders. He was part of the Bavarian 6th Army under the command of Crown Prince Rupprecht of Bavaria, seen here, second from left, standing next to Kaiser Wilhelm II (third from left) at a weapons review. (IWM)

Members of the German Army wounded behind the Western Front mingle with enemy wounded. Note the length of the bayonets on the guards' rifles! During the war, Sepp was wounded by a piece of shrapnel in the lower right leg, as well as cut by an enemy lance over his left eye. Sometime during 1915–16, he received a shell splinter on the right side of the head after being buried alive in an explosion. (HG)

"All Quiet on the Western Front" as reflected in the grave of a soldier who didn't come back. The wartime loss of comrades in combat was a powerful bond linking those leaders of the Nazi Party who had seen action: Hitler, Göring, Hess, Röhm, Strasser, and Sepp Dietrich. This set them apart from the younger tier who had not been in combat, men like Goebbels, Bormann, Himmler and Heydrich. (HG)

1923

Bearing München license tag on the cab roof, this truck contains the members of the Adolf Hitler Shock Troop *en route* for German Day in Bayreuth on September 2, 1923. The unit's first commander, Josef Berchtold, is leaning on the cab roof, while Ulrich Graf holds the First World War Imperial German War Flag. Seated just behind the cab at right, wearing wind goggles, is Schreck. (HH)

Exactly what role Sepp did play in the Nazi Beer Hall Putsch of November 8–9, 1923 has never been clarified. Here, in a scene from the American wartime propaganda film *The Hitler Gang*, Bavarian police open fire on Hitler's marching column, stopping the coup in its tracks. (BT)

Hitler was almost killed by München police bullets when his marching column was dispersed on November 9, 1923, a scene depicted here in the American wartime propaganda film entitled *The Hitler Gang*. (BT)

1926

Above left: Hitler was only one of many Nazi leaders protected by the early SS men. Here Dr. Paul Josef Goebbels stands guarded while speaking in 1926 in Berlin. Hitler appointed Goebbels Gauleiter, a post he held until his death by suicide in 1945. In 1926 the SS also solicited advertisers and subscribers to the Party's newspaper, *Volkischer Beobachter*, as well as recruited new members for the Party itself. (CER)

Above right: Wearing lederhosen, Hitler appears in an early photo with four of the five first SS men, from left, Julius Schaub, Schreck, Maurer and Schneider. States SS historian Andrew Mollo in *A Pictorial History of the SS, 1923–45*, "The fifth man was Emil Maurice, who was thrown out of the SS in 1935 when found to be a Jew, but later allowed to retain his appointments and privileges, and wear SS uniform. His blacked-out figure is between Schreck and Hitler, and his feet are still showing! (HH)

Below: A carload of early Hitler bodyguards, all wearing the initial SS uniforms of black cap, tie and trousers with Nazi Party brown shirt. They are, from left, Rudolf Hess, Julius Schaub and a lean Julius Schreck at the wheel. Hitler sits in front, talking with Christian Weber (1883–1945) a member of the Stosstrupp Hitler later responsible for Hitler's safety during the annual Beer Hall Putsch Commemorations in Münich each November 8–9 from 1933-on. Note the pre-1930 armband worn on Weber's left sleeve of red band, silver or gold-edge swastika on white field, and silver or gold horizontal braid to indicate rank. (HH)

1927

Sunday, August 21, 1927, the party Day of Awakening, Hitler (top, center) salutes a parade containing all 30,000 members of the SA. In front of him stands former First World War air ace Captain Hermann Göring, wearing his Pour le Merite /"Blue Max" at the throat and an early Nazi Party brassard or armband on the left tunic sleeve of his SA uniform. At far left is Ulrich Graf, wearing the first type of SS uniform: brown shirt with black kepi cap, tie and breeches. Born on July 6, 1878 at Bachhagel, Graf was an ex-butcher and amateur wrestler when he became Hitler's bodyguard at age 42 in 1920. He is credited with saving Hitler's life by bold action on November 9, 1923 in the waning moments of the Beer Hall Putsch. At right is a rarely photographed Gottfried Feder. (HH)

1929

Above: An early SS unit wears the black cap, tie and trousers, plus the Party brown shirt that became one of the Nazis' most famous trademarks. Upon his release from Landsberg Prison, Hitler founded the SS in 1925. (CER)

Julius Striecher (1885–1946), stands here with hands on hips, a favorite pose of his. Standing next to him, at left, is Ulrich Graf. At his left elbow stands one of the first SS men, Schneider. Nazi Gauleiter for Nuremberg and Franconia, Streicher was hanged on October 16, 1946 by the International Military Tribunal after his conviction as a war criminal for helping to incite the Holocaust against the Jews. (HH)

Early SS men guard Hitler's car during The Party Day of Composure, September 1929 at Nuremberg. Hitler is in the car, while standing on the running board and wearing lederhosen is an early SA leader, Franz Felix von Pfeffer und Salomon. At left center is Streicher, and next to him (pointing) is Nazi publisher Max Amann. Note the flower-strewn street. (HH)

One of the many Hitler residences guarded by the SS was a site still standing in Münich today, his apartment on the second floor of No. 16 Prinzregentenplatz. Hitler rented this apartment from October 1, 1929, until his death on April 30, 1945. It contained nine rooms, two kitchens, two storage rooms, two bathrooms and bedrooms. For a time Dietrich lived here, as well as Hitler's niece Geli Raubal, who died in the apartment in 1931. (HH)

Ulrich Graf was Hitler's personal bodyguard during 1920–23. He was seriously wounded while throwing himself in front of Hitler to protect him from police gunfire during the crushing of the Beer Hall Putsch on November 9, 1923. Here he wears the collar tabs of an SS Sturmbannführer, but ultimately was promoted to Gruppenführer in the General SS. The cap has an early-style (1929–36) eagle-and-swastika adorning its peak. (CER)

1932

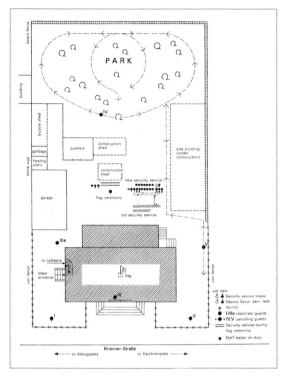

Sie kämpften und bluteten für Deutschlands Freihei

Above left: An outstanding map of the 1932 Brown House Nazi Party Headquarters buildings and park in Münich, City of the Movement. Pre-war, Sepp and the LSSAH also guarded Hitler here, and Sepp even lived here occasionally. (Dr. Peter Hoffmann, LC, Wash., DC/USA)

Above right: The caption to this cover picture on the August 15, 1932, edition of the *Illustrated Observer*, a Nazi paper, reads, "They fight and bleed for Germany's freedom:' This was clever propaganda on the part of Dr. Goebbels to elicit public sympathy for Himmler's "heroic" SS men during the on-going street battles against the German Reds. Ironically, the earliest duties of the SS not only were protecting Party speakers, but also selling subscriptions to keep the cash flowing into the Party coffers. (Peterson)

After Hitler's falling out with chauffeur Emil Maurice, a rival for the affections of his niece, Geli Raubal, Schreck succeeded him, holding the post for five years. Here he is seen at the wheel of one of Hitler's early open touring cars during a Nazi electoral campaign. Waving from the back seat is Wilhelm Frick, and next to him is Dr. Goebbels. (HH)

Above: After the Second World War, Sepp stated that he first met Hitler in 1921, when the latter was addressing the men of Schutzenbrigade 21, but still didn't join the Nazi Party until May 1, 1928, as well as the SS. States Charles Messenger in *Hitler's Gladiator*, "It was probably at about this time that Dietrich learnt to fly. Certainly, Hitler later recalled that during the election campaigns of 1932, 'Often I had to use a little Junkers single-motor that had belonged to Sepp Dietrich. It was rather an unstable aircraft. Dietrich was also awarded the very rare Pilot's and Observer's Badge in gold and diamonds. Wolf-Dieter Dietrich, Sepp's eldest son, now possesses it." Here, Sepp and Hitler are seen during that time; is this the airplane in question? (HH)

Below: During the German Presidential campaign of 1932, candidate Hitler alights from the door of his Ju-52 aircraft as a detachment of SS men stand at attention at right. (HH)

1933

Above: Giving an informal, bent-at-the-arm Nazi salute—and not a wave!—Hitler, clutching a coffee can-style kepi cap introduced into the SA Storm Troops and then the SS by Franz von Pfeffer und Salomon—is followed by 1920–23 SS bodyguard Ulrich Graf, seriously wounded protecting Hitler while throwing him to the ground during the police volley of fire that ended the November 9, 1923 Beer Hall *Putsch* march. (HH)

Below left: SA men at top left face SS in caps at left and steel helmeted SS in the Berlin Sports Palace during a Nazi rally before the war. (Previously unpublished HHA)

Below right: Himmler (left) and Hitler (center) at a pre-war NS Nüremberg Party Congress rally. (Previously unpublished HH)

Above left: From left to right, unknown SS man, Sepp Dietrich, Heydrich, unknown SS, Hitler, Führer aide Albert Bormann, Himmler, and two more unidentified SS stand in the doorway of the Old Reich Chancellery in Berlin during a musicale by the LSSAH band on a pre-war Hitlerian birthday. (Previously unpublished HHA)

Above right: Black-uniformed SS standard bearers carry their banners at a pre-war Nüremberg Party Congress. In 1929, they numbered but 280 men nationwide, but a decade later had 240,000 men both in regimental and divisional units. By 1945, there were 39 Waffen SS divisions under arms as well. (Previously unpublished, HHA)

Hitler (right) wearing tuxedo and carrying opera glasses at an annual pre-war Wagner Festival at Bayreuth. At far left is SS bodyguard Karl Wilhelm Krause, and at center SA Adjutant General Wilhelm Brückner. (HH)

Above: Hitler left gives an informal backhand salute to an airport honor guard (right) of LSSAH men, his aircraft seen at center background. (HH)

Right: The first Mrs. Dietrich—Betti—bore a resemblance to Mrs. Heinrich Hoffmann, wife of Hitler's longtime personal photographer. Here, she poses for a shot seated at a traditional German heating unit at the Führer's alpine chalet, *The Berghof.* (EBH)

Hitler (left) with the first Mrs. Sepp Dietrich—Barbara Betti Seidl of Münich—whom he married on February 17, 1921. They were still married when Sepp began seeing another, younger woman, whom he married in 1942 after his divorce. Betti was the sister of Sepp's lawyer during his various war crimes trials post-war, Alfred Seidl. (EBH)

LSSAH trainee enlisted men in fatigue uniforms grinning with mess kits in hand. (HH)

Hitler renders an informal Nazi salute as he sits next to his final and most famous chauffeur, Erich Kempka (1910–1975). In the rear seat sits another SS guard at left and Nazi Labor Corps Leader Dr. Robert Ley. (HH)

In 1933, LAH men are ready to leave Lichterfelde in vehicles taken over from the Prussian Regular Police, with LAH logo on the front cab door. Note, too, the sides that lift up and down for easier deployment of their riders in a hurry. (HH)

Happy pre-war racer Sepp (left) with driver. (HH)

Hitler (center) greets NS Party officials (right), while at far left Sepp watches, and next to him is the Führer's personal SS adjutant, Julius Schaub. (HH)

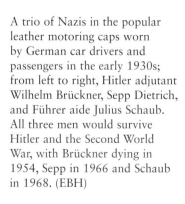

A trio of Nazis in the popular leather motoring caps worn by German car drivers and passengers in the early 1930s; from left to right, Hitler adjutant Wilhelm Brückner, Sepp Dietrich, and Führer aide Julius Schaub. All three men would survive Hitler and the Second World War, with Brückner dying in 1954, Sepp in 1966 and Schaub in 1968. (EBH)

Above left: Sepp Dietrich (far right) with the national leadership of the SS in 1933. At center stands Himmler, and to his right Kurt Daluege. The circled man is Reinhard Heydrich, whom Sepp detested. (CER)

Above right: "The Commander" followed by an aide emerges from a doorway at the Lichterfelde Cadet Barracks outside Berlin. (CER)

Below: SS men wearing 1929–36 issue uniforms hold back an enthusiastic German crowd bent on reaching their idol, Hitler. Initially, Hitler said later, even though small his SS "would be unconditionally loyal to me, and would march even against their own brothers. Better only 20 men from a city—under the condition that one can depend upon them absolutely—than an unreliable mass." (HH)

To commemorate the burning of the Reichstag Building, these SS men wear black armbands over their traditional black-white-red swastika brassards as they enter the new Nazi Reichstag. Until 1933, street fighting and beer hall brawls against the German Communist Party blooded the SS for repression and, later, wartime conquest. (CER)

Above left: SS men on the march before "Red Berlin's" famous Brandenburger Tor. (CER)

Above right: : In April 1932, German Chancellor Heinrich Brüning banned Nazi political uniforms, causing these Pfalz SS men to parade shirtless in opposition. The gesture was effective, and the ban was lifted. (CER)

SS men were expected to be physically fit—and were. Notes Weingartner in *Hitler's Guard*, "These men were carefully selected for their imposing physiques, membership in the Leibstandarte being contingent upon a minimum height of five feet eleven inches, a requirement which, however, had been waived in the case of the barrel-chested, squat Dietrich. He was five feet six inches. (HH)

Left: With SA men in front and on the platform, Hitler speaks at a Berlin rally in 1933 while his own LSSAH form a semicircle behind the stage. Note the photographer at bottom center. (HH)

Below left: States Charles Messenger in *Hitler's Gladiator*, "Sepp Dietrich had given up his München apartment at the end of April 1933, but retained his room in the Brown House until toward the end of September 1934." From 1931 onward, the Brown House had been Nazi Party Headquarters at Briennerstrasse 45. The Party bought the building in 1928, and Hitler's first architect—Paul Ludwig Troost—remodeled it. It was from here that Hitler directed the second phase of the Blood Purge on June 30, 1934, in which Sepp played a still-controversial role. (Peterson)

Above left: Hitler (left) gives the Nazi salute as the SS sentries presents arms and Grimminger (right) dips the 1923 Blood Flag in salute to the dead whose names are listed on the plaque at top center. (Peterson)

Above right: The Leibstandarte was intimately involved with all aspects of the memorials to the failed 1923 Beer Hall Putsch that took place each November after the Nazis gained power in 1933. At left, Hitler lays a wreath to the dead at the Putsch Memorial at the Feldherrnhalle, where there was installed a bronze plaque (seen here just above the wreath at top center). Two SS sentries stand guard at shoulder arms, while a trio of others help their Führer place the wreath. The Field Lord's Hall was at the southern end of Ludwigstrasse in old München, on the Odeonsplatz. The "arcaded war memorial had been completed in 1844," according to a book entitled *Hitler and München*, by Brian Deming and Ted Hiff (no date of publication given). (HH)

In the photo at right, Goebbels watches a Labor Corps review at one of the carefully-staged annual Nüremberg Party Day Rallies. At far left is another rabid Nazi propagandist and early political ally of Hitler, editor of *Der Stürmer* (*The Assailant*), Franconian Gauleiter Julius Streicher. At far right is Nazi publisher Max Amann, who lost his arm in a post-war hunting accident. Dr. Goebbels was a strong Sepp backer until almost the very end of the war, when even the LSSAH failed to stem the Red Army steamroller. In March 1943, he wrote in his diary, "In case there were ever an attempt at revolt in Berlin by foreign workers, the Führer would send his Leibstandarte to the capital. It would make an example of them all that would make every lover of such excesses lose all itch for them." (HH)

Above: Nazis celebrate the annual Beer Hall Putsch over their steins at the Münich Bürgerbräukeller. From left are: Reichsleiter and Chief Judge of the Nazi Party Walter Buch; Party founding member Hermann Esser; Party National Treasurer Franz Xavier Schwarz; Labor Front Leader Dr. Robert Ley, and Dr. Goebbels. Of these five key Party associates of Sepp's, three would die by suicide: Goebbels by shooting himself in 1945; Ley by hanging in his cell from a toilet pipe, also in 1945; and Buch by drowning and slashing his wrists in 1949. (HHA)

Below: Buch and Schwarz relax in a cell in the Nuremberg Palace of Justice after the war. Schwarz died on December 2, 1947, age 72, in an internment camp, while Esser, edged out by his more powerful rivals during the high days of the Third Reich he'd helped create, outlived them all, dying at age 80 on February 7, 1981. He had witnessed the entire rise and fall of Nazi Germany, and the first several decades of the chronicling of its final place in history. (US Army Signal Corps photo by Ray D'Addario)

Above left: Two men Sepp Dietrich knew well were Deputy Führer Rudolf Hess (left) and Hitler Youth Leader Baldur von Schirach, later wartime Gauleiter of Vienna. Both men would be convicted of war crimes at Nuremberg and be jailed at Spandau Prison outside Berlin—Hess for life and von Schirach for 20 years. Schirach completed his term in 1966, published his memoirs and died on August 8, 1974. Hess hanged himself in Spandau Prison in 1987 at the age of 93. (HH)

Above right: Named Defense Minister in Hitler's first Cabinet by Hindenburg was General Werner von Blomberg, seen here in steel helmet with an aide standing between the top-hatted Chancellor (right) and Hitler's Vice Chancellor and rival, Franz von Papen. Although von Blomberg was basically pro-Nazi, he told Hitler the Army would act against Röhm and the SA if the Führer didn't—a veiled threat that the former corporal never forgot. (HH)

Below: What a difference a year makes in terms of "politically correct" personages! SA Chief of Staff Ernst Röhm is a featured speaker atop the lectern at the 1933 Rally, the first since the Party had come to power the previous January. Behind the flag stands Hess in SS black, and Hitler stands at far left. Down in front are the men of the SS Staff Guard. Middle:

At the same spot in the Congress Hall at the 1934 Rally, the slain Röhm is gone, and the security detail has been beefed up considerably, as Hitler feared an SA delayed reaction to his murder of Röhm and the other high Brownshirt leaders; none occurred, though. Hess speaks, but this time in SA brown, perhaps to mollify the SA men. At left, from left to right, are Schwarz, Himmler, Lutze, Brückner, Hitler, Martin Bormann and Streicher. (HH)

Above left: Another annual event in the Nuremberg Party Day Rally scenario was the march past of all the Party paramilitary formations before Hitler's Mercedes-Benz parade car in the old town market place. Here, massed General SS location unit standards pass Hitler's outstretched arm (left) (HH)

Above right: The one man Hitler feared above all others during 1933--34 was the Weimar Republic's aging President, First World War Field Marshal Paul von Hindenburg, seen here reviewing a German Army color guard in Berlin. He had the military power to crush Hitler and the Nazis. (HH)

Above: A squad of SS "asphalt soldiers" drawn up for review. Note the officers with drawn sabres at left. (HH)

Below left: Bitter rivals within the SS were Sepp and this man, SS Reichsführer Heinrich Himmler. Sepp was a combat veteran of the First World War; "Heini" was not. Sepp was blunt, gruff, straight-forward and loved; Himmler was secretive, devious, hated and feared. Himmler's constant battles to have Sepp and the LSSAH placed under his command always failed, and the reason was both simple and obvious: Hitler didn't fully trust him. Thus, the heads of Hitler's security forces— Sepp and Rattenhuber— reported to him directly, not to Himmler, their nominal superior. Himmler poses in SS black in 1933, age 33. Born October 7th, 1900, he was just over three months younger than his friend and rival for power, Martin Bormann. (HHA)

Below right: Himmler wears the Blood Order Ribbon on his right pocket and the Golden Nazi Party Membership Badge on his left. In January 1929 Himmler was named Reichsführer SS by Hitler and held this post until almost the very end of the war. Caught trying to make peace with the Allies, Hitler fired him and condemned him to death, but Himmler survived the war only to commit suicide as a British POW on May 23, 1945, and today is still buried in a secret grave in Germany. In the photograph he appears in Waffen SS gray and spectacles, as opposed to his more famous pince-nez glasses. (HH)

LSSAH cadets in formation. (HH)

The 11A Company of the LSSAH, standing from left Graf, unknown, Moser, unknown, Linge, four unknowns, Weidner, Koster, Kath; sitting, left to right, Pattberg, Görgens, Zechmeister, Sarnow, Cissy, Hansen, Stenwedel, Boysen. On ground: unknown and Böhnke. (CER)

Below: LTG Hans Baur (seen here in the uniform of an SS Colonel with the early pattern Death's Head and eagle on his soft cap) was Hitler's pilot from the German Presidential election campaign of 1932 until the end. Here he sits at the controls of a Junkers 52. States Charles Messenger in *Hitler's Gladiator*, "Sepp controlled key members of the Führer's personal staff including Hitler's chauffeur and his personal pilot, Hans Baur, whose names were on the books of the Leibstandarte." A fighter pilot in the First World War, afterwards Baur flew for Germany's civilian airline, *Lufthansa*, before joining Hitler's staff. Hitler counted him not only a colleague, but also a friend, and gave him his prized Lenbach portrait of Frederick the Great as the war wound down. Baur was wounded trying to escape from the Berlin Führerbunker after Hitler's death, had a leg brutally amputated by the Russians and spent a decade in their prisons. His memoirs—*Hitler's Pilot*—first published in 1956, are available in English now as *Hitler at My Side*, and are very interesting reading, indeed. (HH)

LSSAH men fire a salute in honor of a dead comrade, 1933. (HH)

Above: Hitler (center) salutes the LSSAH honor guard at right, followed by Sepp Dietrich (left) and SA Chief of Staff Ernst Röhm at Berlin's Tempelhof Airdrome in 1933. Note that Hitler still carries his then-trademark hippopotamus hide whip, which shortly thereafter he abandoned as an affectation no longer desired. (HH)

Right: Reporting directly to Sepp Dietrich concerning the Führer's airborne safety was Hitler's longtime pilot, Hans Baur (second from right). Here, at Tempelhof Airfield with Hitler (left) and Deputy Führer Rudolf Hess. (HH)

Above left: Hitler receives a bouquet as Wilhelm Frick (center) and Rudolf Hess (over Hitler's left shoulder) watch, as does the nervous-looking SS Technical Sergeant at far left. To the right of Hess is SS Reichsführer Heinrich Himmler, and at far left can also be seen Hitler Youth Leader Baldur von Schirach. (HH)

Above right: Someone gives the Führer a bouquet of flowers, as here, during an evening at the opera. Might there be a bomb hidden in them, or poison? (HH)

Above and below: In a revealing statement made to his architect, Albert Speer, in November 1936, at Obersalzberg, the Führer said, "There are two possibilities for me: To win through with all my plans, or to fail. If I win, I shall be one of the greatest men in history. If I fail, I shall be condemned, despised and damned." His photographer, Heinrich Hoffmann, was careful to pose him with children. The last scene takes place in Jagerndorf Marketplace in the Sudetenland, October 8 1938, as an SS Escort Commando ushers the little girl forward. (First 3 HH, last HG)

Above left and right: The earliest SS men were also chauffeurs doubling as bodyguards, such as Schreck and Maurice, and later, Kempka. It was these men, and Sepp's coolness in leading them to fight the German Reds, that impressed Hitler enough to order the formation of a special SS guard for the Old Reich Chancellery on March 17, 1933. Right: A back-up car full of LSSAH men. In both cases the vehicles are Mercedes-Benz touring cars. (Peterson, HH)

The Führer personally greets the first LSSAH detail assigned to guard him at the The Berghof at Obersalzberg, July 1933. He trusted these men with his life, and Bormann gave orders that no one would be admitted onto the "holy mountain" without the proper papers and cards. "A government Minister's uniform was no exception." (HH)

Above left: An SS man stands watch on the famous terrace of The Berghof, his 1916-style helmet in silhouette against the magnificent mountain view. (HH)

Above right: An extremely rare shot of the new Chancellor Hitler in top hat and tails being saluted in a corridor of the Old German Reich Chancellery Building in Berlin by a guard of SA men. These guards reported to SA Chief of Staff Ernst Röhm—no wonder Hitler appears somewhat nervous! Behind him is Führer aide Wilhelm Brückner, and at right is then-German Foreign Minister Baron Constantin von Neurath. Note the pistols on the Brownshirts' belts. The sentries armed with rifles at both left and right in the foreground are also SA men. (HH)

Once, Hitler told his shocked aides that it would be a simple matter for someone to "stall" a truck packed with explosives outside the Old Reich Chancellery and blow the building up—with all of them inside. When his architect Albert Speer designed this balcony on the Old Reich Chancellery, the bottom was reinforced with steel to guard against such an explosion when Hitler and his entourage were standing on it. (HH)

1934

Himmler's "asphalt soldiers" at Nüremberg. (Previously unpublished, HHA)

LSSAH men taking their oath of allegiance to Hitler on the blade of an officer's sword during the war. (HH)

Vehicle license plate (right) 1A203126 of an LAH BMW motorcycle detachment at Lichterfelde Cadet School Barracks, Berlin, at the end of 1934 with police vehicles. The trio of men standing at left are, from left to right, Hoffmann, Wagner, and Flechner. (HH)

BMW LAH motorcycle company troops in 1934, their commanding officer standing and saluting at right. (HH)

The Führer (center) proudly reviews the men of the LSSAH at Lichterfelde Barracks, December 17, 1934, six months after the Röhm Purge that they conducted for him. Sepp wears a steel helmet at far right. (Previously unpublished, HHA)

Hitler (right) and Sepp troop the line of the LSSAH presenting arms at left at Lichterfelde on December 17, 1934, the famed asphalt soldiers standing in a light snowfall. (Previously unpublished, HHA)

With Sepp at his side, Hitler reviews his Bodyguard Regiment on December 17, 1934. (HH)

"Hitler's Gladiator" participates in the annual February Winter Relief program by collecting donations from passers-by in the streets of Berlin. Note the Adolf Hitler cuff band on his left overcoat sleeve. (CER)

Above left: Sepp in SS black. An autographed photo, signed while he was an SS Lieutenant General. Note the Golden Party Membership Badge underneath the row of ribbons on his left breast pocket. (CER)

Above right: Sepp in pre-war SS black headwear, the 1916-style steel helmet, later replaced for a more streamlined model that was used throughout the Second World War.

Below: Sepp (second from left) appears in black soft cap and overcoat. All the cap eagles are of the first pattern, worn 1929–36 with the first pattern Deaths Head, 1923–34 as well. The two officers to Sepp's right and left are SS Sturmbannführers, while the one at far right is a Brigadier General. (CER)

Above left: On February 17, 1921, Sepp married his first wife, Barbara "Betti" Seidl, of Münich, seen here (left) with him and Eva Braun, then Hitler's mistress, at one of the annual Nuremberg Nazi Party Rallies. "Betti" was four years younger than Sepp. Charles Messenger writes in his 1988 biography, *Hitler's Gladiator*, "She was still officially his wife until at least April, 1937." Sepp's lawyer in the various war crimes trials he endured was Dr. Alfred Seidl: "It is certain that he was a relation to his first wife, probably a brother." (EBH)

Above right: SS Maj. General Josef "Sepp" Dietrich (center) at a Nazi Party meeting with Hitler and Göring behind him and at left. (HH)

Left: Hitler mounts the wooden steps of a Nuremberg arena during the somber September 1934 Party Rally there, the first after the Blood Purge. Hitler is followed by Hess, Amann and Goebbels, and they are all preceded by the two SS men in the foreground, a 2nd Lieutenant at left and a Standartenführer at right. (HH)

Only 37 at the time of his death, Julius Schreck was Nazi Party Member #53, a member of the SA, and a co-founder of the Strosstrupp Hitler as SS Man #5. An important member and the shaper of Hitler's early entourage, here Schreck is seen being lionized at the Nuremberg Party Rally in September 1934 during the filming of Leni Riefenstahl's *Triumph of the Will*. Note that he wears a ceremonial dagger at his side, the 1923 Blutorden, the collar tabs of an SS Oberführer and, on his cap, the 1929–36 eagle and first pattern Death's Head of 1923–34. The inverted silver V-patch on his right coat sleeve marks him as a veteran of service in the armed forces (or police). Julius Schreck wore a Hitler moustache and sometimes was considered a double for Hitler, perhaps drawing away would-be assassins. (HH)

At one of the annual Berlin Auto Shows, held in February, photographer Heinrich Hoffmann (left) and Hitler listen to Schreck as he explains the engine of this Mercedes-Benz parade car. Hitler once lauded his driver thus: "Schreck is the best driver you can imagine! Our supercharger is good for over 100. We always drive very fast, but in recent years, I've told Schreck not to go over 50. How terrible if something had happened to me!" (HH)

Göring, wearing a Luftwaffe General's uniform, greets Hitler upon his arrival at the ceremonies marking the reburial in Germany of Hermann Göring's first wife, the former Swedish Countess Carin von Kantzow. The ceremonies took place on June 19, 1934, eleven days before the Blood Purge against the SA began. Sepp looks on at left, as does Hitler adjutant SA Maj. General Wilhelm Brückner at right. In the center are (left) Himmler (who claimed his car had just been fired on) and Führer aide Julius Schaub, both in SS black. (HG)

A well-known snap of Sepp (left) and Hitler's longtime Adjutant to the Fuhrer Gen. Wilhelm Bruckner (1884–1954), seen here wearing a civilian suit. (*HA*)

Left: A typical LSSAH box formation surrounding the speaker's platform completely on all four sides, front, back, right and left. This is May Day, 1934, on the Maifeld outside Berlin. (HG)

Below left: Only a glass door separates the pensive Führer from his adoring SA Stormtroopers. Their two pre-1933 revolts ultimately led him to purge their unruly leadership in 1934 in favor of the more disciplined SS as the sentry posted here. After the purge, Hitler was warned by his Interior Minister, Dr. Wilhelm Frick, that he now also should purge the SS. A careful student of history, Hitler was well aware that the Praetorian Guards of old had overthrown many Roman Emperors. The question was: who guards the guards? In Hitler's case, both the LSSAH and the RSD reported to him alone, and he personally approved and met every single applicant before the war. (HH)

Above: Hitler's speaking platforms in halls were routinely guarded by his LSSAH, but as can be plainly seen, a bullet fired from a pistol easily could have hit the exposed Führer. He relied instead on the loyalty of his people and troops, on an ever-changing travel schedule and on just plain luck. (HH)

Right: Behind the SS guards, Hess sits next to Hitler and Brückner behind. (HH)

Below: The SS and the leaders' travel arrangements were always closely connected. Here, as Reich Aviation Minister, Göring deplanes at Belgrade in 1934 for the funeral of the assassinated King Alexander of Yugoslavia, he is cordoned off by his contingent of SS manner. (HG)

In order to better protect Hitler and other top Nazi leaders, Sepp worked closely with these two men: German Regular Police Chief General Kurt Daluege (center) and Reich Interior Minister Dr. Wilhelm Frick (right). Both were hanged after the Second World War, Daluege by the Czechs and Frick by the Allies. (HH)

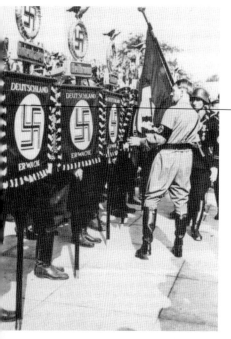

States author James Weingartner in *Hitler's Guard*, there was an "annual ritual conducted at Nuremberg of consecrating the standards of new Party units by sacramentally touching them with the banner carried by the Nazis in the abortive Beer Hall Putsch of November 1923." This ceremony was captured on film in German director Leni Reifenstahl's 1935 documentary of the 1934 Nuremberg Rally, *Triumpf des Willens*. One man always carried that flag, a shadowy, little known SS man named Jakob Grimminger. Who was he? Charles Hamilton, in his work *Leaders and Personalities of the Third Reich*, notes that Grimminger was born April 25, 1892, and "served with distinction in the First World War. An early member of the Nazi Party and the SS, Grimminger took part in the Beer Hall Putsch...The flag was drenched with the blood of those killed on November 9, 1923 ... Grimminger was an SS Colonel and a City Councillor of München. He died in München in obscurity and poverty on January 28, 1969, age 77." Grimminger wears a steel helmet and stands by Hitler as the Führer consecrates SA banners at Nuremberg. (HH)

Above: Besides the Führer, the LSSAH provided guard detachments for other Nazi bigwigs, such as Himmler, Göring and Goebbels, who is seen here in the front passenger seat of this Mercedes-Benz touring car in 1934. These men reported to Hitler through Dietrich, and thus the Führer could arrest the men the LSSAH "protected" anytime he wished. (HH)

Below left: Ironically, the man who most wanted the resolution of the Röhm–SA problem—von Blomberg, Germany's vaunted "Siegfried with a monocle"—was also the man who helped fulfill Röhm's dream: an armed Party army, but the SS, not the SA. States Weingartner, "As the early history of Leibstandarte had indicated, the Army was not opposed in principle to a militarily-armed and trained Party organization, as long as it remained relatively modest in size and the Army's primacy as weapons-bearers of the nation remained unaffected. On July 5, 1934, with the destruction of the SA as a threat to this primacy still fresh in mind, the malleable Defense Minister Werner von Blomberg offered the SS a quantity of arms sufficient to equip a division." In the bottom left photo, von Blomberg—wearing his First World War Blue Max, Iron Cross and Wound Badge—chats with the man who helped bring him down, SS Maj. General Reinhard Heydrich.

Below right: Blomberg (left), whom his critics called the "Gummilowe" (Rubber Lion) because of his flexibility, talks with Hermann Göring (center, in SA uniform) and the latter's adjutant, Luftwaffe General Karl Bodenschatz, during the September 1934 Nuremberg Party Rally, just a few months after the Blood Purge. In 1938, Göring plotted to succeed Blomberg as Defense Minister, but Hitler fooled him and, in effect, took the post himself. (Both HG)

Above left: Nazi politics in the early summer of 1934 was a curious blend of comradely loyalty and deadly rivalry—that flowered forth into murder. Most of the top Nazis involved had fought the common enemy in the First World War, and then the German Communists afterward. In the top photo, deadly enemies Röhm and Göring stand behind Röhm's Berlin SA leader, Karl Ernst (right) at his wedding. He never made it on his honeymoon, however, as SS killers arrested him *en route* and had him shot. In his 1937 book, *I Knew Hitler*, German author and former Nazi Kurt G. W. Ludecke wrote, "Sepp Dietrich, leader of SS Obergruppe Ost and commander of Hitler's Leibstandarte, shot Röhm in his cell, to be rewarded a few days later for his heroic deed by promotion to the post of Obergruppenführer". Sepp's biographers in later years deny this charge that he shot Röhm himself and, indeed, state that he regretted the LSSAH role in having to purge these Nazi Party comrades after the years of political struggle. (HH)

Above right: In 1933, after the Party took power, are seen, left to right, SS aide, SA Stabchef Ernst Röhm, his subordinate, SS Reichsführer Himmler, SS aide, Sepp Dietrich and SA leader Viktor Lutze. (HH)

THEY SALUTE WITH BOTH HANDS NOW

A famous drawing by British cartoonist David Low, that appeared the day after the Blood Purge ended. It shows Hitler and Göring as the chief killers, with a spineless Goebbels cringing beneath them. Actually, Goebbels had played a dual role, trying to keep credibility with all sides, and in the end stayed close to Hitler to avoid being shot by any faction; he survived. (LC)

July 2, 1934: The end for deposed SA strongman Ernst Röhm, confronted in his cell by SS assassins Maj. Michael Lippert and Maj. General Schmausser in cell #474 at Stadelheim Prison outside Münich. Here Röhm is given the chance to shoot himself. When he refused, the two SS men pumped a trio of bullets into him. This is a scene from the American wartime propaganda film, *The Hitler Gang.* (BT)

One of the most feared men in Nazi Germany during 1933–34 was SA Chief of Staff Ernst Röhm, seen here at his desk, in front of a tapestry of the Austrian Empress Maria Theresa. (HH)

The results of the June 30, 1934, Nazi "Blood Purge" are slain SA men, as depicted here in the wartime American propaganda film, *The Hitler Gang.* The shootings always bothered Sepp, asserts biographer Charles Messenger. (BT)

Above left: An immediate beneficiary of the Blood Purge as Röhm's successor as SA Chief of Staff was Hanover SA leader, Reichsleiter and SA Lieutenant General Viktor Lütze (1890–1943). Lütze is seen here as an aide holds open his briefcase for him at Berlin's Tempelhof Airfield before the war. States Charles Hamilton, "An uninteresting and colorless leader, Lütze died in an automobile accident on May 3, 1943." The accident is still considered mysterious. (HH)

Above right: Following the Putsch's suppression, Dr. Goebbels' propaganda apparatus did its best to put a good face on the killings between killer and killed in this heroic photograph of SA and SS men standing together. Both organizations survived until the very end of the war. (HH)

In the spring of 1934, the men of the SA, seen here at the annual Nuremberg Nazi Party Rally, were a grave threat to the Führer's regime. These SA band members have with them a "Jingling Johnny," common to all European armies of the day. A "Jingling Johnny" was known in Germany as a "schellenbaum; or "bell tree" device with bells to accompany a military band of Turkish derivation. Note the letters "SA." (HH)

Above left and right: Much of the world's pre-war perceptions of the LSSAH came from newsreels of the annual Nazi Party Day Rallies at Nuremberg, held each September of 1933–38. The 1939 Rally—the Party Day of Peace!—was cancelled because Germany invaded Poland. One of the rituals in which the LSSAH participated was the ceremony for the Commemoration of the Dead, with music written by Ernst "Putzi" Hanfstaengl, who was forced to flee the Reich for his life in 1937. Held on the Zeppelinwiesse, it began with a long walk down serried ranks of SA and SS men from the speakers' platform left, to a huge wreath at the other end of the field. From left, the trio of Nazis includes Himmler (SS), Hitler (Party and State united) and Lutze (SA). The salute duly rendered to the fallen comrades, the three men would about-face and walk back, in what must have seemed an eternity to the waiting troops! Note the standard bearer detail and honor guard from the LSSAH. (HH)

Reifenstahl's 1935 documentary of the 1934 rally, *Triumph of the Will*. As the LSSAH files by, Hitler salutes from his touring car, while standing before him are Hess and Himmler. (HH)

The first SS man to pass in review by his Führer is the Reichsführer SS, Heinrich Himmler, seen here in mid-goosestep, sabre drawn, and Sepp right behind him. Drawn up in front of the car are, from left, Hess, Göring and Franz Pfeffer von Salomon, an early SA commander. (HG)

Sepp Dietrich (center, left) leads the LSSAH standard and color guard down the broad steps of the Luitpold Arena during the annual Nazi Party Rally at Nuremberg in September 1934. (HH)

Here are gray-clad Army generals whom Hitler feared so much in the spring of 1934. In the front row center are (second from left) General Gerd von Rundstedt and (right) War Minister General Werner von Blomberg. Later, Hitler would promote both men as Field Marshals and also fire both—von Rundstedt several times over. (HH)

By the spring of 1934 the German Army commanded by Baron General Werner von Fritsch (facing camera, with hand on hip) was demanding that Hitler do something about curtailing the growing might and numbers of his unruly SA—or the Army would. It was not an idle boast, as Hitler well knew. (HH)

The Regular German Army parades past Hitler and Generals von Fritsch and Blomberg during spring maneuvers. Hitler knew that the Army had the military might to bring down the Nazi regime if he did not curb SA excesses. (HH)

Hitler and his entourage (on platform) review an Army war games demonstration at the annual Nuremberg Nazi Party Rally, Monday, September 10, 1934, "The Day of the Army." The Army would later train Sepp's Leibstandarte men to be real soldiers. Note Hitler's armored cap lying on the garlanded railing at lower right and the LSSAH men drawn up in front of the reviewing stand. (HH)

A famous picture from the rear cover of George H. Stein's ground-breaking 1966 study entitled *The Waffen SS: Hitler's Elite Guard at War, 1939–45.* These are the famed "asphalt soldiers"—the SS Verfugungstruppen presenting arms. (HH)

A young architect, Speer sits at the table center at bottom, and Sepp sits in almost exactly the same position at the table at lower right, 1934. (HH)

SS Brigadeführer Reinhard Heydrich. After the war, Sepp Dietrich would describe him as "a great pig" to the Allies. Only 38 when he died, Heydrich was Head of the Reich Security Main Office (RSHA), administrator of the concentration camps and a major architect of the Holocaust against the Jews, gypsies and others in Nazi-occupied Europe. (HH)

Above left: The fearsome Death's Head skull and crossbones—associated for centuries in other lands with piracy—in Germany symbolized the famed Hussar cavalry of Frederick the Great's era, and under the SS came to personify concentration camps and crematoria. Here the emblem is seen on LSSAH trumpet banners, as well as on the kettledrum, played by an SS bandsman private. (CER)

Above right: The embroidered skull on the banner is of the second pattern. (CER)

Below: At his famous speech defending his murderous actions in the Röhm Blood Purge on July 13, 1934, the Führer felt it necessary for the first and only time in his 12-year reign to place black-garbed LSSAH men in steel helmets in the chamber, and here there are four visible. Göring salutes from the Reichstag President's chair at top, under the swastika banner, while from the Government Bench are seen, from left to right, unidentifiable, Frick, Hess, von Neurath and Hitler. (HH)

Seen here at the annual Beer Hall Putsch commemorative march are from left: unknown, Hermann Göring, Dr. Walter Schultze, Hitler, Alfred Rosenberg, Graf, two unknowns, and Col. Hermann Kriebel. (HJ)

Above left: The LSSAH unit standard, as seen in two events. At left, color guard detachment with drawn sabers and the Regimental Standard. The Führer's name is on the plate underneath the Nazi eagle and swastika, while the Party battle cry—*Germany Awake*—appears on the banner itself. (HH)

Above right: Lt. General Dietrich framed against his banner. (HH)

Symbols of Prussian glory to inspire Hitler's elite were evident at Lichterfelde. As the Nazis had linked the glories of Germany's martial past to the new Nazi saviours of the nation at Frederick the Great's Potsdam Garrison Church in March 1933, the SS sought to inspire its new recruits with dreams of future accomplishments with the evocation of history. At top left is *Der Isteder Löwe*, the Prussian trophy called *The Isted Lion*, which overlooked the parade grounds used by the LSSAH's 1st and 2nd Battalions. Note the circled SS runes at the base of the statue. (CER)

The crowned Prussian eagle at top right stood watch over the entranceway to the officer cadets' church. That building's rear façade featured four statues of famous Prussian monarchs. They were Frederick William I, father of Frederick the Great, whose tall grenadiers were the talk of Europe; "Der Alte Fritz," Frederick II (the Great), conqueror of the Austrian province of Silesia in the Seven Years' War and Adolf Hitler's personal hero; Frederick William III, the monarch in power when Napoleon I was overthrown in 1813–15 during the German War of Liberation; and Kaiser Wilhelm I, the unifier of modern Germany in 1871 and the first German Emperor, revered by the Nazis along with Bismarck. (CER)

Above: Sentries real and imagined. Above left, a set of twin stone guardians greeted recruits arriving at Lichterfelde for induction into the LSSAH, and, indeed, remained in place even during the American Army occupation of the site after the war! By then, however, both the sentry at right and the Nazi eagle atop the main building were long gone, and the legend inscribed underneath removed. (CER)

Below: Sepp Dietrich, in full military regalia (center) inspects the unit of which he was the first and most famous "Commander." States his biographer, Charles Messenger, in *Hitler's Gladiator*, "Whatever faults can be laid at Dietrich's door, there is no doubt that he was a colorful character, and, in many ways, larger than life ... He fought on every front in 1939–45 except North Africa, was a key figure in what was probably the most controversial war crimes trial in Europe and finally became a victim of the guilt which wracked the West German nation in the 1950s. In truth, the menu is rich and varied." (CER)

Two views of the parade ground and main building of the LSSAH Barracks at Lichterfelde. The left photograph is a close-up of the Main Entrance of the new Administration Block Building, while the shot below shows the SS Artillery Reserve Battalion in formation in 1940. It should be recalled that, during the shootings of the SA at Stadelheim Prison in Münich in the 1934 Blood Purge, Göring ordered other executions to be carried out here, at his old alma mater. (CER)

Parading LSSAH troops at Saarbrucken in the Saar, 1935, when it voted to return to Germany after having been occupied by the French since 1918. (HHA)

Above left, right and below: December 17, 1934: Six months after the Röhm Purge, Hitler inspects his bodyguard truppen in their new feldgrau winter overcoats at Lichterfelde, accompanied by Dietrich and Maj. Jurgen Wagner. (Some sources state the year as 1935) (HH)

A famous shot, used in virtually every study of Sepp and the LAH, and included here for the sake of continuity: Hitler and Dietrich inspect a man's personal effects locker, an ordeal dreaded by all soldiers in all armies, time immemorial. In the doorway stands Reich Press Chief Dr. Otto Dietrich, wearing SS black. The others, except Hitler and SA Chief of Staff Viktor Lutze (far right, partially obscured) are in field gray. Note the unit name cuff bands. Sepp was adored by his men, particularly those enlisted, and he made a point of eating with them in their mess halls. "It makes them happy to see me," he often said, and he retained the survivors' respect until his own death in 1966, two decades after the lost war, no small measure of the man. (HH)

Above left: Troops in training, July 1934, at the Jüterbog depot. Seen here are a dozen Sergeants-Major, from left they are C. Hansen, two unknowns, Heinz Clausen, von Benthen, Wendt, Lehmann, Hansel, Vogt, Sandig, Hilbert and Diederichs. (CER)

Above right: Hitler's plane—D-2600—over the Zeppelinwiese on the Nuremberg Party Rally grounds in 1934. The tri-motored Ju-52 was a highly reliable aircraft, nicknamed "Auntie Ju" by the German paratroops who jumped from it in the Second World War. (HH)

Secretary to the Führer Martin Bormann (far right) is seen here arriving with Hitler (left) and (center) Deputy Führer Rudolf Hess, whom he succeeded in duties, if not in name, when the latter flew to Scotland in May 1941. (HH)

Above left: An interesting aerial view of Hitler striding to his parade car during the Nazis' May Day 1934, festival, followed by Dietrich, and, farther back at left, the rest of his entourage, including Dr. Goebbels (center). An LSSAH man holds open the car door at right, while the street on both sides is cordoned off for the Führer's security. *Right:* Krause closes the door as Hitler is greeted by *Hitler Jugend* leader Baldur von Schirach (right) and an SS officer salutes, before a Führer review of the Hitler Youth at a Nuremberg Party Rally. Note the photographer with ladder at middle right. (HH)

The Führer's inner circle at the Old Reich Chancellery in Berlin listens as he tells a funny anecdote. From left are seen pilot Hans Baur, in the uniform of an SS Brigadier General; Dr. Wilhelm Frick, Interior Minister (in civilian suit), Deputy Führer Rudolf Hess, Alfred Rosenberg, unknown, Luftwaffe General Karl Bodenschatz, Reichsleiter Martin Bormann and SA Chief of Staff Viktor Lutze (also in civilian clothes). At far right is Dr. Phillip Bouhler, head of Hitler's Private Chancellery. Hitler sits on a step, his back to the camera. At top left are Labor Minister Dr. Franz Seldte (left) and aide Albert Bormann (right). (HH)

LSSAH Members guard the corridors of the Old Reich Chancellery in Berlin. Note their Adolf Hitler cuffbands. They have not yet been awarded their distinctive white cross belts. (HH)

Hitler and Göring greet the Berlin crowds from the newly built balcony of the old Reich Chancellery Building on Wilhelmstrasse. So far as is known, no one ever took a shot at the Führer there, but when Albert Speer designed this balcony, he reinforced its bottom with steel to guard against a bomb explosion from below. (HH)

1935

Parading LSSAH troops at Saarbrücken in the Saar, 1935, after it voted to return to Germany after having been occupied by the French since 1918. (HH)

Left: Pre-war LSSAH field training still photo. (CER)

Below: Pre-war LSSAH field training fire control section, with the man at left using a range finder. (CER)

Above: Sieg Heil! Sepp Dietrich (right) reviews his men on a muddy Lichterfelde parade ground. Dressed in SS black, he wears white gloves and an ornate dress sword. His men wear full marching gear, including rifles with fixed bayonets. (HH)

Below left: Clad in spotless white driving togs, Sepp (left) and German Regular Police General Kurt Daluege chat with two fellow SS drivers at right, both Obersturmführers (first lieutenants). States author James J. Weingartner in his excellent book *Hitler's Guard*, "Dietrich had a passion for hunting and auto racing and was sought after by the Daimler-Benz and Auto Union motor companies as a driver for their cars in road races." (HH)

Below right: Sepp as a passenger in this Auto Union racer of the mid-1930s. Note the swastika flag on the right front of the hood and the license plate, which indicates this car was registered in Berlin. (HH)

Above left: Dashing racer Sepp poses, hands on the wheel, cigarette clenched between his teeth, in command of Auto Union racer #107. The Vier Ringe symbol is still used by Audi, the last of the four German auto companies still in existence that merged to form Auto Union in 1931; Horch, DKW and Wanderer were the other three. (HH)

Above right: Sepp Dietrich (top) at the very epicenter of Nazi power, mingles at a cocktail party in Berlin in 1935. (HH)

Sepp enjoyed hunting throughout his long life, as did his Nazi colleagues Himmler, Göring and von Ribbentrop—but not the Führer. (LC)

Hitler, Sepp and Schreck listen to a concert by the LSSAH Band in the courtyard of the Old Reich Chancellery in Berlin, 1935. (HH)

Hitler arrives at a Nuremberg rally followed by (left to right) his military aide, Army Col. Friedrich Hossbach; a naval aide; Nazi Party Deputy Führer Rudolf Hess; and adjutant Julius Schaub, wearing SS black. Reich Photo Reporter Prof. Heinrich Hoffmann walks down the steps at right. Behind Col. Hossbach (hands on belt) is Nazi Reichsleiter Martin Bormann. Behind the naval aide, wearing SA dress uniform, is Führer adjutant Wilhelm Brückner, fired in 1940. (HG)

This time wearing Luftwaffe blue general's uniform, Göring affably escorts bushy-browed Rudolf Hess (left). They are followed by Hess' then-deputy, Martin Bormann, and Göring aide Erich Koch, who died in Polish captivity at age 90 in 1986. The man in SS black to Göring's left is Dr. Walther Darré, Reich Farm Leader and Minister of Food (1895–1953). (HG)

The LSSAH and later the RSD were always present when Hitler spoke outdoors, as these two examples illustrate. Left, the scene is Berlin, and at right, at Nuremberg's Day of the Army. Atop the platform, left to right, stand Göring (in Army General's uniform), Hitler, unknown, War Minister Werner von Blomberg, Army Commander-in-Chief Baron Werner von Fritsch, and Army General Wilhelm Ritter von Leeb. (HH)

Right: The doomed march of 1923 that aimed to overthrow the German Republic ended in police gunfire. It was memorialized each November 9th after 1933 with a march down the exact same route, with massed SS unit standards drawn up in front and at right. (HH)

The Honor Temples on the Konigplatz in downtown Münich, where an SS sentry always stood guard, wreaths were presented each year to remember the Nazi fallen and an SS march past the Führer was held. Thus, a humiliating defeat was transformed by Nazi propaganda into a magnificent spectacle and political victory. (HH)

Dietrich's military exploits were highly touted in the German press and newsreels by Nazi Propaganda Minister Dr. Josef Goebbels (second from right), seen here aboard the cruiser *Scharnhorst* clowning with a cigar and wearing sunglasses. The Naval officer at left center holds his overcoat, while Joachim von Ribbentrop looks on at right. (VR)

The five men appear in 1935, and are from the 6th Company of the Leibstandarte. From left, they are Schiller, Kummert, Krause, Schmidt (in front) and Skomrock. Among the LSSAH's more noted marching songs were *The Adolf Hitler Bodyguard March* and the Führer's favorite air, *The Badenweiler March*. (CER)

As with the January 30th celebrations, Hitler's parade car is parked on the walk outside his Old Reich Chancellery, again with the band at right. (HH)

Above left: Göring, in Air Force greatcoat, salutes an SS detachment in 1935, at what is believed to be one of the German Imperial or Royal Palaces in Berlin, possibly Sans Souci (Without Cares), the famed estate of Frederick the Great. (HH)

Above right: SS men flank a column of SA men marching across a bridge in downtown Nuremberg, on their way to parade past Hitler during the September 1935 Nazi Party Rally. The previous year, it was the SS who purged the leadership corps of the far more numerous Sturmabteilungen. (HH)

Hitler's architect and wartime Minister of Armaments and War Production, Albert Speer, testified before the International Military Tribunal at Nuremberg after the war in 1945 that he tried to kill the Berlin Bunker occupants by funneling poison gas through the air conditioning system, but the plot failed. Here, a decade earlier, he looks into the camera lens as Air Force General Hermann Göring (left) hoists a beer stein in a toast to German construction workers. (HH)

Above left: Wearing full pack, marching gear and overcoats, SS men board a train bound for the annual Nazi Party Rally at Nuremberg, September 1935. (HH)

Above right: A famous shot of the Leibstandarte presenting arms in Münich on November 9, 1935, under the command of Capt. Theodor "Teddy" Wisch, commander of the LSSAH 1st Company. In later years, he became an SS Brigadier General and Divisional Commander of the 1st SS Armored Division LSSAH, the first successor to Sepp Dietrich. Born December 13 1907, before the end of the Second World War, he had been awarded the Knight's Cross with Oak Leaves and Swords. HH)

Below: Here the annual commemorative march for the 1923 Beer Hall Putsch is beginning on November 9, 1935, in Münich. From left are seen Hitler adjutant Julius Schaub, the Führer, Himmler, Deputy Führer Rudolf Hess, SA Chief of Staff Viktor Lutze, Hitler Youth Leader Baldur von Schirach, Labor Front Leader Dr. Robert Ley, Party Judge Walter Buch, Party Treasurer Franz Xavier Schwartz and Phillip Bouhler, head of Hitler's Private Chancellery. In time, Hitler, Himmler, Hess, Buch and Bouhler all committed suicide. The man with the Blutfahne at right is Jakob Grimminger. (HH)

Above left: SA Chief of Staff Viktor Lutze was the commander of the Sturmabteilung succeeding Ernst Röhm as Stabschef. He died from injuries received in an automobile accident. Lutze was given an elaborate state funeral in Berlin on May 7, 1943. Hitler ordered Joseph Goebbels to convey his condolences to Viktor's wife Paula and son Viktor, Jr. Goebbels, in his diaries, had already described Lutze as a man of "unlimited stupidity" but at his death decided he was a decent fellow. (HH)

Above right: Wearing SS black once more, von Ribbentrop (right) has a chat aboard ship with General Karl Bodenschatz. Bodenschatz was Manfred von Richthofen's last adjutant in 1918, then went on to fulfill that same function for Göring until the end of the Second World War in 1945. Under Göring, he served particularly as liaison officer at the Führerhauptquartier, where he was severely wounded and nearly killed by the bomb blast of July 20, 1944. He was buried October 19, 1979, in Germany, age 80. (VR)

Below: Despite his detractors both within and without the German Foreign Office, Joachim von Ribbentrop served as Hitler's private foreign affairs advisor before being named Ambassador to Great Britain in 1936, and was his last Foreign Minister from 1938–45. His friend was Heinrich Himmler, whom he nonetheless feared. As was his way, the Reichsführer co-opted both his friends and potential rivals by making them honorary SS men, as he did with von Ribbentrop. Here, Ribbentrop, at center with folded arms, stands with others in SS black awaiting the annual September parade through Nuremberg of the various Nazi Party paramilitary formations. With him are, left to right, Weitzel, Erich von dem Bach Zelewski, Rediess and Moder; at far right in the third row, wearing soft cap, is Party Press Chief Dr. Otto Dietrich (no relation to Sepp). (VR)

Left: Although Heydrich (center) was nominally Himmler's deputy in the SS, the latter (seen here at middle, behind Himmler) actually feared him—as did almost everyone—and with good reason. (Peterson)

As designed by Hitler himself, the Standarte appears above two white-belted LSSAH men at an annual Nazi Party Day at Nuremberg. This, states author Brian Leigh Davis in his detailed 1975 work *Flags and Standards of the Third Reich*, is "the right side of the Führerbegleitbataillon standard ... based on the design used for the Führerstandarte." Note the standard bearer's gorget. Not to be confused with either the LSSAH or the RSD, the battalion was a German Army unit from the Greater Germany Regiment to guard the various FHQ. LSSAH men swear their oath of allegiance on a staff-mounted version of their unit standarte. (HH all)

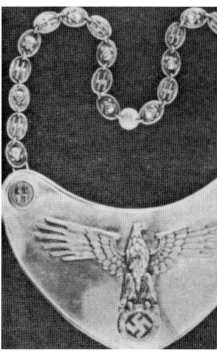

Above left: A trio of LSSAH drum majors drilling in September 1935 on the Lichterfelde parade ground. (CER)

Above right: A SS standard bearer's gorget. (CER)

The LSSAH Band serenades Hitler and Göring in the courtyard of the Old Reich Chancellery in Berlin. (HG)

Led by its Jingling Johnny, the Band leaves the Hradschin Castle in Prague during the war. (HH)

Two ceremonial usages of the LSSAH unit standard: left, on review at Lichterfelde, December, 1935. (Right) On parade past the Führer, September, 1936, with Dietrich once more leading the way. (HH)

An important part of Göring's police organization was sheltered in Berlin's Lichterfelde Barracks. In Imperial times, the stark walled complex (top photo) of brick buildings had housed Germany's most prestigious military academy, the so-called Hauptkadettenanstalt. Göring had attended the academy before the First World War. After the First World War, Lichterfelde had been converted into a police barracks, which purpose it continued to serve immediately following the Nazi seizure of power as the base of operations for a heavily armed state police unit under the command of Police Major (later Colonel) Walter Wecke, as well as auxiliary police formations controlled by him. It was Wecke's police group which was to be used as a cover for the expansion of the Stabwache into a sizable, Party-based military force, one of the nuclei of the wartime Waffen-SS. The building in the bottom photo is the Leibstandarte classroom structure. (Both CER)

According to Weingartner, following the Röhm Purge, on July 5, 1934, an agreement "placed emphasis on the militarized SS (now designated SS-Verfuhgungstruppe or 'disposal troops' in the sense of their being at the disposal of the régime), as an instrument for the preservation of internal order, although the possibility of its commitment on the battlefield in wartime was also envisioned." Here some of these men look at a target on a firing range. (HH)

A German Army officer looks over an LSSAH machine gun position, while Sepp (center) watches with his staff officers. (HH)

On pre-war maneuvers, Sepp (right) and his officers go over maps. States Weingartner in *Hitler's Guard*, "Two new militarized SS units of roughly regimental strength, later to be designated *Germania* and *Deutschland*, and a communications detachment were planned." (HH)

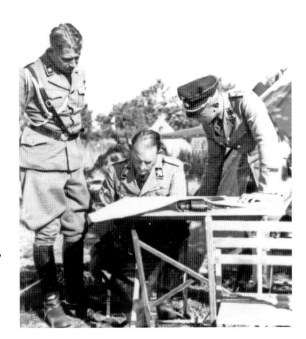

Wearing the coveted feldgrau uniforms formerly reserved for the German Army, Sepp Dietrich and his staff officers pore over a map during LSSAH maneuvers. Sepp wears the collar tabs of a Waffen SS Lt. General. Note the binoculars on the table underneath the maps. (HH)

Hitler joins Sepp (with tripod) on pre-war LSSAH maneuvers in 1935. During the war, the unit would establish a combat record that was admired by friend and foe alike. (HH)

SS Maj. General Sepp Dietrich stands at the top of the steps and directs his LSSAH men carrying memorial wreaths as they prepare to board a Junkers 52 aircraft in 1935. At his side Dietrich wears a ceremonial sword. (HH)

All of the Führer's pre-war and wartime train trip routes were screened and protected by the LSSAH and the RSD. Here Hitler detrains after one such pre-war journey. (HH)

One man who reported to Sepp Dietrich was Hitler's third and final chauffeur, SS Sturmbannführer Erich Kempka, seen here at the wheel of one of Hitler's many Mercedes-Benz armored touring cars, at Nuremberg in September 1935. It was Kempka who both supervised the Reich Chancellery motor pool and doused Hitler's dead body with gasoline in the NRC garden on April 30, 1945. (HH)

Hitler felt perfectly secure taking long walks— either alone or with members of his entourage—along the snowy paths of the Obersalzberg as here in 1935. The nine-mile long enclosure of the complex was entirely secured by the LSSAH. (HH)

Right: An LSSAH Acting Corporal stands guard outside a government building in Berlin, 1935. Note the LSSAH cuff-band Adolf Hitler on his left jacket sleeve. (HH)

Below: Hitler and Dr. Goebbels (in front of open doorway) gather with the assembled Nazi Party Gauleiters in the park of the Old Reich Chancellery in Berlin in 1935. Ironically, both men would be buried in this garden a decade later and their corpses burned with gasoline. The Russians discovered the half-buried corpses. (HH)

1936

Above: Fully equipped Elite Guard LSSAH men move into position during an event on Nüremberg's Zeppelinwiese parade ground, pre-war. (Previously unpublished, HHA)

Below left: The Führer consecrates an SS banner by touching it with the 1923 Blutefahne, then shakes the bearer's hand, as seen here. (HG)

Below right: A favorite scene of mine showing Hitler fastening his rain cape after leaving the Zeppelinwiese at Nüremberg, followed by SS bodyguard Karl Wilhelm Krause (born 1911), nicknamed "Hitler's Shadow" for always being immediately behind his Leader. Note also the massive Führerstandarte behind them on the walled façade. (HH)

Above: Sepp with drawn sword at far right leads his parading LSSAH past Hitler, saluting from his car at far left on an annual birthday pre-war. Himmler stands immediately under Hitler's right arm. (HH)

Right: LSSAH in black overcoats parade past Hitler unseen here at far left, pre-war. Note their distinctive—and unique to them—white cross belts. (HH)

Trumpeters with SS rune flags. (HH)

Above: The public are held back in Wilhelmstrasse by uniformed security as Hitler salutes the marching Leibstandarte-SS. (CER)

Left: Sepp Dietrich at the Berghof, Obersalzburg, Berchtesgaden. As an old colleague and close confidante, Sepp was a frequent guest at the Berghof and presumably took the occasional opportunity to visit the nearby SS barracks a little further up the mountain. (HH)

Left: A Heinrich Hoffman photograph of Heinrich Himmler. Himmler a slightly-built, bespectacled chicken farmer from Waltrudering who had never seen active combat service in the First World War, unlike virtually everyone (except Goebbels) in the upper leadership strata of the Nazi Party. This difference—as well as those of temperament and approach—created a lifelong gap between Sepp and Himmler that would never be bridged. In addition to that, even though he was Dietrich's nominal superior in his role as SS Reichsführer (National Leader), "Heini" fumed over the fact that Dietrich always enjoyed instant access to Hitler and, as head of the Leibstandarte, reported direct to the Führer, not to Himmler. Hitler kept it that way, perhaps fearing too much Himmler—control of the SS men responsible for his personal safety and maintenance in power after 1933. (HH)

Below: Although Sepp and Himmler did not get along, there was a degree of socializing as this hunting party shows. Sepp, with dog on leash is in conversation with Himmler, binoculars at his front. To the far right is Reinhard Heydrich. (BT)

Sepp's rapport with "other ranks" was legendary. Here, during maneuvers in 1936, he examines an SS private's rifle, as another private looks on at left. This was a popular picture postcard sold during the Third Reich to glorify Sepp's soldierly virtues. (CER)

Born July 13, 1898, in München, Schreck died at age 37 on May 16, 1936, of cerebrospinal meningitis. At least one report links his death to an auto accident in which Hitler was not involved. Here, Dr. Goebbels—a black mourning band over his swastika armband—gives Schreck's bier a Nazi salute. (HH)

Schreck is perhaps the only bodyguard and chauffeur in history to have his government give him a State Funeral with full honors. Here, a cordon of men wearing early SA uniforms surround an inner cordon of helmeted SS manner. The SA man in front carries a pillow bearing the deceased's wartime and Party decorations. (HH)

All the top members of the Nazi government turned out to revere Schreck in death. From left, Streicher, Schaub, Hess, Goebbels, Lutze, Hitler, Amann, Todt, Ley, Dr. Otto Dietrich, Huhnlein, Himmler, Heydrich, and center, Sepp Dietrich. (HH)

Draped in a red-white-black swastika banner, Schreck's coffin is borne from its bier by an SS Honor Guard. Asserts author Charles Hamilton in his superb 1984 volume, *Leaders and Personalities of the Third Reich*, "Schreck is remembered with fondness by the surviving members of Hitler's entourage." (HH)

Wearing an early-issue SA uniform, Hitler adjutant Julius Schaub comforts the stricken Schreck family. The SS Honor Guard commander stands with back to camera, and at far right, wearing black mourning band over his swastika brassard, is Nazi Party official Martin Bormann. (HH)

Above left: Above: Sepp, far right, has a place of honor accompanying the Führer at the opening of the 1936 summer Olympic Games in Berlin's newly built Olympic Stadium. Just behind Hitler's left shoulder walks Dr. Walther Funk, and in the background (center) is Army General Wilhelm Keitel. The Olympic Torch has not yet lit the brazier at the top of the photo. (HH)

Above right: Again Brückner follows Hitler; note the long SA overcoat. Just over Hitler's right shoulder is Reich Press Chief Dr. Otto Dietrich, wearing SS black. The man at far left is Hitler's personal orderly and bodyguard, Karl Wilhelm Krause, (1911–2001) who served in that post during 1934–39. States Charles Hamilton in *Leaders and Personalities of the Third Reich*, "Krause's most important job was to protect the Führer from assault or assassination by following directly behind him at public appearances and on tours. Hitler often jokingly called him Schatten since, at times, he appeared to blend in with the shadow of the Führer." (HH)

Club-footed Dr. Josef Goebbels, Nazi Minister of Propaganda and Public Enlightenment (left), Brückner (turning his head), and Dr. Lammers (right, in SS black) follow behind Hitler. (HH)

Above left: Sepp Dietrich (right) looks aside, and an LSSAH sentry stands with his rifle at port arms as Hitler emerges from the home of a famous Blue Max winner, General Karl Litzmann, born January 22, 1850. He received his *Pour le Merite* for his service on the Eastern Front on November 29, 1914, and later received the Oak Leaves as well for his successful assault on Kovno on the Niemen River against the Russians. He died shortly after this photo was taken, on May 28, 1936, age 86. (HH)

Above right: Right: In 1936, Hitler named von Blomberg the first Field Marshal of the Third Reich, and here he is seen saluting with his omate baton at the September 1936 Nuremburg Party Rally. At right is the Army Commander-in-Chief, General Baron Werner von Fritsch and at center the Navy's Commander-in-Chief, Admiral Erich Raeder. Göring, Himmler and Heydrich combined forces to bring down both Army officers on sex scandal charges—von Blomberg for taking a Berlin prostitute as his second wife, and Fritsch for alleged homosexuality. Both lost their posts early in 1938, and 22 years later Raeder, in his book *My Life*, still professed himself shocked over the incidents. (CER)

Below: March 1936: Hitler (center, cap in hand) enters the Berlin Sports Palace (Sportspalast) for a Nazi Party rally, flanked by RSD Chief Johann Rattenhuber at far left and Sepp Dietrich at right (second from right). Note how the LSSAH men handle the crowd on either side: one man facing in, two facing out. (VR)

Heinrich Himmler was proud of the Dachau concentration camp, and here he shows the facility to Deputy Führer Rudolf Hess on a rare visit. (BT)

Above left: Hitler with two former commanders of his rowdy SA battalions, at the September 1936 Nazi Party Rally at Nuremberg: Hermann Göring (center) and Franz Pfeffer von Salomon (right). (HG)

Above right: Former SA Leader Hermann Göring was ordered arrested by the SS at Berchtesgaden on Hitler's orders when he telegrammed that he was willing to open peace negotiations with the Allies in 1945. His enemy at Hitler's court in Berlin—Martin Bormann—wanted him shot, but Hitler backed away from this. Here, Göring gives the Nazi salute at a pre-war Nazi rally. (HG)

Above left: One of the many top Nazi leaders Dietrich was assigned to protect was his friend, fellow hunter and Party comrade, Hermann Göring (left), seen here wearing an early Luftwaffe (Air Force) dress uniform and ceremonial sword. The occasion is the 1934 funeral of Yugoslav King Alexander I in Belgrade. Göring's aide General Karl Bodenschatz is second from right, and the other two men are Serbian Army officers. Göring was one of the prime movers of the June 30, 1934 "Blood Purge" of the SA. (HG)

Above right: The RSD gradually began taking over the duties of the LSSAH around the time of the Olympic Games in 1936, replacing Sepp's men as bodyguards to Hitler and other Nazi leaders, such as Hermann Göring, seen here after having signed an autograph for a fan at the games. His second wife, Emmy Sonnemann Göring, is at left, the logo of the Olympics emblazoned on their box below. This is at the Winter Games, held that year at Garmisch-Partenkirchen outside München. (HG)

Below left and right: A close-up view of the Zeppelinwiese reviewing stand showing Hitler addressing massed steel-helmeted SS at the September 1936 Rally. *Right:* This is perhaps the most famous photo known of the SS, usually cropped for publication well above the three backpacks. This is the full image. (HH)

Massed General SS in soft caps and packs assembled next to SA men. (Peterson)

7 March 1936. The LSSAH men are gone, and so is the banner behind the Speaker's Chair. It is replaced by the final, huge Nazi swastika featured in so many pre-war and wartime newsreels. (HG)

Top: A guard detail in front of the guardhouse at Lichterfelde's main gate. *Below:* A pre-war changing of the guard ceremony at Lichterfelde, complete with kettle drummer at left. States James Weingartner, "Lichterfelde Barracks was developed by Dietrich, with Hitler's encouragement, into something of a military showplace.... One entered the barracks from a pleasant, tree-lined street." (CER)

Hitler arrives for the funeral of Luftwaffe General Walter Wever at the German Air Ministry, June 17, 1936, greeted by Göring (center) and Field Marshal von Blomberg, with baton (left). Sepp prepares to close the door, as an Army officer steps out of a car registered in München, according to its license plate. The building is still used. (HG)

One of several personal residences of Adolf Hider guarded by Dietrich and his elite LSSAH was The Berghof, the Führer's Alpine chalet at Obersalzberg above the village of Berchtesgaden in Bavaria. The LSSAH Barracks were to the rear at the left and farther up the mountain. (HH)

Above left: The fireplace in the main salon of The Berghof. Hitler received Sepp Dietrich here many times. (HH)

Above right: A view of the Berghof. (HH)

Above left: An SS sentry stands guard at Obersalzburg. The SS barracks at Berchtesgaden. (HH)

Above right: The SS barracks at Berchtesgaden.

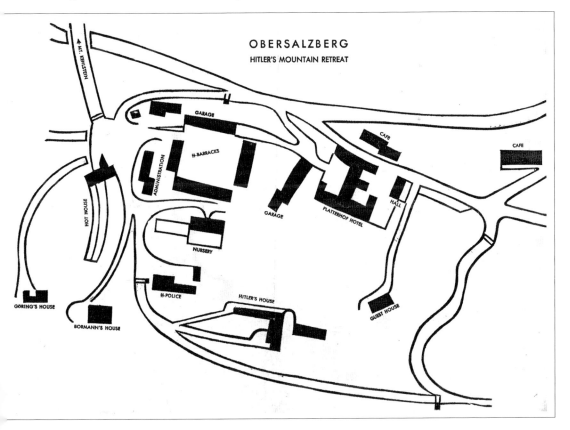

A map of the Obersalzberg complex on April 23, 1945. Note the homes of Hitler, Göring and Bormann, and the proximity of both the RSD and SS barracks to them at center. Nevertheless, states Dr. Peter Hoffmann, "Rattenhuber was worried in November 1937 after Hitler had ordered a number of Leibstandarte sentries withdrawn, and he urgently pointed out to Bormann and Brückner that it was now possible for anyone to drive around on Obersalzberg when Hitler was there. Many SS men of LSSAH patrolled the grounds around the Berghof, but this activity was largely ineffective." (BT)

The Führer inspecting the table arrangements. The bottom photo—from Eva's home movies— shows a light moment enjoyed during a meal. (EBH)

The road from The Platterhof to the Führer Area on the Obersalzberg. At left is the motor pool, the LSSAH Barracks and Bormann's greenhouse. (HH)

An aerial view of the LSSAH Barracks in the Obersalzberg, above The Berghof (not seen here, but would be at lower left in picture). 1) Haus Bormann, 2) Bormann's greenhouse, where the area's vegetables were raised, 3) The Barracks, 4) Gymnasium, 5) Motor Pool, and 6) Kitchen and storehouse building. (HH)

1937

Sepp Dietrich shakes hands with Hermann Göring (left) on the occasion of his birthday, January 12, 1937, at his Berlin residence. At far right stands SA Chief of Staff Viktor Lutze, the successor to Ernst Röhm. (HH)

The LSSAH's own Adolf Hitler standard at the German Museum at Münich, 1937. Note the white gloves as well. (HH)

Hermann Göring receives pre-war birthday greetings from the RFSS and his staff, from left to right: unknown, Karl Wolff, two more unknown SS officers, Heydrich, Himmler, Regular Police General Kurt Daluege, (1897–1946), Göring in Luftwaffe uniform, and his secretary, Paul "Pilli" Korner. (HG)

Above: The head of Dwight Eisenhower's Secret Service detail told *Look* magazine in the late 1950s that he always cringed when the President was around armed soldiers, fearing one might shoot him. Adolf Hitler, however, was almost constantly around them. Hitler, Himmler, Karl Wolff, Wilhelm Brückner and an unknown SS officer next to the swastika banner have just reviewed an LSSAH honor guard and are trooping the line of a detachment of regular German police. The scene is at the opening of the House of German Art in Münich in 1937. (HH)

Below left: Serenaded by the LSSAH Band, Hitler stands in the doorway of the Old Reich Chancellery on his 48th birthday, April 20, 1937, flanked by Sepp Dietrich (left) in full regalia, and by Himmler, wearing the 1923 Blood Order over his left breast pocket and the ordinary brown leather strap of the General SS. (HH)

Below right: The view from the Leibstandarte band's vantage point across the street. As always, Hitler uses his car as a reviewing platform, while before him, left to right, are Deputy Führer Rudolf Hess, LSSAH Commander Sepp Dietrich with drawn saber, and Reichsführer SS Himmler. Note the white facings on the black overcoats. Dietrich would lead the march past at the head of his men, stride up to the car, salute Hitler, then take his place below the Führer and watch the rest of the parade from this spot. (HH)

Above: When Sepp's LSSAH took the arrested SA leaders to Münich's Stadelheim Prison for execution on June 30, 1934, they met an unlikely Nazi opponent, Hans Frank, the Bavarian Minister of Justice. States Charles Messenger in his 1988 work, *Hitler's Gladiator,* "Frank was at the prison and Dietrich showed him the list, but Frank said that no executions could be carried out without a legal warrant." After a flurry of telephone calls to Hitler and Hess, Frank stood aside when told that the ultimate authority for the murders without trial came from none other than Reich President von Hindenburg. Adds Messenger, "Dietrich himself later testified at his Münich trial in 1957 that he had left after the 'fourth or fifth shot: not being able to stand any more." In the left photo, Frank (left) puffs on a cigar as Benito Mussolini, hands in pockets, listens intently to a Göring anecdote during the Duce's September 1937, visit to Göring's estate Carinhall outside Berlin. For turning over Röhm and the other SA men to the LSSAH for execution, Frank was roundly condemned by his son, Niklas Frank, in his scathing 1991 biography of his father, *In the Shadow of the Reich.* (HG)

Below: After the war, particularly at the trial of the major German war criminals before the International Military Tribunal at Nuremberg, few German leaders had anything good to say about the much-maligned von Ribbentrop. They were friendly enough with him during and before the war, however, as here he chats with the notorious Gauleiter of Nuremberg, Julius Streicher; both were hanged by the Allies on October 16, 1946, their bodies burned and their ashes scattered. (VR)

The Standard of the SS Leibstandarte Adolf Hitler Division (LSSAH), as personally designed by Hitler. The standard was modeled on those of ancient Rome, Napoleon's Imperial eagles and those of Fascist Italy. (HH)

Despite the fact that he had been shot at, verbally threatened and even had a rock once graze his head, Hitler insisted throughout his pre-war political career in standing bolt upright in his cars, believing that it would both impress his own men and cow his opponents; he was right on each count. Typical pre-war car arrival of the Führer Column. Kempka is at the wheel, as Krause starts to get out behind the standing Führer. In the back sits, left to right, Martin Bormann, Julius Schaub, Wilhelm Brückner and Col. Schmundt. Hoffmann stands on the curb at the far right. (HH)

The column is halted by an LSSAH honor guard (bottom center). Hitler salutes and behind him are Martin Bormann, Schaub and Schmundt. Peering anxiously at far right in SS black is Rattenhuber. (HH)

One of the big annual events in the Nazi calendar was the Fall Bückeberg Harvest Festival that drew over a million people. In the top photo from the Hugo Jaeger Collection, Rattenhuber (back to camera) and his RSD men restrain the crowd as Hitler greets them. In the bottom photo, Hitler's delegation is in the center of the walkway. RSD men stand there and line it to left and right. (Hugo Jaeger, Peterson)

Above left: SS men attempt to hold back these enthusiastic German girls as they shake hands with Hitler at the annual Bückeberg Harvest Festival in 1937. (HH)

Above right: Aside from the ever-present bouquet of flowers threat, all of Hitler's various bodyguards over the years—LSSAH, RSD, SS-Begleit Kommando, and others—feared the crush of the delirious crowds that mobbed their Führer wherever he went, as seen here at the 1937 Bückeberg Harvest Festival. As usual, the Führer is at the center of it all. (HH)

While photographer Heinrich Hoffmann snaps a shot at right, Hitler, followed by Sepp Dietrich (left), Heinrich Himmler and SS General Karl Wolff (right), mounts the steps at the annual Harvest Festival at Bückeberg, 1937, guarded on both sides by LSSAH and SA standard-bearers. (HH)

1938

January 12, 1938: The Nazi coalition that cost the Army its top leadership in the Blomberg–Fritsch Crisis, just two months before the events unfolded. The trio gained substantially. From left: Luftwaffe General Hermann Göring, who became the Third Reich's second Field Marshal after von Blomberg resigned, and who established Air Force field divisions during the war as well; SS Reichsführer Heinrich Himmler, who saw his Waffen SS divisions grow beyond Röhm's wildest imagination, and was himself named an Army Group Commander by Hitler near the end of the war; and Reinhard Heydrich, who felt himself somewhat revenged for having been kicked out of the German Navy some years earlier for a sex scandal of his own. The previous year, 1937, Heydrich's intrigues had led Soviet dictator Josef Stalin to purge his own Red Army General Staff, believing it disloyal. The other two men are Pilli Korner (between Göring and Himmler) and Daluege (between Himmler and Heydrich). (HG)

Himmler and his entire police staff congratulate Hermann Göring on his birthday, January 12, 1938, at his home. The Luftwaffe commander-in-chief stands at left. Greeting him at right are, from left: Himmler, Sepp Dietrich (center) and SS General Reinhard Heydrich (second from right), the latter wearing SD (for Sicherheitsdienst for Secret Police) on his left sleeve cuff. Sepp would survive all these men, dying in 1966. (HG)

Above left and right: The German Regular or Criminal Police also guarded the high leaders of the Nazi Third Reich, although, prior to 1933, it had been their job to keep an eye on them! In the left photo, Göring reviews an honor guard of these men to celebrate his 45th birthday, January 12, 1938. In the right photo, a motorized unit passes Göring's stand at left, on the side of which are positioned from left Kurt Daluege, Reinhard Heydrich and Paul Korner. (HG)

Celebrating the Nazi accession to power was the first event on the Nazi calendar of official Party celebrations, and the annual march past the Führer by the Leibstandarte was the highlight of the day. Here, their standard color guard is at center. At left, under Hitler's outstretched arm, is Himmler, dressed in overcoat and soft cap. (HH)

Easy to be confused! This is the same spot, but with different troops on two separate occasions. The photo at left was taken on January 30, 1938, the fifth anniversary of Hitler's appointment as Reich Chancellor by President von Hindenburg. The white belts identify the men as LSSAH, reviewed once more by Hitler, Hess, Dietrich and Himmler. The shot at right is of a parade of General SS men (minus the white accoutrements) on Hitler's 50th birthday, April 20, 1939. (HH)

Arrival at the Krolloper Reichstag, the Kroll Opera House in Berlin, selected by Hermann Göring as the replacement for the charred original building, set afire February 27, 1933. Here, the LSSAH presents arms to Chancellor Hitler as he arrives for a session of the Parliament on February 20, 1938. With him are Sepp, Brückner, Albert Bormann, Schaub, von Below and Schmundt. Bayonets are fixed. (HH)

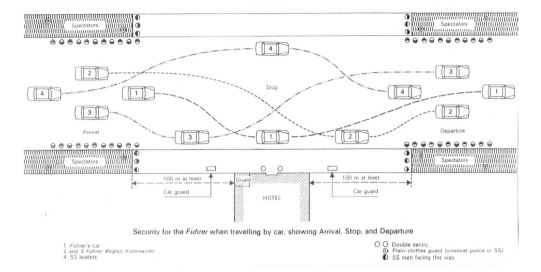

Security for the *Führer* when travelling by car, showing Arrival, Stop, and Departure

1 *Führer's car*
2 and 3 *Führer-Begleit-Kommando*
4 SS leaders

○ ○ Double sentry
⊙ Plain-clothes guard (criminal-police or SS)
❶ SS men facing this way

Above: "Security for the Führer when traveling by car, showing Arrival, Stop, and Departure." (Dr. Peter Hoffmann, LC)

Standing at parade rest is Hitlerian chauffeur SS Erich Kempka. (HH)

Hitler's G-4 Mercedes-Benz touring car entering Vienna in triumph, March 15, 1938 as the RSD cars follow. (HH)

Above: March 1938: Hitler enters Vienna in triumph, guarded by men of the RSD. The RSD commander, Johann Rattenhuber, walks behind the Führer's G-4 parade car at right, while another RSD man sits in the rear of the car. Hitler stands in front, while behind him rides Austria's new Nazi Chancellor, Artur von Seyss-Inquart. (HH)

Below: "Jingling Johnnys" were used by the SA and SS and are still used today by most European army bands. At right is a line drawing of a SS Standarte 36 of the Free City of Danzig, now known as Gdansk, Poland. Note the horsehair tails, evocative of the Mongol Horde of Genghiz Khan. (CER & Anne S.K. Brown Military Collection, Providence, RI/USA)

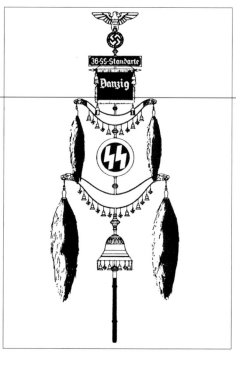

Above left: During the LSSAH's peaceful occupation of Austria on March 15, 1938, the men pose in front of the statute of Frederick the Great's former nemesis, Empress Maria Theresa. Among them is Kurt Meyer, of whom states LTC Angolia in *On the Field of Honor*, volume 1, "was later tried as a war criminal, convicted and sentenced to be shot. Following many appeals, he was released on September 6, 1954 to return to his home." (CER)

Above right: Massed SS standards pre-war. (HH)

Below: Guarded by white-belted and helmeted LSSAH men, the top Nazi leadership corps is assembled. From left to right, on the ground level are Lt. General Josef "Sepp" Dietrich, SS Reichsführer Heinrich Himmler, Adolf Hitler and Luftwaffe Chief Hermann Göring. on the first step, left to right, are Interior Minister Wilhelm Frick, Propaganda Minister Dr. Josef Goebbels and Reichsleiter Martin Bormann, named in 1943 as Secretary to the Führer. Sepp would outlive them all—Himmler, Hitler, Göring and Goebbels would commit suicide; Bormann was killed by Russian gunfire in Berlin, and Frick was hanged by the Allies at Nuremberg. (HG)

Comments noted author James Weingartner in his 1979 study, *Hitler's Guard*, "Always prominent in these (Nuremburg Party Day Rally) pageants were the black-uniformed formations of the SS, who appeared to march with significantly greater precision and purpose. Their favored position *vis-à-vis* the person of Hitler was reflected in the body of SS men who accompanied him to Nuremberg (and virtually everywhere else ...) The banner carried by the Nazis in the abortive Beer Hall Putsch of November 1923, the so-called *Blutfahne*, was always borne by an SS man, Jakob Grimminger." The top shot shows Grimminger standing behind SA Chief of Staff Viktor Lutze as he speaks in the Nuremberg Congress Hall, September 1938. Below, at the same annual event four years before, Grimminger stands behind Lutze, who is under Hitler's outstretched arm in front of the Super Mercedes, as their SA men march past on the main market square downtown. In the top photo, behind Grimminger, left to right, are Rosenberg, Frick, Goebbels, Ley, Himmler, Koch, Hitler, Streicher, Hess and Göring, clutching his Luftwaffe Marshal's baton. (HG top & HH bottom)

The steps lined by wary members of his LSSAH (at left), the Führer and his entourage descend a flight at the September 1938 annual Nazi Party Rally at Nuremberg. The Führer is at center, behind him, left to right in the first rank, are Reichsleiter Martin Bormann, Reich Sports Leader Hans von Tschammer and Osten, and SA Chief of Staff Viktor Lutze. Behind them, in the second rank in black SS uniforms, are SS General Karl Wolff, SS Reichsführer Heinrich Himmler and Adjutant Julius Schaub. The officer in the field gray uniform at right is Hitler's longtime Army adjutant, Col. Rudolf Schmundt. (Hugo Jaeger, LC)

Luftwaffe Field Marshal Hermann Göring hoists his bejeweled baton to return the salute of a General SS honor guard as he arrives in Nuremberg at the railway station for the September 1938 rally. Walking behind him from left to right are Streicher, Paul "Pilli" Korner (Göring's aide for the Four-Year Economic Plan) and Air Force General Karl Bodenschatz, seriously wounded in the bomb blast of July 20, 1944, at Ft. Wolf FHQ at Rastenburg. (HG)

During the Czechoslovakian crisis Sir Neville Chamberlain met Hitler at the Berghof, 15 September 1938. From left to right: Sir Neville Chamberlain, Adolf Hitler, Dr Paul Otto Gustav Schmidt, Hitler's interpreter and Sir Nevile Meyrick Henderson, British ambassador to Germany. (HH)

Two views of Martin Bormann in the feldgrau uniform of the Waffen SS, wearing the rank collar tabs of a Major General at left and a Lieutenant General at right. The left photo was taken during the Münich Conference on September 28, 1938, and shows Hitler in front of the Führerbau, the site of the Four-Power meeting that still stands today intact. At far left stands Himmler's aide, Karl Wolff, wearing SS black, while, at center, holding leather attaché case, is Führer adjutant Maj. General Julius Schaub. Schaub also wears SS feldgrau and sword, as does Bormann, who is whispering in Hitler's left ear. The right photo shows, left to right, Hungarian Regent Adm. Nikolaus Horthy, von Ribbentrop, Field Marshal Keitel and Bormann at Rastenburg, 1941. (HH)

Chamberlain's arrival at Münich Airfield for the start of the Four-Power Conference that sealed Czechoslovakia's doom, September 29, 1938. Bottom: Having alighted, Chamberlain starts his review of the SS honor guard as von Ribbentrop gives the Nazi salute. (VR)

Two views of the arrival of French Premier Edouard Daladier at Münich Airfield for his participation in the Four-Power Conference of September 29, 1938. Greeting him are Bavarian Gauleiter Adolf Wagner (left, in Party brown uniform and cap), and Reich Foreign Minister Joachim von Ribbentrop (dark civilian overcoat). Daladier reviews first the SS band and then (below) the honor guard itself, their rifles at fixed bayonets, blades unsheathed. Daladier has been presented to history as a weak man but, in fact, he had served in the French Foreign Legion and fought in the First World War. He hated the part he played at Münich and was ashamed for France. (Both VR)

Above left and right: : Sir Neville troops the line with Ribbentrop, Wagner and Franz Ritter von Epp, a hero of the First World War and holder of the Blue Max. *Right:* The delegation includes from left Wagner, von Epp, von Ribbentrop, Chamberlain and Henderson. Behind Chamberlain is German Regular Police Chief Kurt Daluege, hanged by the Czechs later as a war criminal; and SS General Reinhard Heydrich, assassinated by the Czechs in 1942 at age 38. (Peterson)

Below: Hitler's 770K Grosser-Mercedes open touring parade car at Münich's Führerbau during the 1938 four-power conference there. Kempka drives, and Hitler's personal bodyguard SS Karl Wilhelm Krause sits directly behind the Führer in the mid-car right hand side jump seat. An LSSAH Honor Guard is drawn up in front, and the flags of France (left) and Great Britain (right) hang from the structure's left front balcony of two. Actually, the proportions of the main cross at center of this Union Jack are way out of sync. (HH)

Above left and right: The leaders of Fascist Italy and Nazi Germany arrive for the start of the Münich Pact Conference, September 30, 1938. In the top photo, an anxious RSD 2nd Lieutenant looks over his shoulder, while Hitler bodyguard Karl Wilhelm Krause keeps his eye on the Führer's back. Middle: The SS guard of honor (right) has been reviewed as Hitler and Mussolini lead the procession. Behind them, left to right, are Himmler, Göring, Ciano, unknown, and Reich Press Chief Dr. Otto Dietrich. (VR)

Hitler crosses the German-Czech frontier into the newly acquired Sudentenland at the town of Widenau in WH-32288, an Army vehicle. At far right the G-4 is Rattenhuber and other RSD men, like Hitler wearing overcoats. (HH)

States James Weingartner in *Hitler's Guard*. "Foreshadowing the role it was to play in Hitler's war of aggression, Leibstandarte had been the first German unit to enter the Saar district in March 1935 ... and later with other elements of the SS Verfungstruppe took part in the occupation of Austria, the Sudetenland and Bohemia-Moravia." Saluting the crowd, Hitler enters his newest bloodless conquest in Mercedes-Benz G-4 touring car license plate WH-32288— an Army vehicle on October 1, 1938, the Sudetenland. (HH)

Singing as they come, the Leibstandarte enters the Führer's newest bloodless conquest: the German Südentenland in dismembered Czechoslovakia. (CER)

A good pre-war view of RSD men carrying German children from an excited crowd to greet their Führer. This time, the throng is held in check not by SS men, but by the SA. Again, both the cars are Mercedes-Benz touring autos, and the second vehicle carries a typical contingent of alert RSD men ready to spring out at a moment's notice of danger. (HH)

At bottom, a nervous Himmler scans the crowd (center) while his SS men hold back the multitude of happy Germans upon the occasion of Hitler's return to Berlin from the recently acquired Czech Sudetenland in October, 1938. At center, the German Army honor guard commander reports to the Führer, whose entourage includes, from left, Ley, Goebbels, Albert Bormann, Bernhard Rust, Army General Walther von Brauchitsch, SA Chief of Staff Viktor Lütze, Karl Bodenschatz, Julius Schaub, Hitler, Göring, Col. Rudolf Schmundt (behind Göring with his baton), Luftwaffe adjutant Col. Nikolaus von Below and German Foreign Minister Joachim von Ribbentrop. (HG)

The RSD man at left screens the girls' bouquet as they give it to Hitler, while in the car behind, two more RSD scan the area for trouble. (HH)

Hitler's triumphant arrival at Freudenthal in the Sudentenland on October 7, 1938, in pictures in exactly the same order as they appear in Hermann Göring's personal albums in the Library of Congress, Wash., D.C. In the top photo, the Führer salutes, while behind him sit Schmundt, Krause and Schaub, with Kempka driving. Anxious RSD men trot along behind the car, a Mercedes-Benz G-4 cross-country tourer. In the right photo, Göring, swagger stick informal Field Marshal's baton in his right hand (lower left), stands to greet his Führer. An RSD man starts to open the door and Hitler waits to step down. Standing behind him are Schaub and Air Force adjutant Col. Nikolaus von Below. (HG)

As Hitler toured the Czech Sudeten fortifications surrendered to him without a shot fired in accordance with the Four-Power Münich Pact agreement, Sepp (second from left), was there, wearing Waffen SS feldgrau, although here with an infantry Colonel's collar tabs. The two Army officers at center are Generals Gerd von Rundstedt (holding map) and Wilhelm Keitel, both future Field Marshals closely associated with Sepp's wartime military career. (HH)

On November 9, 1938, in Münich, just before the annual Beer Hall Putsch commemorative march to the Feldherrnhalle are seen, from left, Hitler, Graf, Philip Bouhler, Hermann Göring and Bernhard Rust (1883–1945). Hitler and Graf wear the Nazi Blutorden on their right uniform pockets. Begun in 1933, it was given to the 1,500 Nazis who marched a decade earlier. Elected to the German Reichstag in 1936— the equivalent of the US. Congress—Graf survived the Second World War, and died at age 78 in 1950. (HG)

1939

It is January 7, 1939—almost five years after the Röhm Purge against the SA—and the Brownshirts have long since been replaced by black-coated LSSAH men, averaging in age from 18–22. The building is the New German Reich Chancellery in Berlin, and the Führer is having his first inspection of the just-completed Marble Gallery. From left are seen Hitler's valet Kramer, Hitler in overcoat, architect Albert Speer (who designed the building), SS ordnance adjutant Ludwig Bahls (who died in September 1939 from an appendicitis attack nine months after this picture was taken), Dr. Morell, surgeon Dr. Haase, photographer Heinrich Hoffmann and an unknown aide. Speer also designed the high-backed chairs. Note the high ceilings, marble doorways, carpets and tapestries on the walls. (HH)

The Mosaiksaal of the New German Reich Chancellery at Berlin was 150 by 60 feet wide, and 45 feet high. The date is April 20, 1939, Hitler's 50th birthday, and he is seen receiving newly commissioned SS officer candidates, just four months before they would be waging the Second World War. (HH)

The Honor Courtyard of the New German Reich Chancellery in Berlin. The statues were designed by noted sculptor Arno Breker, still alive in 1990. The statue at left was entitled *The Party*, and carried a torch of enlightenment, while that at right, called *The Army*, brandished the sword of war, and is shown. (*Signal,* Peterson)

Doorways in the New German Reich Chancellery in Berlin. Standing with their rifles at order arms are two LSSAH men in the left photo, on guard outside Hitler's study off the Marble Gallery, which was nearly 500 feet long! The AH monogram over the archway was designed by Hans Vogel. The picture at right is an often-used and famous view of the Voss St. entrance, with the largest of several Nazi eagles designed by Kurt Schmid-Ehmen. (*Signal,* Peterson)

The Honor Courtyard doorway of the New German Reich Chancellery in Berlin, 1939. In the top left photo, the sentries stand at shoulder arms as the Führer emerges. Two footmen flank the party which includes von Ribbentrop in formal diplomatic attire, and (right) Army General Wilhelm Keitel. In the right photo, the sentries present arms. This time the group consists of (left to right) Army C-in-C General Walther von Brauchitsch, Luftwaffe Field Marshal Hermann Göring and Navy Adm. Erich Raeder, Bodenschatz is just behind von Brauchitsch. Note, too, that this time the footmen stand at the bottom of the steps and give the Nazi salute. (HH, HG)

Heil Hitler! The Führer is saluted by an officer of the Leibstandarte in the ornate Mosaic Hall of the New Berlin Reich Chancellery on the occasion of his 50th birthday, April 20, 1939. (HH)

Above left and right: On his 50th birthday on April 20, 1939, Hitler appears in the doorway of the New Chancellery with the children of his architect, Albert Speer. At left center are Albert Bormann and Dr. Hans Heinrich Lammers, while Sepp grins in both photos. (HH)

Outside, other children appear with smiling members of the Führer's young Elite Guard. (HH)

April 20, 1939: Close-up of steel-helmeted Reichsführer SS Heinrich Himmler in front of the Führer's car for the birthday march past. His Leader's aiguillettes are white, as is the belt, trimmed in silver. This is not to be confused, though, with the white belts of the LSSAH; since he was not a member, the National Leader of the SS was not entitled to wear them! (HH)

An LSSAH honor guard in the New Reich Chancellery Courtyard of Honor presents arms with fixed bayonets on their rifles in salute to Italian Fascist Foreign Minister Count Galeazzo Ciano (fourth from left) as he arrives in Berlin for a meeting with Hitler in the spring of 1939. This meeting led to the signing of the Axis Pact between the Third Reich and Italy. At far left is the German Foreign Office Chief of Protocol Baron Alexander von Dornberg, while the German Ambassador to Italy, Hans-Georg von Mackensen, is partially hidden behind Ciano. (HH)

The only known picture of Sepp as a member of the German Reichstag, which corresponds to the US. House of Representatives, British Parliament's House of Commons and the Japanese Diet. With arms folded Sepp sits behind Martin Bormann's father-in-law, Party Judge Walther Buch. (HH)

Above left: Like Sepp, another colorful personality within the top strata of the Third Reich was former First World War air ace General Ernst Udet (center). Udet is seen here talking with Hitler and Hermann Göring during an air weaponry test at Rechlin Airfield outside Berlin in June 1939. At far left is Army General (later Field Marshal) Wilhelm Keitel and at far right Navy Grand Adm. Erich Raeder. Of this group, only Raeder did not die violently: Keitel was hanged by the Allies, Göring took cyanide, and Hitler and Udet shot themselves. (HG)

Above right: Possibly LSSAH Bandmaster SS General D. von Reinhard (center) greeting his musicians. (Previously unpublished, HH)

A famous wartime snapshot of Himmler (right) sharing a laugh with the commandant of Hitler's military Führer Headquarters in Poland in September 1939, Army General Erwin Rommel (left) in the dining car of the Führer Special Train, *Amerika*. (HH)

LSSAH Regimental Engineer troops ferry across the Warthe River in Poland a Mercedes Stuttgart staff car on a raft with pontoons. The car is license plate # SS-1074. (LSSAHA, LC)

LSSAH troopers lug a stalled truck by rope across Polish sand, September 1939. (Previously unpublished LSSAH Albums, LC)

Hitler (left) causes liberated German nationals in conquered Poland to weep with joy at meeting him during the September 1939 campaign. Watching at center and wearing goggles with inverted V on his right jacket sleeve is RSD commanding officer Johann Rattenhuber, during a car tour stop. (HH)

Rattenhuber (left, standing) grins for the camera as he holds a submachine gun in Warsaw, September 1939. Note also the machinegun mounted on a bar at mid-car with Führer SS adjutant Julius Schaub riding up front in the right car passenger seat. (HH)

Above left: The scene was always the same in the Bürgerbräukeller when Hitler gave his long anniversary tirade—except on November 9, 1939, when he cut short his address and left abruptly. A few minutes later a bomb exploded. (HH)

Above right: Seemingly unending columns of armed LSSAH men on the march, Berlin, 1939. (HH)

Major General (Gruppenführer in the General SS) Joachim von Ribbentrop in SS black uniform, wearing also the Golden Nazi Party Membership Badge as a tie stickpin. (Photo from the Heinrich Hoffmann Albums, US National Archives, College Park, MD/USA)

Above left, right and below right: States author James Weingartner in *Hitler's Guard*, "Together with 4th Panzer Division, Leibstandarte was ordered north to the Bzura River sector to prevent strong Polish forces being driven southeast by Army Group North, from crossing the river and falling back on Warsaw." These photographs depict the German crossing, as seen through the lens of an SS combat photographer. The two tanks shown are of the PanzerKampfwagen I-class. (SSA, LC)

An interesting cross-section of German transport modes in Poland, from left, motorcycles, a tank, car and horses. States Weingartner, "Leibstandarte had indeed participated in a great victory. In addition to the enormous quantities of equipment, the Bzura (Zora in German) battles had yielded approximately 105,000 prisoners, of which 20,000 were claimed by 4th Panzer and Leibstandarte." (SSA, LC)

Above and below: The various combat accounts of the Leibstandarte's early advance phase into Poland mention "the sandy soil, which was difficult for vehicles to negotiate" as seen in this series of photos. The middle left shot, shows SS vehicles 998 (right) and 999 (left), their men armed with rifles and pistols. In the middle right photo, SS vehicle 003 includes a trooper with two stick grenades tucked into his belt. "To the Front" proclaims the sign at bottom left, while another SS vehicle (bottom right) enters a Polish town hit by artillery fire. (SSA, LC)

Above left and right: The German advance continues into conquered Poland, as (left) a Polish wagon is passed by a car and truck. At right, close on the heels of the soldiers came the first war criminals of the SS: Heydrich's Einsatzgruppen killers, routing out Jews, gypsies and possible guerrillas. (CER)

Middle right: Stacked LSSAH arms and grounded steel helmets on September 9, 1939, as the men examine captured enemy tanks aboard a Polish armored train destroyed not by the Luftwaffe, but by gunfire. The site, according to author Rudolf Lehmann's 1983 work, *The Leibstandarte in Pictures*, is "to the west of Warsaw and south of Oltarew." (SSA, LC)

Above and below: The destruction rent by the Polish-German war, as seen in the destroyed combat vehicles of both sides. At top left is, according to Rudolf Lehmann, "the first armored scout car ... knocked out by three anti-tank hits on the southern boundary of Boleslawez" on the first day of the fighting, September 1, 1939. It is a SdKfz vehicle, of the type also used by the LSSAH in Greece in 1941. At top right is a knocked-out Pzkpfw model, as is the one at bottom left, seen from another angle. The first three armored vehicles are German, but the last is a captured Polish tank, proudly viewed by a trooper in the bottom right picture. Of the scout car, Weingartner writes in *Hitler's Guard*, "Leibstandarte suffered its first casualties as an armored reconnaissance car struck a Polish mine. Boleslawiec was found to be stoutly defended, but shortly after 10 o'clock, Leibstandarte had taken the village after heavy fighting." (SSA, LC)

Above left and right: SS weaponry dug into Poland's sandy soil. At left is a light Pak gun, while at right there is an SMG machine gun (center). (SSA, LC)

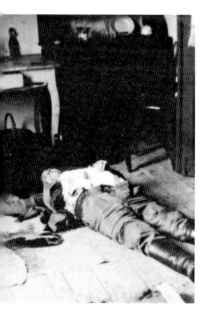

The German captions are (left) "Before Panjonice" and (right) "Burning Modlin." States the *Time-Life Third Reich* volume *The SS*, "At the town of Panianice, Polish troops surrounded Dietrich's men, who had to be rescued by a regiment of the regular army." Adds Weingartner in *Hitler's Guard*, "Twice Leibstandarte launched frontal attacks on the Polish defensive positions, and twice its attacks were repulsed ... Leibstandarte found itself surrounded by the Polish defenders and was extricated by Infantry Regiment 55 of 10th Division." (SSA, LC)

Hitler in conversation with Himmler in Poland, 1939. The officer on the left appears to be General Walter von Reichenau, (1884–1942). He issued the notorious Severity Order concerning fighting on the eastern front, which made him a war criminal. (BT)

Hitler observed, but did not direct, the ground war in Poland— the first and the last time that he would not interfere in such operations. Here, the Führer makes a point to the commander of his Führer Escort Battalion, Maj. General Erwin Rommel. In 1944 Rommel was Sepp's superior in Normandy. (HH)

A G-4 Mercedes-Benz cross-country touring car of Hider's Führerkolonne (Leader Column), filled with RSD officers. (HH)

Above left: Hitler comes calling, September 25, 1939. In the left photo the Führer is greeted by Sepp (left), and watched by Hitler's SS ordnance officer, Max Wünsche at center and his Army adjutant, Infantry General Rudolf Schmundt (right), seen here at age 43. Schmundt died as a result of his wounds in the attempt to kill Hitler in 1944. (HH)

Above right: SS rivals in Poland, September 1939, as the LSSAH received its baptism of fire in its first combat against the Polish Army, which it helped defeat in record time. Here, Sepp Dietrich (left) smiles while listening to the only man he ever said he hated, his nominal boss, Reichsführer SS Heinrich Himmler. Himmler is seen with collar turned up against the wind. (HH)

Time out for a cigarette by LSSAH men during the Polish campaign. (SSA, LC)

Hitler boards his Ju-52 in wartime Poland, followed by a grimy, solemn Dr. Karl Brandt, his travelling SS Escort Physician. (HH)

Hitler survived two bomb blasts meant to kill him, the first being here, on November 9, 1939, during the annual Beer Hall Putsch commemorations. He cut his speech short and left just before the explosion. Were Sepp and Himmler somehow involved? The question remains unanswered to this day. (Hugo Jaeger, LC)

The Führer travelled by car extensively during both the Polish campaign in 1939 (as above, entering conquered Warsaw, with guards on the deserted streets and RSD backup vehicles behind) and in France the following year. Note the headlamps blocked-out with night driving canvas covers that featured a small rectangular slit in the center to emit a concentrated beam of light that would both show the roadway and conceal the car, a Mercedes-Benz G-4 cross-country tourer, from Allied aircraft. Linge stands in the car in 1939. At top right, Hitler's standard is seen on the mudguard at FHQ Ft. Wolf next to an SS Master Sergeant, 1941. (HH)

States Weingartner in *Hitler's Guard*, "The primary responsibility of Dietrich's unit remained the protection of Hitler's person, and elements of Leibstandarte were always on duty ... at Hitler's retreat at Obersalzberg, where, clad in white vests and black trousers, they also waited on the Führer's table." In his superb 1979 study, *Hitler's Personal Security*, author Dr. Peter Hoffmann states, "The Führer's valets were instructed to carry guns at all times .. . The valet Wilhelm Schneider claims that personal valets who served at the table did not actually carry their guns, but this implies a serious violation of the Führer's orders—an unlikely story ... Insiders such as cooks (including a Jewish cook for a number of years), valets, and SS bodyguards had every chance of assassinating the Führer, but it so happened that none of them felt motivated to do so." Hitler greets his waiters in the Great Hall of the Berghof. States Hoffmann, "Hitler never tired of personally looking after the wellbeing of his servants, making certain that they received generous pay and the same food served at his table, that each of his employees had his own room and quarters were provided for married servants." (HH)

Sepp Dietrich returns the salute of an SS man of the 28th SS Panzer Grenadier Division Wallonien in Brussels, Belgium. Belgian SS Maj. Léon Degrelle, author of the 1985 book *Campaign in Russia: The Waffen SS on the Eastern Front*, watches to Sepp's left. (CER)

THE ANGELS OF PEACE DESCEND ON BELGIUM

"The Angels of Peace Descend on Belgium," wartime cartoon by David Low, from *Years of Wrath: A Cartoon History, 1931-45*, David Low, text by Quincy Howe, 1946, LC)

From Left: German Foreign Minister Joachim von Ribbentrop, Dr. Theo Morell, Reichsleiter Martin Bormann and Adolf Hitler at Führer Headquarters Wolfsschlucht in May 1940. Dr. Morell was responsible for Hitler's health, while Bormann, here adjusting his belt (unseen) and wearing the collar tabs of a Waffen SS Major General, was in charge of all the Führer's residences, headquarters and travel arrangements. (VR)

Left: Dr. Theodor Morell (1886–1948) was Hitler's personal physician from 1936-45; prior to this, Dr. Morell practiced his questionable medical skills on German movie stars and Heinrich Hoffmann, Hitler's photographer. It was this latter connection that led him to the Führer. Attests author Charles Hamilton in his 1984 book *Leaders and Personalities of the Third Reich*: "Over a period of nine years, Morell continued to shoot serums made from bull's testicles and cows' intestines into Hitler. Over 28 drugs—including some untested amphetamines—were injected into the Führer." He made a fortune from his connection to Hitler via drugs he sold and a patented lice powder for German troops on the Russian Front, but he died despised and penniless in Allied captivity after the war on May 16, 1948, at Tegernsee, age 64. His medical rival at Hitler's court was SS Dr. Karl Brandt (right), another of Hitler's physicians from 1929. Brandt (1904–48) was a Waffen SS Brigadeführer and in 1942 was named Reich Commissioner for Sanitation and Health. In this latter capacity Dr. Brandt would be tried and convicted as a war criminal by the Allies and hanged on June 2, 1948, having survived his rival Morell by a mere seven days. An attempt to overthrow Morell by informing Hitler of the phony and dangerous drug injections he was getting backfired, and the Führer fired him instead. He was later condemned to death for sending his family to surrender to the U.S. Army. Morell was fired by Hitler on April 21, 1945, because the Führer feared being drugged in a Bormann/SS plot to remove him from Berlin. (HH & USASC photo by D'Addario)

Above and below: Hans-Georg Schulze, top photo, was Hitler's SS ordnance officer from October 1939—August 1941, when he was killed in action serving in Russia with the LSSAH. He was popular with everyone, particularly the future Mrs. Adolf Hitler, Eva Braun, whose friend and skiing companion he was. He had replaced Max Wünsche as ordnance officer. Top: Eva photographed him, wearing the SS collar tabs of rank as 1st Lieutenant. Bottom: Hans-Georg Schulze (center), looking trim and dapper in France with Hitler in 1940, is watched at far right by the man he replaced, Wünsche. (EBH)

Above left: "RSD detail waiting for Hitler at Brussels Airport, June 1, 1940 (from left), Paul Leciejewski, Karl Weckerling, Hans Kuffner, Josef Jorg, Peter Högl, Josef Hausner, and Franz Grill," RSD men all. Note also the pair of barrels skyward of mounted machine guns. (Dr. Peter Hoffmann, LC)

Above right: Hitler's personal RSD detail posing for a tourist snap in front of one of the monuments to Imperial Germany's 1918 defeat at Compiegne, France on June 21, 1940. Fourth from left is the unit's commander, Johann Rattenhuber, and at his left is the Führer's famous cross-eyed bodyguard, Bruno Gesche (1905-80), well-liked by Hitler, but not by Himmler, who detested both his independence of command and his chronic drinking. Both Rattenhuber and Gesche survived the war, while neither Hitler nor Himmler did, both committing suicide in 1945. (Previously unpublished photo, HHA)

Above left: Waffen SS guards present arms to Italian Duce Benito Mussolini (closest to lens) and German Foreign Minister Joachim von Ribbentrop as they enter the Fuhrerbau in Münich on June 21, 1940. The sentry at right is a Staff Sergeant. (VR)

Above right: LSSAH on June 24, 1940, Unit 15./Kradschützen at rest at St. Étienne, France. (CER)

Exhausted Waffen SS troopers during the 18-day campaign in France in June 1940. (CER)

Father and son, SS men both, greet each other in France during a lull in combat in 1940. At right, wearing the uniform of the German Foreign Office that he helped design, is Joachim von Ribbentrop, and at left his son Richard. Richard would go on to fight in Russia and again in France in 1944 as a Panzer commander in the LSSAH. (VR)

Exhausted SS drivers catch some roadside "sack time." (CER)

A previously unpublished view of German Foreign Minister Joachim von Ribbentrop (center) visiting the Front in the West, surrounded by Waffen SS. (VR)

Hitler and Sepp take time out to pet and feed a horse. (HH)

Above left and right: The Reichsführer SS first salutes and then reviews Sepp's LSSAH in France in 1940 at the conclusion of the Western Campaign. Ironically, both men ended their military careers as Army Group Commanders, but Himmler's short-lived 1945 stint with Army Group Vistula was a total failure. (HH)

Above: Hands-on-belts, LSSAH men wearing wartime field gray uniforms hold back delirious Berliners upon Hitler's July 6, 1940 victory return from the Western Front after the defeat of France. (HH)

Below: The LSSAH steps out on flower-decked streets for the gigantic Victory Parade in Berlin of July 19, 1940, as Waffen SS victories are publicly acknowledged for the first time. The soldier at left with the sabre is SS 2nd Lt. Hans Becker. (CER)

States author Rudolf Lehmann in his excellent work *The Leibstandarte, 1/1st SS Panzer Division*, "In August of 1940, Himmler (lower left), acting as the agent of Adolf Hitler, transferred the Standarte des Führers, the unit's new field insignia, to the Regimental Commander (Dietrich) at Ft. Alvensleben in Metz. The banner was a replica of the pennant displayed on the official car of the Führer and Reichskanzler and raised at the Reich Chancellery to signify his presence." Top Right: The ceremony. (CER)

Above left: July 19, 1940: Hitler arrives at the Kroll Opera House in Berlin in his wartime Mercedes-Benz parade car for his victory speech to the Reichstag following the successful conclusion of the Western Campaign. This campaign saw the fall of Denmark, Norway, France, Holland and Belgium and the evacuation of the British Expeditionary Force at Dunkirk back to England. Here Sepp Dietrich strolls along at left while his LSSAH men line the sidewalk guarding the Führer's arrival. German police are lined up behind them. Hitler's SS valet, Heinz Linge, holds the door open for Hitler, who can be seen through the windshield, while his military adjutant, Col. Rudolf Schmundt (left), and SS adjutant Julius Schaub (right) are already exiting the car's back seat. (HH)

Above right: July 19, 1940: Following his Reichstag speech offering Britain peace, the Führer leaves from the main entrance of the Opera House. He shakes hands with newly promoted Reich Marshal Hermann Göring (still in his old Luftwaffe Field Marshal's uniform, however), while SS Reichsführer Heinrich Himmler stands between LSSAH men in Waffen field gray at either side of the doorway, and officers salute on both sides. SS valet Heinz Linge is by the car door, ready to open it for Hitler, while chauffeur Erich Kempka is at the wheel of this heavy Mercedes-Benz parade car, IAV148697. (HH)

Above left: Like other high leaders of the Third Reich, Ribbentrop had SS guards and chauffeurs, as here in France in 1940, an SS Scharführer. The other man outside the car belongs to the Luftwaffe. Sitting in the front seat is a Spanish diplomat of the Franco regime, while the man in back is Dr. Paul Schmidt, a German Foreign Office interpreter whose postwar memoirs, *Hitler's Interpreter*, painted unflattering portraits of the Nazi leadership, particularly of his former boss, Joachim von Ribbentrop. (VR)

Above right: Luftwaffe commander-in-chief Field Marshal Hermann Göring (center, white cap) walks with German construction czar Dr. Fritz Todt (left center) and his Air Force liaison officer to Führer HQ General Karl Bodenschatz (right). Todt died in a mysterious air crash at Rastenburg in East Prussia in February 1942 that fanned the Führer's fear of air travel. (HG)

From raw recruits to precision marchers—scenes common to all armies. Top Left: trainees in fatigues with mess kits. Top Right and Middle: checking in for inductions. Bottom: Boot call on the double! The LSSAH was allowed to recruit from all over the Reich. (CER)

Sepp (left) inspects his LSSAH in their barracks outside Berlin, 1940. The other man is Richard Schulze-Kossens, a Hitler SS aide later, during the war. (HH)

Victory in France, 1940 is observed as the Führer celebrates Christmas with Sepp (left, next to the Führer at table) and his men in winter quarters at Metz on December 26, 1940. (HH)

Sepp believed in personally decorating his men whenever possible, and thus once again gained their admiration, affection and respect. At top left, the scene is November 17, 1941. At top right, he presents the Knight's Cross of the Iron Cross to (left to right) Max Hansen, Hans Becker and Hermann Weiser. In the bottom left shot, he pins the Iron Cross 1st Class on the tunic of 1st Lt. Albert Frey, 1940, after the victorious French campaign. (CER)

1941

Field informational sign (right) for the 40th SS Panzer Grenadier Regiment in the 18th SS *Freiwilligen* Panzer Grenadier Division, an SSLAH sister unit, with mobile troopers carried here by truck. (CER)

Above left: Vehicle LSSAH unit identification sign, wartime. (CER)

Above right: SS Obergruppenführer Josef "Sepp" Dietrich (1892–1966), wearing at the throat his Knight's Cross of the Iron Cross with Oak Leaves. (HH)

LSSAH in action, Second World War , in Russia. (CER)

Wartime medals award ceremony at the Berghof in Bavaria, with SS Max Wünsche and Sepp Dietrich at center. (EBH)

Sepp (center, facing lens) with surrendered Greek Army officers in Greece, April 1941. (EBH)

Above left: LSSAH motorcycle scouts and backup motorized infantry at a halt, 1941. (CER)

Above right: "Volunteers in the foreign legions of the Waffen SS, left to right: Danish, Norwegian, and Dutch." All joined to fight the Red Army in Russia. (CER)

WSS unit in Yugoslavia, April 1941. (CER)

WSS in Yugoslavia in April 1941 receive a jubilant welcome from civilians. (CER)

Sepp in Waffen SS feldgrau, wearing the collar tabs of an Obersturmbannführer. As Commander of the Motorized Infantry Regiment LSSAH, Sepp won the Ritterkreuz on July 5, 1940, at the age of 48; the Eichenlaub on December 31, 1941, of the same unit on the Eastern Front; the Schwerter on March 16, 1943, after the LSSAH had been designated 1st Panzer Division; and the Brillanten on August 6, 1944, as Commander of the 1st Panzer Corps LSSAH and Chief of the 5th Panzer Army. (CER)

As a German newsreel photographer records the event, Hitler greets Sepp in the summer of 1941 at his Wolfsschanze FHQ at Rastenburg, East Prussia. Note the steel-shuttered windows and camouflaged walls of the FHQ's above- ground bunkers. Contrary to popular belief, none but the Reich Chancellery bunkers in Berlin was below ground. (HH)

SS Reichsführer National Leader Heinrich Himmler was named commanding general of Army Group Vistula near the end of the war. Himmler was a disappointment to the Führer in his new role. Here he is seen on the Russian Front in 1941 interviewing a young Russian boy with what were thought to be Aryan features. Between them stands SS General Karl Wolff, former SS liaison officer to Hitler's headquarters. Wolff later served as Himmler's Higher SS and Police Leader in Northern Italy, keeping a watchful eye on Mussolini, and fighting both the Allied armies and the indigenous Italian Communist partisans as well. (Peterson)

Eicke shares a laugh with comrades at FHQ in 1941. From left are Karl Wolff, Eicke, Führer adjutant SS 1st Lt. Richard Schulze-Kossens, Army Field Marshal Wilhelm Keitel and Hitler aide SS Lt. General Julius Schaub. A veteran of the First World War and the German border police afterwards, Eicke was also a member of the post-war Freikorps that preceded the Nazis in fighting the Communists. (HH)

Hitler's dog Blondi among a strange assortment of Germans at the Berghof. From left they are: a photography shop salesgirl, a former army corporal and sergeant, and an architect—Eva Braun Hitler, Adolf Hitler, Sepp and Albert Speer. In 1945, Blondi would be murdered on Hitler's orders, to see if the cyanide capsules worked; they did. Then Hitler and Eva took their own lives. Sepp died in 1966, Speer in London on September 1, 1981, the 42nd anniversary of Hitler's invasion of Poland. (EBH)

Himmler visits his sometime deputy and now rival in Prague after Heydrich's takeover as Reich Protector of German-occupied Czechoslovakia in the fall of 1941. Here, the smiling Reichsführer (center) greets Heydrich's immediate staff. Himmler is watched by Heydrich at right and his own rival at left, just over his right shoulder, SS Brigadeführer Karl Hermann Frank. (CER)

Wolff, Heydrich and Himmler (left to right) inspect an Honor Guard of the Waffen SS (SS under arms) in the courtyard of Hradcany Castle in Prague, the Reich Protector's formal seat of government. (CER)

Leibstandarte sentries stand outside their guard boxes at the Hradcany Palace's gate. The Czech parachutists concluded that it would be impossible to kill Heydrich here and decided to attack him *en route* from his country home outside Prague. (CER)

Dr. Hans Heinrich Lammers was head of the Führer's Reich Chancellery in Berlin, as well as a State Secretary and Minister. Born in 1879 during the Bismarckian Reich, he had a hunchback. During Göring's attempt to succeed Hitler as Head of the State in the spring of 1945, Dr. Lammers sided with the Reich Marshal—leading an enraged Hitler to order his arrest for high treason on April 23rd. Here (center) he is talking with the Sudeten German Nazi Leader Karl Hermann Frank, seen (right) in the uniform of an SS Gruppenführer. At left is Professor Jaroslav Krejci, Premier and Minister of Justice under the Nazis' Reich Protectorate of Bohemia and Moravia. (HH)

Prominent members of the High Command of the Luftwaffe assembled at the Wolfsschanze FHQ in 1941, from left: General (later Field Marshal) Wolfram von Richthofen, SS aide Richard Schulze-Kossens, Col. Nikolaus von Below, Chief of Staff General Hans Jeschonneck, unknown Air Force officer, and General Kurt Student, founder and wartime commander of Germany's Luftwaffe paratroop forces. (HH)

Above: Göring (white jacket) and German General Dietrich von Choltitz (center) of the German Army. Choltitz is most famous in the Second World War for the capture of the Black Sea port of Sevastopol in the Crimea on July 27, 1942, and for surrendering Paris to the Allies two years later despite Hitler's orders. He also, however, saved Student's life from the Leibstandarte in Rotterdam in Holland in May, 1940, States Charles Messenger in *Hitler's Gladiator,* "Student was supervising the surrender of the Dutch troops, using the Dutch Kommandanteur as his headquarters. Leibstandarte elements passed by, saw armed Dutch troops farther up the street and immediately opened fire. Student had gone to the window to see what had happened and was chipped by a bullet in the head. Only when Lt. Col. von Choltitz, commanding a battalion of the 16th Infantry Regiment, which was under Student's command, dashed outside and herded the Dutch into a church did the firing cease." Gravely wounded, but never blaming the LSSAH, Student recovered in time to win his greatest victory, at Crete a year later. Attests Messenger, "From the evidence available, the blame must rest with Dietrich's men." Both Choltitz and Student survived the war. Student died in 1977. (HG)

Below: The Leibstandarte achieved outstanding successes in the Greek campaign of Spring 1941 that was undertaken to rescue the Germans' battered Fascist Italian ally, Mussolini. The LSSAH's timely victory at the Klidi Pass opened the road to the heart of Greece for the Nazi panzer steamroller. It was in this campaign that the SS discovered that the 88 mm anti-aircraft gun made an, excellent antitank weapon as well— and quickly knocked out eight British tanks. When the British evacuated Greece from the Gulf of Corinth in what was termed a "second Dunhkirk," "Panzer" Meyer's men were in hot pursuit via fishing craft. Here a light gun is unloaded at the port of Patras. The motorcycle of the type seen at right enabled German cycle troops armed with rifles to take the Klidi Pass. (CER)

A moment of blazing military glory for Sepp and the LSSAH occurred when he accepted the surrender of two entire Greek Armies—some 16 divisions—on Hitler's 52nd birthday, April 20, 1941. Dietrich is at right, SS 1st Lt. Max Wünsche at left, Greek General Tsolakoglu at left bottom center. The Klidi Pass operation drew special praise in the form of an Order of the Day from Cavalry General Georg Stumme, later briefly the successor to Rommel before El Alamein. (CER)

Above and left: Sepp unwittingly created a diplomatic incident between Axis Pact partners Nazi Germany and Fascist Italy when he accepted the Greek surrender without Italian participation. Mussolini demanded, and got, a second surrender, much to the disgust of the LSSAH. At left, on April 20, 1941, at Metsovon Pass, a Greek delegation comes under a flag of truce to begin surrender negotiations. Nevertheless, (above) Sepp found time to smile (right), alongside a captured British officer. (CER)

Above left: The end of Hitler's Greek War, 1941: An LSSAH private on sentry duty. (HH)

Above right: A ceremonial usage of the "Führer's own" Standard. In Campulung, Rumania on March 16, 1941, Heroes' Memorial Day is observed on foreign soil as Sepp delivered the main address. (CER)

On September 30, 1941, General Erich von Manstein became one of many German Army commanders to use the LSSAH as a "military fire brigade." "At the crucial joint where the 170th Rumanian Infantry Division met the left flank of the 30th Corps, and where a new Russian breakthrough threatened," the LSSAH was brought in, asserts Weingartner in *Hitler's Guard*. Born November 24, 1885, Manstein wears the shoulder boards of a Field Marshal. He attained that rank from Hitler on July 1, 1942, for his conquest of the Crimea in the USSR. On his left sleeve he wears that campaign badge. A former Royal Page, Manstein was wounded on the Eastern Front in November 1914, after which he became a staff officer in Poland, Serbia and France. A son born in 1920 was killed in Russia in 1942. Named General of Infantry in 1940, it was his joint plan with Hitler that same year that won the stunning Western victory. Named commander of Army Group South in 1943, Hitler honorably dismissed him in March 1944, and he surrendered to the British in May 1945; they tried him as a war criminal, but he was released in 1953, and died 20 years later, on June 10, 1973. (CER)

Above left: Reich Marshal Göring with German Army Field Marshal Sigmund List (right), overall commander of *Operation Marita* in Greece in the spring of 1941, in which both Sepp and the Leibstandarte garnered victor's laurels. This photo was taken at the premiere of the documentary war film, *Sieg im Westen,* held at Vienna the same year.

Field Marshal List was born May 14, 1880, and fought in the First World War in France, Belgium, the Balkans, and with the Turks; in 1930, he commanded the Infantry School at Dresden and was named lieutenant general in 1932. He took part in the occupations of both Austria and Moravia and the invasion of Poland. After service in France once more, List defeated the Yugoslavs, Greeks and Australians, but he fell out with Hitler over Russia and was fired in 1942. He died at age 91 on June 18, 1971. (HG)

Above right: Sepp went to bat for German Army Panzer Col. General Heinz Guderian on two different occasions when he had been fired by the Führer. Here, Guderian combs his hair before a meeting with Hitler at Führer Headquarters, while an enlisted man holds the mirror. Hitler's Army adjutant, Col. Gerhard Engel looks on at left. (HH)

Heinz Wilhelm Guderian was a pioneer in the development of armored warfare, and was the leading proponent of tanks and mechanization in the Wehrmacht. He died in 1954 aged 65. (CER)

Two famous shots of one of the more renowned SS combat leaders, Kurt "Panzer" Meyer, 1910-1961, the second commander of the HJ Division (12th SS Armored) after the death of Fritz Witt in 1944. At left he is seen barking a command in Greece in May 1941, in the rank of Sturmbahnführer, in a photo that was used on the cover of *The SS*, the first in the *Time-Life Books Third Reich* series. At right Meyer is seen in Russia in 1941, somewhat less well groomed! After a series of mild strokes, he died of a heart attack in Hagen, Westphalia on December 23, 1961, his 51st birthday. Fifteen thousand people attended Kurt Meyer's funeral in Hagen. A cushion-bearer bore his medals. The holder of the Knight's Cross with Oak Leaves and Swords, Meyer was an SS Major General when he was captured in France on November 17, 1944. (CER)

During a wartime leave from the Eastern Front, Sepp poses with Führer adjutant and LSSAH member Max Wünsche on the terrace of the Berghof overlooking the Bavarian Alpine village of Berchtesgaden. Both men wear black wrap-around, wool panzer crew uniforms. Sepp's collar tabs are for his rank as a Waffen SS Col. General, the highest rank he would attain, while those of Wünsche denote him to be a Major at this time. Wünsche was captured by the Allies in 1944 during the Normandy fighting. (EBH)

Several members of Hitler's inner circle share a laugh at his wartime Führer Headquarters, from left Hans Baur, Hitler's pilot; Propaganda Chief Dr. Josef Goebbels; Press aide Heinz Lorenz (behind Goebbels); SS General and Führer Adjutant Julius Schaub; Führer aide and SS man Richard Schulze-Kossens (behind Schaub); and Reich Chief Photo Reporter Heinrich Hoffmann. Sepp Dietrich knew and worked with them all. Baur's collar tab is a Colonel's rank, while that of Schaub indicates an SS Lt. General. (Hugo Jaeger, LC)

Later in the war, the comparatively tiny Junkers 52 was replaced for Hitler's travel by the giant Condor aircraft shown here. This time the Condor is in occupied Ukraine in August 1941. Himmler is preceded down the exit ladder by an SS officer. On the ground, from left to right, are Hitler, Dr. Paul Schmidt, Walter Hewel, Mussolini, SS aide Günsche, and Linge, carrying the dictators' overcoats. (HH)

German Army Field Marshal Gerd von Rundstedt (left), greets Hitler as the Führer alights from his private Junkers Ju-52 aircraft in the USSR. (HH)

Throughout his political career, Hitler often traveled by air, although he hated to fly and feared drowning should his plane go down in the water. Here, his Ju-52 taxis to a halt on an airstrip on conquered Soviet territory, as German Army Field Marshal Wilhelm Keitel, swagger stick baton held behind him, waits for it to halt. (HH)

An LSSAH machine gun team sizes up a target in the Soviet Union, 1941. Note the rangefinder being used by the man in front. (CER)

Waffen SS Lt. General Paul Hausser is seen here being awarded on August 8, 1941, the Knight's Cross of the Iron Cross by Panzer General Heinrich von Veitinghoff (right). He was later awarded both the Swords and Oak Leaves to the Ritterkreuz, although he angered Hitler several times during the war. After fighting in both Poland and France, he lost an eye on the Eastern Front, took the city of Kharkov in March 1943, and was severely wounded during the Battle of the Falaise Gap in France in 1944. He returned to active duty and was captured by the Allies in April 1945. He outlived virtually all of his top SS comrades—with the exception of Karl Wolff. (HH)

In charge of everything at the Berghof complex at Berchtesgaden was Secretary to the Führer and Reichsleiter Martin Bormann (left of Hitler), seen here arriving with the Führer (center) and Reich Marshal Hermann Göring (light-colored overcoat) at a train station. The "shattered" effect of this photograph is due to the original cracked glass negative. (HH)

Rattenhuber's RSD men on duty. At left, two of them sit chatting on a park-style bench outside a camouflaged bunker. In the right photo, a guard stands outside Hitler's own bunker. The view is from just inside the screened-in porch, for the East Prussian swamps were notorious for their pesky mosquitoes. (HH)

The outside view of the same bunker, but this time seen from the guard's perspective. Reich Marshal Göring (left) and Luftwaffe General Karl Bodenschatz chat at right; Hitler's Air Force liaison officer, Col. Nikolaus von Below (right) talks with an unidentified officer in the doorway. Note the iron shutters on the windows to be closed in case of an attack. This is in the summer of 1941. (VR)

An LSSAH Captain wears protective headdress to guard against mosquitos at the Führer's principal wartime military Headquarters, Wolfsschanze at Rastenburg, East Prussia. (HH)

The man in charge of Hitler's daily regimen both before and during the war was Nazi Reichsleiter and Secretary to the Führer Martin Bormann. Bormann is seen at right at age 40 in 1940, and above in 1941 with Hitler and NSKK chief Lt. General Erwin Kraus, on a rain-swept walkway at Wolfsschanze, Hitler's principal wartime military headquarters during 1941–44. Note the one-story, camouflaged buildings and shuttered windows. (HH, left. Hugo Jaeger, right)

Above: Hitler's valet and SS Major, Heinz Linge (center), appears in many photographs with the Führer either carrying his coats or hanging them up. He enlisted in the SS in 1933 and, notes Charles Hamilton, "Was soon attached to the SS-Begleitkommando, the SS detachment entrusted with the Führer's personal safety. In July, 1935, he became Hitler's ordnance officer, and in 1939, after the departure of Karl Krause, was appointed as Hitler's head valet." His last mission for the Führer was to wrap his dead body in a brown army blanket, place it in the Chancellery park, burn it with gasoline with the help of SS chauffeur Erich Kempka and then bury it. Captured by the Russians, Linge was imprisoned for 10 years. He died a prosperous Hamburg businessman on March 9, 1981, age 68. Here he follows Hitler and Mussolini at train side during the Duce's August 1941 visit to Rastenburg. The others are, left to right, interpreter Dr. Paul Schmidt, Julius Schaub and Army Col. Rudolf Schmundt. (HH)

Below: A rare shot of the two brothers, SS 1st Lieutenants and Führer adjutants together, Richard Schulze-Kossens at left and Hans-Georg (nicknamed "Frettchen") at right. "Frettchen" wears the Iron Cross and the Wound Badge. (EBH)

All smiles, Sepp decorates SS Untersturmführer Hans-Georg Schulze-Kossens, Hitler's SS Ordnance Officer from August 1939–August 1941, when he was transferred to the Russian Front. An extremely popular officer at The Berghof, he was killed in action. Saddened, Hitler offered his job to his brother, SS officer Richard Schulze-Kossens, on October 3, 1941, and he accepted. (CER)

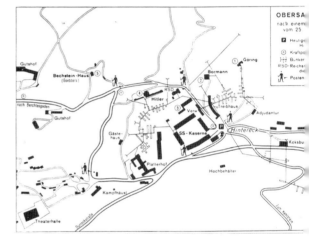

A plan of Obersalzberg, a mountainside retreat situated above the market town of Berchtesgaden in Bavaria, showing the site of the Berghof, Göring's house, Bormann's house etc. (BT)

Typical arrivals and departures at the Berghof in which LSSAH honor guards took part. In the two photos the guest is Japanese Ambassador Hiroshi Oshima (center, in Army uniform and samurai sword). Oshima survived the war, conviction and imprisonment as a war criminal, and died in 1978. At left, he is seen with Ribbentrop, at right with the towering German Foreign Office's Baron Alexander von Dornberg, right. (VR)

In April 1941 the visitor is Croatian Ustacha (Fascist) Poglavnik (Leader) Dr. Ante Pavelic (saluting). Others from left to right include Air Force General Karl Bodenschatz, Foreign Office liaison Walther Hewel, Albert Bormann, a rarely caped Adolf Hitler, von Ribbentrop and Göring. A newsreel photographer, Walter Frentz, at right records the scene. (VR)

The Haus Türken on the Obersalzberg, above and behind The Berghof and at the foot of the hill upon which sat the Bormann House. At left, the men of the guard company stand at-ease behind their stacked arms, while right, a relieved guard company leaves the building guard house entrance on its way back to barracks. (CER)

1942

IN OCCUPIED TERRITORY

Above left: "In Occupied Territory," cartoon by David Low. Hitler asks, "Why don't they like us, Heinrich?" (LC)

Above right: On January 19, 1942, Sepp, the national hero of the Third Reich, married his second and final wife, Ursula Moninger, whose father owned the famous Moninger Brewery in Karlsruhe that is still in business. She was 22 when they met at Horcher's Restaurant in Berlin in 1937. Sepp was 45, more than twice her age. The marriage endured the end of the war and his long imprisonments for 24 years, until his death in 1966. (CER)

Sepp's second marriage, to Ursula on January 19, 1942 is celebrated with dinner. The smiling new bride sits at his left at table in the left of this photo. The union produced a trio of sons. (Previously unpublished, HH)

The newly married Dietrichs—Ursula and Sepp—on January 19, 1942, as they leave the ceremony. (HH)

Above left: Barechested, Sepp performs his daily morning shave. (CER)

Above right: In his splendid 1988 biography, *Hitler's Gladiator*, author Charles Messenger asserts that this is Sepp clowning around as a Russian peasant woman in a photo taken by Eva Braun Hitler; the current writer, however, is doubtful that this is so. (CER)

After the rescue of the deposed Italian Duce in September 1943 by SS man Otto Skorzeny, Benito Mussolini (seen here, right, with Reich Marshal Hermann Göring on January 28, 1942) was grateful. (HG)

Eicke has come down in Nazi history as one of the SS men who helped murder SA Chief of Staff Ernst Röhm in his jail cell at Stadelheim Prison in Münich at the conclusion of the June 30, 1934 Blood Purge—but he was much more than that. Known as "Papa" Eicke to his men, he was born October 17, 1892 (the same year as Sepp) and was shot down by the Russians behind their lines in his Fieseler Storch (Stork) recon plane on February 26, 1943; thus, he was only 49 at the time of his death, one of the youngest of the senior Waffen SS field leaders to die in the Second World War, and by enemy action. In these two photos, he wears the collar tabs of his rank, SS Obergruppenfuhrer and General der Waffen SS, as well as the Knight's Cross with Oak leaves, the Golden Party Membership Badge and the First World War Wound Badge. He was a tough and brutal man, even by the standards of the SS. (HH)

Above left: Sepp and Speer—by now Reich Minister of Armaments and War Production (right)—inspect captured British Churchill tanks after the failed Allied assault at Dieppe in France, 1942. (CER)

Above right: In his 1970 book *Inside the Third Reich: Memoirs*, Speer writes, "Sometime in the autumn of 1943, the staff of Sepp Dietrich's SS army had held a drinking bout ... in Himmler's opinion, Speer was dangerous; he would have to disappear ... Later, after the (D-Day) invasion, Sepp Dietrich gave me a vivid account of the demoralizing effect of massed bombings on his elite divisions ... Dietrich ... persistently took issue with Hitler's layman opinion, but ... only brought down anger on (his) head, since he took all this as an attack on his military expertise and technical intelligence ... At a simple supper in a small back room of the Chancellery furnished in peasant style, I by chance heard from Sepp Dietrich ... that Hitler intended to issue an order that ... no prisoners were to be taken. In the course of advances by SS units, it had been established, Dietrich said, that the Soviet troops had killed their German prisoners. Hitler had then and there announced that a thousand-fold retaliation in blood must be taken. I was thunderstruck ..." Speer (left) and Sepp (right) at Dieppe, 1942. (CER)

Below left: Sepp walks with German Cavalry General Eberhard von Mackensen (third from left, with whom the author corresponded in 1967) past some destroyed Russian rail rolling stock. He was the son of the famed Field Marshal August von Mackensen of the First World War and the brother of the German Ambassador to Italy. Born September 24, 1889, he achieved the rank of Colonel General and the command of an army. His highest decoration was the Oak Leaves to the Knight's Cross, awarded May 26, 1942, for his Russian Front service. (CER)

Below right: Hitler greets his Chief of General Staff, Col. General Franz Halder (left), as Field Marshal Wilhelm Keitel looks on (at right). After the war, Halder would testify that he often attended meetings with Hitler with a loaded pistol in his pocket—but never drew it to shoot his Führer. Born June 30, 1884, he was an artillery officer and interpreter of French before being selected for the Great German General Staff in 1917 during the First World War. After the war, Halder taught tactics and conducted field maneuvers. Fired in 1942, he died at age 88, on April 2, 1972. (HH)

Above and below: SS Lt. Col. Max Wünsche (1914-1995) was the Führer's ordnance officer during 1938-40, after which he was transferred to front-line duty with the LSSAH after a complaint was lodged against him by Hitler's butler, Arthur Kannenberg. States author Charles Hamilton in *Leaders and Personalities of the Third Reich*, "He was awarded the Knight's Cross on February 28, 1943, the Oak Leaves on August 11, 1944, and was captured in France on August 27, 1944. On May 27, 1941, when the Greek Army surrendered to Sepp Dietrich, Wünsche was present. *Top Left:* After the victory at Kharkov, Wünsche is personally congratulated by Goebbels in Berlin." As Wünsche watches at left, Dr. Goebbels shakes hands with Sturmbannführer Kross. He beams in Russian fur cap at top right, and stands to Sepp's left in the bottom photo. Note the wraparound tanker jackets. (HH)

Above left: Most of Hitler's life during the Second World War was spent at various military headquarters. During the Polish campaign, it was aboard his special train *Amerika* and at Zoppot Hotel. The 1940 Western Campaign found him at a series of above-ground bunkers in forest settings: Felsennest (Eyrie) near Bad Nauheim in Germany; Brûly-de-Pesche in Eastern France (Wolfsschlucht, or Wolf's Lair); Tannenberg in the German Black Forest. The Balkan Campaign of April 1941, was again directed from *Amerika* at Mönichkirchen in Austria. For most of his Russian war, his best-known FHQ was at Rastenburg in East Prussia at Wolfsschanze during 1941-44. For a brief time in 1942, his FHQ was on Ukrainian soil at Winnitza at Werwolf. At top left, Hitler walks outside one of the camouflaged bunkers. Rattenhuber and his men trail behind the group. In the middle, left to right, are Heinrich Hoffmann; Ribbentrop's FHQ liaison officer Walther Hewel; Himmler, Lammers; Ribbentrop; auto designer Dr. Ferdinand Porsche; Dr. Robert Ley; an SS orderly; Dr. Morell; Hitler; Albert Speer (behind Hitler); and German Navy Grand Adm. Erich Raeder. Summer 1942. (VR)

Above right: According to his press chief, Dr. Otto Dietrich, Hitler feared dying in an air crash like the kind that killed *Alpenkorps* General Edouard Dietl, seen here with the Führer at Leader Headquarters at Wolffschanze, Rastenburg, East Prussia. (HH)

Below: Battlefield glory and Nazi heroism aside, this was the reality of the bitter, protracted fighting on the Eastern Front: death and graves all over the Soviet Union, as at Lake Ilmen (right) and as witnessed by the LSSAH men at the final resting places of some of their comrades (left). (CER)

States the official German wartime caption to this photo, "Members of the Waffen SS have reached the homes on their entrance to the city of Malgobek, located in the most significant area for petroleum, south of Torek... has been captured on October 7, 1942, during the thick of the fighting by Army Medical teams (!) and the men of the Waffen SS.— SS Inspec. Control Mobius." (CER)

Above left and right: Born October 7, 1880, in Brandenburg-Havel, Germany, Paul Hausser was Sepp's foremost military rival within the Waffen SS and outlived him, dying at age 92 on December 21, 1972, in Ludwigsburg. Awarded the Knight's Cross with Oak Leaves and Swords for his wartime exploits, Hausser saw action as Division, Army and Army Group Commander, and lost his right eye in battle. At top left, he chats with Sepp in Russia, as two white-jacketed LSSAH waiters look on and General Gille talks with Maj. Kurt Meyer at right. (CER)

Waffen SS Col. General Paul Hausser is seen here with Adolf Hitler at FHQ during the war, while an aide holds a decoration box at right. (HH)

Hitler inspects a new model troop carrier, as Kempka stands ready in the doorway at centre to answer questions. Note the wartime headlamp covers, with their nighttime driving light slits at center of each. (HH)

Linge hangs up Hitler's coat as the Führer shakes hands with an Army officer at FHQ Rastenburg. (HH)

SS Col. Richard Schulze-Kossens (1914–1988) was an SS Lieutenant Colonel and the surviving brother of Hans-Georg Schulze. Originally von Ribbentrop's aide, he was kidded by Soviet dictator Josef Stalin himself during the signing of the Nazi-Soviet Non-Aggression Pact in Moscow in August 1939. States Charles Hamilton in *Leaders and Personalities of the Third Reich*, "In 1942 the Führer made Schulze (Kossens) responsible for all men serving in the SS-Begleitkommando, the SS men entrusted with Hitler's personal safety. Schulze finished up the war as the last commander of the SS training school at Bad Tolz." In this photo, Schulze-Kossens "helps arrange the Führer's birthday reception," states author John Toland; the date is probably 1942 at FHQ Rastenburg. (HH)

Sepp with and without his Hitler-style moustache, which appears to have gone sometime late in 1942 or early in 1943. At left, he is seen with SS Captain and company commander Jochen Peiper on the Eastern Front. Of Sepp Hitler once said, I've always given him the opportunity to intervene at sore spots. He's a man who is simultaneously cunning, energetic and brutal." (CER)

Adolf Hitler was always keen to see new military developments. Here an SS officer gives a demonstration to top brass, more particularly Hitler and Himmler. Sepp Dietrich is at the far left. (CER)

1943

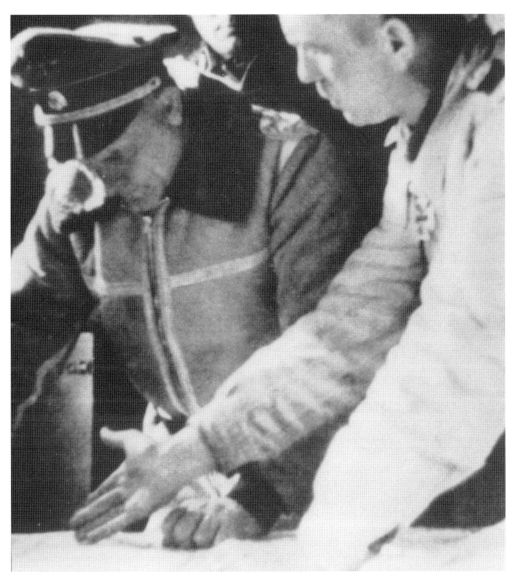

Above: Wearing winter parka, Sepp (left) receives a map briefing from Kurt Meyer (right). (CER)

Right: Austrian SS man Ernst Kaltenbrunner succeeded Heydrich as Head of the Reich Central Security Office on January 30, 1943, the apex of his career. Like his fellow Austrian, Otto Skorzeny, Kaltenbrunner wore his student dueling scars proudly. He was tried, convicted and hanged at Nuremberg on October 16, 1946, as a war criminal. (USASC photo, D'Addario)

At Stalingrad, German Field Marshal Friedrich von Paulus and his 6th Army were caught in a Russian vise. Here, von Paulus and his senior staffers are seen surrendering to the Russians—the first German Field Marshal to do so. Born September 23, 1880, he was named commander of the 6th Army in January 1942, and was awarded the Knight's Cross with Oak Leaves by Hitler, as well as given a Marshal's baton. After his surrender, he made anti-Hitler broadcasts for the Russians, and the Führer had his family arrested. He never saw his wife alive again and was held by the Reds until 1953—a full 10 years. After a stint as an inspector of the Communist East German People's Police, von Paulus died of cancer in Dresden on February 1, 1957. *Right:* The defender of Nazi Vienna in 1945 was Alpenkorps General Lothar Rendulic, seen here wearing a Hitler moustache. A Colonel General, Rendulic won the Oak Leaves of the Knight's Cross on August 15, 1943, "for his role in the surrender of the 9th Italian Army," states Angolia. (Both CER)

Like Hitler, Sepp preferred German Shepherds as pets. The picture at left was taken in the spring of 1943; that at right in the summer of 1941. Note Sepp's wristwatch and Adolf Hitler cuff band in the left photo, as well as the second pattern eagle, worn 1936-45. (HH)

Right and below: Two views of Sepp in different winter apparel on the Eastern Front in the Second World War. In the upper shot, he listens to SS Obersturmbannführer Kurt Meyer (pointing finger) from his command vehicle on March 14, 1943, at Kharkov. Significantly, this victory, the last clear-cut German victory of the Second World War, was won by the LSSAH. With him is Capt. Fend in the city's tractor works. The lower shot shows, left to right, Lt. Col. Keilhaus, Dietrich and Kurt Meyer, all wearing non-German issue Russian fur caps on the Ssambek. (CER)

The last SS—and German—victory in Russia was at Kharkov, in March 1943. At left, a soldier puts up a sign declaring the site "Bodyguard Plaza," but the designation was short-lived. At right, weary men of the new SS Panzerkorps—that consisted of LSSAH, *Das Reich* and *Totenkopf* divisions— watch Luftwaffe dive bombers pound the city. Soon, however, the Red Air Force as well as those in the West would overwhelm Göring's men and planes. (CER)

Two famous photos of Waffen SS non-coms in the Kharkov street-fighting, armed with both an MP-40 sub-machinegun and the famed "potato masher" stick grenade. (CER)

Dressed as warmly as possible to ward off the chill of the Russian winter, LSSAH Division commander Col. General Sepp Dietrich (left) congratulates SS officer Kurt "Panzer" Meyer on his victory in the taking of the city of Kharkov in March 1943 — the last such clear-cut German victory in the Second World War. (CER)

April 1943: Sepp and his LSSAH Division staff pose for a formal picture on the Russian Front at their headquarters. Sepp stands with clasped hands at center, with Kurt Meyer on his right. Dietrich's successor as commander of the division, Theodor Wisch, is second from left in the second row, while his Chief of Staff, Rudolf Lehmann (later a chronicler of the Waffen SS in several post-war books) is just behind Sepp's left shoulder, looking down. (CER)

SS General Hausser decorates an SS 2nd Lieutenant during the war as a photographer checks his camera. Angolia writes in *On the Field of Honor* (1979), volume 1, "Few men of the SS brought the leadership qualifications with them as did Paul Hausser ... He retired from the Reichswehr as a Generalmajor in 1932, only to be reactivated again in 1934, when he transferred to the SS Verfugungstruppe. In 1936, he was made Inspector of that organization, which permitted him to formulate the training directives and code of standards. Even before his leadership role of the SS during the Second World War, he was accorded the affectionate title of 'Papa Hausser' by his men." A hero of both world wars, Hausser captured Kharkov in 1943. (HH)

Sepp in animated conversation on the Eastern Front with a trio of Waffen SS officers, from left, Priess, Gille and Kruger. Born March 8, 1897, in Gandersheim, Germany, SS Obergruppenführer and General der Waffen SS Herbert Otto Gille won his Knight's Cross on October 8, 1942, commanding 5th Artillery Regiment in SS Division Viking the Oak Leaves on November 1, 1943, as the divisional commander, the Swords on February 18, 1944; and the Diamonds on April 19, 1944, in the same role. He died December 26, 1966, age 69. (CER)

Above left: Linge wears the collar tabs of a 1st Lieutenant. (HH)

Above right: Günsche wears the collar tabs of an SS 1st Lieutenant. (HH)

Above left: Baur in SS black and wearing the collar tabs of a Lieutenant General. (HH)

Above right: Army Field Marshal Walter Model, another Western Front commander, was called "The Führer's Fireman." Model was sent wherever the front was in danger of cracking under enemy pressure. Here he is greeted by a grateful Hitler, along with German Army Field Marshal Wilhelm Keitel, (center) and the Führer's Army adjutant, Col. Rudolf Schmundt (right). (HH)

Above and right: The Russian steppes seemed endless to the Waffen SS—as indeed they were from a Central European geographic perspective—and that was why Hitler wanted to conquer them for future German "lebensraum," or living space. In his 1970 book, *Memoirs: Inside the Third Reich*, Albert Speer wrote of his flight over Occupied Russia in February 1942: "Beneath us the dreary, snow-covered plains of Southern Russia flowed by. On large farms we saw the burned sheds and barns. To keep our direction, we flew along the railroad line. Scarcely a train could be seen; the stations were burned out, the roundhouses destroyed. Roads were rare, and they, too, were empty of vehicles. The great stretches of land we passed were frightening in their deathly silence, which could be felt even inside the plane. Only gusts of snow broke the monotony of the landscape, or, rather, emphasized it. This flight brought home to me the danger to the armies almost cut off from supplies." His companion on the flight was Sepp Dietrich: "Huddled close together, we sat in a Heinkel bomber refitted as a passenger plane." (CER)

Two wartime views at FHQ of Hitler's chauffeur from 1934–45 and bodyguard, Erich Kempka, 1910–1975. At left, he poses in the snow at Rastenburg with Hitler in 1943, the 10th anniversary of Hitler's coming to power in Germany. In this photo, Kempka wears the collar tabs of a Sturmbannführer. The second shows Kempka after the wedding of Hitler's secretary Traudl Junge, June 1943. From left to right: Otto Günsche, Traudl and Hans Junge, and Erich Kempka. (HH)

Leibstandarte motorized transport in the Soviet Union all marked with the distinctive unit symbol, a skeleton key—"dietrich" in German—from motorcycles to command and staff cars. The blitzkrieg campaigns fought by the LSSAH in Poland, France, Holland, Yugoslavia and Greece simply didn't work well in the Soviet Union; thus, the short war Hitler planned on became the long one he couldn't win. (CER)

Above left: The Russian mud snarled the motorized transport of the LSSAH just as it did that of every other German unit. "General Mud" didn't discriminate! (CER)

Above right: The arrival of fallen Italian Fascist Duce Benito Mussolini at FHQ Rastenburg on September 14, 1943, from left to right: German Army Field Marshal Wilhelm Keitel, Foreign Minister Joachim von Ribbentrop, Mussolini wearing dark civilian hat and overcoat, while Hitler SS valet Heinz Linge takes Hitler's cap from his Führer at far right. (Previously unpublished, HHA)

Below: Apparently murdered by Communists or former members of the French Resistance with long memories, while living in retirement in the French village of Traves on July 14, 1976, Colonel Jochen Peiper became "the last man of the SS 'Bodyguard' to fall," according to unit historian Rudolf Lehmann. Named Commander of the SS Armored Regiment 1 LSSAH in November 1943, Peiper played a key role in both the Battle of the Bulge and the Malmédy Massacre controversy and later the Dachau Trial. Here (left) he appears in black Panzer uniform as a Lieutenant Colonel and (right) in feldgrau as a 1st Lieutenant earlier. In both cases, the Death's Head on his caps is that of the second pattern, 1934–45. Peiper had been a one-time aide to SS Reichsführer Himmler. (CER)

Hitler greets General der Waffen SS Felix Steiner at his Rastenburg military headquarters. Steiner, who died in München on May 17, 1966, less than a month after Dietrich, was rewarded for his wartime services with the Knight's Cross with Oak Leaves and Swords. Born May 23, 1896, of him noted author LTC John R. Angolia writes, "He ranks among the few SS officers of senior rank who had suitable training in leadership for combat." Among his postwar books defending his men was *Army of Outlaws*.

General Steiner looks on as Hitler congratulates Belgian SS Maj. Léon Degrelle (1906–1994), (center) at an awards ceremony at Rastenburg. Hitler once said that if he ever had a son, he wanted him to be a man like Degrelle. The feeling was mutual, and in 1988 Degrelle published the first volume of a pro-Hitler biography. (HH)

Throughout his long career in the Third Reich, Sepp Dietrich worked closely with all these men, seen here in 1943 at a weapons demonstration in East Prussia. From left they are: unknown, Army Field Marshal Wilhelm Keitel (shading his eyes), Foreign Minister Joachim von Ribbentrop, unknown, Karl Otto Saur, Hitler, Hermann Göring, Albert Speer, Navy Grand Adm. Erich Raeder, SS General Karl Wolff and Dr. Robert Ley. (HH)

Above left: SS General Josef Sepp Dietrich, commander of Hitler's SS Lifeguards unit, appears here at the Führer's home, the Berghof, overlooking the village of Berchtesgaden in the Bavarian Alps during the Second World War. He wears the collar tabs of a Waffen SS Obergruppenführer and the Knight's Cross of the Iron Cross at the throat. On his right breast pocket, he wears the ribbon of the Beer Hall Putsch Commemorative Badge and, in his button hole, 1939 Iron Cross eagle pin. Over his right breast pocket are medal ribbons, while below (top to bottom) are the Nazi Party Golden Membership Badge, a First World War armored assault badge (left) and (right) the 1939 Iron Cross pin over top the actual 1914 Iron Cross. On his left sleeve is the cuffband Adolf Hitler for the LSSAH. The German armed forces were near-unique at that time in that their officers and men wore all their orders, medals and decorations into combat. (EB)

Middle: Of Bormann's role in the 1934 Blood Purge, Weingartner had this to say in *Hitler's Guard*, "Dietrich presented himself before Hitler shortly after noon at the Brown House. Around five o'clock in the afternoon, the Führer ordered him to select a firing party from among his men and to proceed with them to Stadelheim Prison, there to liquidate the six SA leaders whose names made up a list given him by Martin Bormann, Chief of Staff to Rudolf Hess." Here, the jovial Bormann plays the role of loving papa to his ever-growing family, as devoted wife Gerda Buch Bormann (lower right) and a white jacketed LSSAH Technical Sergeant waiter stands by in the dining room of Bormann's home, situated on a hill overlooking Hitler's own. Born June 17, 1900, the end of the First World War found Bormann serving as an artilleryman; he joined the anti-Communist Free Corps and was sentenced to a year in prison for his part in a political murder. This made him a quasi-hero to Hitler after Bormann joined the Nazi Party. During 1928–30, he served with the Supreme Command of the SA and was named a Reichsleiter late in 1933. From then until Rudolf Hess flew to Scotland in May 1941, Bormann was Chief of Cabinet in Hess' Office of the Deputy Führer, but in reality was Hess' "liaison" to Hitler himself. He was named Secretary to the Führer in 1943, and had earlier taken over the Nazi Party Chancellery. Many observers compare him to Josef Stalin during Lenin's lifetime. Until 1972, his whereabouts were unknown, but in his 1979 biography, *The Secretary*, German author Jochen von Lang claimed to have finally forensically identified his remains in Berlin, asserting that Bormann had been killed by Russian gunfire in 1945. In 1990, however, the controversy was reopened with the publication of *Quest: Searching for Germany's Nazi Past*, in which it is claimed that he was flown from Berlin in a Fieseler Storch aircraft, escaped into Italy and has lived ever since in Spain, directing a worldwide neo-Nazi organization. In 1966–67, the present writer corresponded from South Vietnam with the tall boy in the center of the photo, then a Catholic priest in the Congo named Father Martin Bormann. He died in March 2013 in Herdecke, North Rhine-Westphalia, Germany. (HH)

Above right: Two controversial Waffen LSSAH commanders shake hands in Belgium during the winter of 1943–44. At left is General Wilhelm Möhnke, suspected by the Allies of SS atrocities against British POWs in 1940, while Sepp Dietrich (right) was charged with being responsible for the murder of 115 American POWs during the Battle of the Bulge in the infamous "Malmédy Massacre." The officers at right are from the new SS *Hitler Jugend* Division, which fought the Allies fiercely in Normandy six months later. (CER)

1944

BE CAREFUL TO
FIX THEM SO THAT
THEY CAN TURN
BOTH WAYS

DEFENSE OF THE NAZI HOME FRONT

Above: "Defense of the Nazi Home Front," in which Himmler instructs, "Be careful to fix them so that they can turn both ways" in this cartoon by David Low. (LC)

Left: An original member of the LSSAH was Fritz Witt, the first commander of the 12th SS Armored Division *Hitler Jugend.* Here, on his 37th and last birthday, May 27, 1944—nine days before the Normandy invasion—Witt celebrates with a basket of flowers given him as a present. He was killed by Allied naval gunfire. (CER)

Like Rommel, Sepp was almost killed when his staff car was strafed by Allied aircraft after D-Day. At top left, two of the Third Reich's most popular soldiers—Rommel (left) and Sepp—share a laugh at the latter's headquarters on July 17, 1944, just before "The Desert Fox" was seriously wounded, and thus out of commission when the attack on Hitler's life occurred three days later. What was Sepp's real position on the attempt? This question is still debated. Some feel that, while he did not take part actively, he would have been willing to accept Hitler's overthrow because he realized Germany had lost the Second World War by that point. *Top Right*: Wearing camouflage of the type used by the U.S. Marines in the Second World War and the U.S. Army today. Sepp (left) chats with a man Charles Messenger calls "an unknown Army general" in *Hitler's Gladiator*, and (Army) tank General Heinrich Eberbach in August 1944. (CER)

The only known picture of Hitler and his would-be assassin together, in front of the Führer's bunker at FHQ, July, 15, 1944. From left Army Col. Count Claus Schenk von Stauffenberg, whose briefcase it was that exploded; Hitler's naval aide Adm. Karl Jesko von Puttkammer; Bodenschatz (shaking hands with Hitler); an RSD man coming up the walk; Army Field Marshal Wilhelm Keitel. The four men other than the Count and the RSD man were all wounded. Note the overhead camouflage netting to protect the site from enemy bombers—but none ever came. The RSD man might be Erich Kempka. (HH)

Top: Ironically, neither Sepp Dietrich nor Johann Rattenhuber had anything to do with putting down the July 20, 1944 Army revolt. An Army man was the key figure in Berlin who, under the orders of Hitler from Rastenburg by phone, and Goebbels in person, quashed the revolt. This was Maj. Otto-Ernst Remer (1912–1997), seen here at left being personally congratulated by a grateful Führer for helping to save the threatened Nazi régime. Prior to July 20th, Remer had been wounded eight times in action and had met Hitler personally when the Führer presented him with the Knight's Cross with Oak Leaves. This played a pivotal role in the post-bomb explosion events. When Remer went to arrest Goebbels on behalf of the plotters, the Propaganda Minister told him Hitler still lived and placed a phone call to Rastenburg. Hitler asked, "Do you recognize my voice?" Remer did, and the men he commanded—the *Greater Germany* Guard Battalion—were used to end the revolt forthwith. In 1990, when Remer was interviewed by Frank Brandenburg for *Quest*, he told Brandenburg that he went to warn Goebbels, not arrest him, as previously believed. (HH)

Middle: The wounded survivors appear after their wounds have been dressed in one of the more famous July 20th photos. From left six unknown Army and SS officers, Martin Bormann, Hitler (his jacket partially unbuttoned, hat pulled down over right eye and left hand clutching wounded right), SS officer, naval officer, General Alfred Jodl with bandaged head, Albert Bormann, Air Force adjutant Col. von Below, and Hitler pilot SS Lt. General Hans Baur. (HH)

Below: Hitler's famous midnight radio broadcast via the Germany Sender from Rastenburg let his people know that he was still alive and in control of the war effort—which would go on. Sitting in front of Hitler as he speaks are, from left Dr. Otto Dietrich, Martin Bormann, Navy Grand Adm. Karl Donitz, General Alfred Jodl, Julius Schaub (in front of Jodl and to the right), and SS General Hermann Fegelein. Note the newsreel lighting technician at far right, and woman at rear. (HH)

A wounded Hitler (left) greets his supporters with his bandaged left hand while holding his injured right arm and hand at his side on July 25, 1944. From left: Dr. Theo Morell, Dr. Hans Heinrich Lammers, hidden man, a Nazi Gauleiter (possibly either Karl Weinrich of Hesse-Nassau-North or Fritz Bracht of Upper Silesia, and most likely the latter), Martin Bormann. Note the steel shutters, air vent and steel door on the bunker. (HH)

The plot has been crushed. From left at Rastenburg: Criminal Police Commissar and SS Maj. Peter Högl; SS General Julius Schaub and SS Reichsführer Heinrich Himmler; the disgraced General Freidrich Fromm's successor as Head of the Replacement Army, later executed as a traitor. (HH)

After the failed assassination plot of July 20, 1944, on the 25th. From left: Julius Schaub, Goebbels aide Dr. Werner Naumann, Dr. Goebbels, Army aide, Hitler, Albert Bormann, Göring, and Heinz Linge, Hitler's SS valet. (HH)

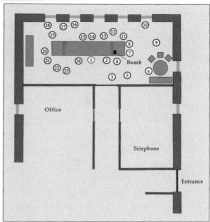

Above left: A telephone close at his side, an RSD man checks the identification card of Hitler's military adjutant, Col. Rudolf Schmundt, who later died of his severe wounds sustained in the attack of July 20, 1944. Note the heavy steel door and handles to secure it fast—from the inside. (HH)

Above right: Of the men standing around the map table when the Army plotters' bomb exploded on July 20, 1944, the briefcase bomb explosion eventually killed Brandt, Korten, Schmundt, Berger and Borgmann, and ended the military career of Bodenschatz. The table support between the briefcase and Hitler may have saved the Führer's life, although he was burned and bruised badly. 1. Adolf Hitler; 2. Lieutenant-General Adolf Heusinger—Deputy Chief of the General Staff of the Army; 3. General Günther Korten—Chief of General Staff of the Air Force; 4. Colonel Heinz Brandt—Aide to General Heusinger; 5. General Karl Bodenschatz—Hermann Göring's liaison officer at Führer Headquarters; 6. Lieutenant-Colonel Heinz Waizenegger—Senior staff officer to Jodl; 7. General Rudolf Schmundt;—Chief of the Army Staff Office; 8. Lieutenant-Colonel Heinrich Borgmann—Hitler's army adjutant; 9. General Walther Buhle—Chief of Army Staff at the OKW; 10. Rear Admiral Karl-Jesco von Puttkamer—Hitler's naval adjutant; 11. Stenographer Heinz Berger; 12. Captain Heinz Assmann—Naval staff officer in the OKW; 13. Major Ernst John von Freyend—Keitel's adjutant; 14. Major-General Walter Scherff—OKW historian; 15. Rear Admiral Hans-Erich Voss—Naval liaison officer at Führer Headquarters; 16.Otto Günsche—Hitler's SS adjutant; 17. Colonel Nicolaus von Below—Hitler's air force adjutant; 18. Lieutenant-General Hermann Fegelein—Waffen-SS representative at Führer Headquarters; 19. Stenographer Heinz Buchholz; 20. Major Herbert Büchs—Jodl's second adjutant; 21. Franz von Sonnleithner—Foreign Ministry representative at Führer Headquarters; 22. General Walter Warlimont—Deputy Chief of Staff of the OKW; 23. General Alfred Jodl—Chief of Staff of the OKW; 24. Field Marshal Wilhelm Keitel—Chief of the OKW. (BT)

After Rommel was wounded in Normandy by a strafing Allied aircraft, Sepp's superior was German Army Field Marshal Hans von Kluge (left), seen here with Hitler. Implicated in the July 20, 1944, Bomb Plot against the Führer, "Clever Hans" committed suicide. (HH)

Above left: A famous SS tanker in perhaps one of the war's more memorable photographs: SS Capt. Michael Wittmann sitting "on the mantelet of his Tiger tank's 88 mm KWK 36 main gun." States Adrian Gilbert in his 1989 book *Waffen SS: An Illustrated History*, "The tank has been coated with Zimmerit paste, a device to prevent the placing of magnetic mines on the tank sides and hull." Wittmann was the holder of the Knight's Cross of the Iron Cross with Oak Leaves and Swords. States Angolia, "Michael Wittmann was the greatest killer of tanks on the ground. The men of his antitank unit were successful in destroying 138 tanks, making him the most successful antitank commander of the German Armed Forces in the Second World War." He was just over 30 when killed in action south of Caen, France on August 8, 1944. (CER)

Above right: : August 6, 1944, Sepp (right) receives the Diamonds to his Knight's Cross from the Führer for his combat record in Normandy that summer. Hitler, still in pain from the Bomb Plot blast of the previous July 20th, shakes with his left hand still clenching the right; also note the white cotton in his right ear. Between the two men is SS General Hermann Fegelein, a dashing cavalry officer who succeeded Karl Wolff as Himmler's liaison officer at Führer Headquarters. Because he didn't fully trust his Reichsführer SS to know the true state of affairs of the war fronts, Hitler would not permit Fegelein to attend military briefings—even though he later married the sister of Hitler's own mistress, Eva Braun. At the end of the war, when Fegelein attempted to flee besieged Berlin, Hitler had him shot outside his Bunker by an SS firing squad for treason, and would've done the same with Himmler had he gotten hold of him. The concrete building at rear is Hitler's reinforced bunker at Rastenburg in East Prussia, not to be confused with the underground Berlin bunker of 1945. (HH)

Below: Left: During Sepp's August, 1944 visit to Hitler's Wolffschanze headquarters in East Prussia, to receive the Diamonds to his Knight's Cross, an impromptu hallway conference is held. Two adjutants are at left, Sepp and Hermann Fegelein are at center, and Hitler gestures at right. When Himmler's peace plot was uncovered in 1945, Hider had Fegelein shot as an accomplice, a traitor and a deserter who failed to escape. *Below:* In August 1944 Fegelein (right), greets his wounded Führer. Fegelein wears SS cavalry tunic in this picture, and Hitler shakes with his unwounded left hand while still wearing cotton in his right ear from the bomb blast of July 20, 1944. A smiling Reischsführer SS looks on. (Both HH)

Above left: SS Brigadeführer Kurt "Panzer" Meyer, commander in 1944 of the 12th SS Panzer Division, the famed *Hitler Youth* that fought the Western Allies during the Battle of Normandy, in which he was captured. Sentenced to be shot as a convicted war criminal, he was sent to life imprisonment instead, but was released in 1954, dying six years later of a heart attack at age 51. He won the Ritterkreuz with Oak Leaves and Swords from Hitler for his wartime service. (CER)

Above right: Left to right, von Rundstedt (holding his swagger stick Marshal's baton), Kurt Meyer, Fritz Witt and Sepp (pointing). (CER)

Above left: A Leibstandarte Royal Tiger tank provides transport for these German paras, with an SS officer just dimly seen behind the man at far right. The Ardennes offensive—named by the Allies for Field Marshal von Rundstedt—started out well, but was stopped when the weather cleared and Allied airpower reasserted itself. (CER)

Middle: "Panzer Baron" General Hasso von Manteuffel served with Sepp during the Battle of the Bulge. Manteuffel, like Sepp, survived the war and later was elected to West German public office. (CER)

Above right: Had he won the Battle of the Bulge against the Americans, Sepp most likely would've been named Hitler's first SS Field Marshal. Here, he is seen in a Volkswagen *Kubelwagen,* talking with his adjutant, Hermann Weiser. (LC)

1945

Above left: For his notorious role as Nazi Governor-General of occupied Poland during 1939–45, Frank was tried, convicted and hanged by the Allies at Nuremberg on October 16, 1946. Here, Frank enters the courtroom in the Nuremberg Palace of Justice followed by a U.S. Military Policeman armed with a baton made from a broom handle. (USASC, D'Addario)

Above right: On June 24, 1945, the victorious Red Army held its parade on Red Square in Moscow—where it was hoped in 1941 that Hitler's banner would one day stand! Now it was dipped to the cobblestones in submission, but without its famed banner, which was reportedly hidden or destroyed by an unknown SS man to prevent its capture. After the parade, Hitler's standard staff was thrown on the red marble steps of Lenin's Mausoleum, and today it still rests in the Museum of the Red Army in Moscow; as of 1993, the banner had never been found or recovered. (LC)

Below: One of the first men to join the LSSAH was SS Col. Wilhelm Mohnke, who commanded the SS forces defending the New German Reich Chancellery during April-May, 1945, as the Russians closed in for the kill. Decorated with the Knight's Cross on July 11, 1944, as the commander of the SS Armored Grenadier Regiment 26 of the Hitler Youth Division, Mohnke also led the LSSAH in 1944-45. *Right:* Hitler shakes hands with the last commander of his Leibstandarte, appointed in February 1945. Formerly, General Kumm—the holder of the Knight's Cross with Oak Leaves—had commanded the Regiment *Der Führer* and the *Prinz Eugen* 7th SS Mountain Division. (CER)

Above left: Sepp served in war twice under this man, on fronts both East and West—German Army Field Marshal Gerd von Rundstedt. Born December 12, 1875, von Rundstedt entered the War Academy in 1902, the General Staff five years later. Named Field Marshal by Hitler, he was fired three times, but brought back twice. (USASC)

Above right: An American Prisoner of War in the witness wing of the Nuremberg jail, Sepp reads a local paper in his cell on November 24, 1945. Never called upon to testify there, he was sent instead to Dachau to stand trial for the events surrounding the Malmédy Massacre of December 1944. (USASC, D'Addario)

Two pictures of the last troop review, identified as taken either on March 20, 1945, or on Hitler's 56th and last birthday, April 20, 1945. It was the former. (HH)

Above left: This photo, found in the ruins of the Reich Chancellery, is believed by experts to be the last ever taken of Adolf Hitler that survived the war's destruction. Hitler is at right, and SS General Julius Schaub is thought to be the man at left. Schaub survived the war, dying as an apothecary in 1967, age 69. Sent by Hitler to Berchtesgaden to destroy his private papers, Schaub was later captured by the American Army. They had taken the man registered as SS #7. (HH)

Above right: The Berghof in ruins. On May 4, 1945 soldiers of the 3rd U.S, Infantry Division captured Hitler's home still smoking from a fire. (USASC)

U.S. soldiers tear down the swastika. (USASC)

April 1945: The Platterhof and LSSAH Barracks area in ruins. (USASC)

1946

The Dachau Trial for which Sepp and the LSSAH were put in the accused's dock for the killing of U.S. Army GIs at Malmédy and elsewhere during the Battle of the Bulge. From left are Dietrich (#11), Kraemer (#33), Priess (#45) and Jochen Peiper (#42). Stated a German Wehrmacht Colonel in a mid-1950s interview, "The Americans were at fault in condemning to death only those who committed the crimes and not Sepp Dietrich. He was the man really responsible for the Malmédy Massacre and the way in which the 1st Panzer— the LSSAH—shot down civilians throughout their advance, particularly at Stavelot. The least that can be said is that the commanders were letting their men run riot." (USASC)

Dietrich stands before the bench with his American Army assistant defense counsel Lt. Col. Ellis. There were 43 death sentences handed down, but none were ever carried out. Of the 31 prison terms mandated, the last man walked free after a decade. (USASC)

1949

Lammers survived the war to be placed on trial by the Allies at Nuremberg, where in 1949 he pleaded not guilty to being involved in the SS murder of Europe's Jews during the war. Like Hitler and Sepp Dietrich before him, he was sentenced to imprisonment at Landsberg, but served only two years of a 20-year sentence, and died on January 4, 1962, age 83, 13 years after this picture was taken of him on the witness stand at Nuremberg. (USASC, D'Addario)

1957 & 1966

After his release from Allied captivity, Sepp Dietrich was arrested and charged by the new West German government with a criminal role in the murder of Röhm and the SA leaders 23 years earlier. Here, on May 10, 1957, Sepp points to the spot in the Stadelheim Prison courtyard where six SA leaders were shot. (BT)

Below left: On April 21, 1966, the day after what would have been Hitler's 77th birthday, Sepp died three weeks short of his own 74th birthday. At top left is the newspaper photo used with Sepp's obituary in the American press. (BT)

Below right: Ludwigsburg, West Germany: Dietrich's final resting place. He was one of the few top Nazis in the post war era to receive a military-style funeral complete with sword, flag and helmet atop his casket. (LC)